American Book Company's

PASSING THE
NORTH CAROLINA EOC TEST

in

Civics and Economics

Kindred Howard

Edited by Devin Pintozz

D1511823

American Book Company
PO Box 2638
Woodstock, GA 30188-1383
Toll Free: 1 (888) 264-5877   Phone: (770) 928-2834
Fax: (770) 928-7483 Toll Free Fax 1 (866) 827-3240
Web site: www.americanbookcompany.com

ACKNOWLEDGEMENTS

The authors would like to gratefully acknowledge the formatting and technical contributions of Marsha Torrens.

We also want to thank Mary Stoddard for her expertise in developing the graphics for this book.

A special thanks to Becky Wright for her editing and formatting assistance.

This product/publication includes images from CorelDRAW 9 and 11 which are protected by the copyright laws of the United States, Canada, and elsewhere. Used under license.

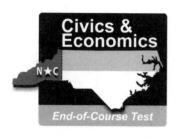

Table of Contents

Preface

Passing the North Carolina End of Course Test in Civics and Economics will help students who are learning or reviewing material for the North Carolina test that is now required.

This book contains several sections. These sections are as follows: 1) General information about the book; 2) A Diagnostic Test and Evaluation Chart; 3) Chapters that teach the concepts and skills that improve readiness for the end of course exam in civics and economics; 4) Two Practice Tests. Answers to the tests and exercises are in a separate manual. The answer manual also contains a Chart of Standards for teachers to make a more precise diagnosis of student needs and assignments.

We welcome comments and suggestions about the book. Please contact us at

American Book Company
PO Box 2638
Woodstock, GA 30188-1383

Toll Free: 1 (888) 264-5877
Phone: (770) 928-2834
Fax: (770) 928-7483
Web site: www.americanbookcompany.com

About the Authors

Kindred Howard is a 1991 alumnus of the University of North Carolina at Chapel Hill, where he graduated with a B.S. in Criminal Justice and national honors in Political Science. In addition to two years as a probation and parole officer in North Carolina, he has served for over twelve years as a teacher and writer in the fields of religion and social studies. His experience includes teaching students at both the college and high school level, as well as speaking at numerous seminars. He is currently completing a M.A. in Biblical Studies at Asbury Theological Seminary, as well as a M.A. in History from Georgia State University. Mr. Howard lives in Kennesaw, Georgia, with his wife and two children.

John Martino graduated from Williams College (MA) in 2003 with a B.A. in economics and mathematics, including an honors thesis in economics. His senior year, he served as a Teaching Assistant for a graduate course at the international Center for Development Economics located at Williams, and he has tutored in various subjects from the 4th grade to college levels. He currently resides in Silver Springs, MD where he is a teaching assistant and student in Theology and Religious Studies at the Catholic University of America.

Perry T. Barrett is from Rockmart, Georgia, where he works as an adjunct online instructor and course developer for several major post secondary institutions. He earned his Masters in Education from Delta State University and enjoys attending historical reenactments throughout the Southeast.

Lisa Bryde is a Curriculum Development Specialist and a Content Developer. She holds a BS degree in Secondary English Education from Georgia State University and a M.Ed. in Curriculum Development from the University of Georgia. She has worked as an educator in the public school system for fourteen years and has served as a consultant for the Governor's Council for Brain Based Curriculum.

North Carolina Civics & Economics
Diagnostic Test

The purpose of this diagnostic pretest is to measure your knowledge of civics and economics. This pretest is based on the **North Carolina Performance Standards** and adheres to the sample question format provided by the North Carolina Department of Education.

General Directions:

1. Read all directions carefully.

2. Read each question or sample. Then choose the best answer.

3. Choose only one answer for each question. If you change an answer, be sure to erase your original answer completely.

4. After taking the test, you or your instructor should score it using the answer key that accompanies this book. Then use the evaluation chart to review and practice for the civics and economics skills tested on the End of Course Test.

1. If one wanted to visit the New England colonies in the late 1600s, which of the following colonies would he/she go to?   1.1

   A   North Carolina   C   Massachusetts
   B   Maryland   D   Georgia

2. Which of the following describes the New England Colonies?   1.1

   A   It was the first region to offer public schools.
   B   Most of the region's rich land owners remained members of the Anglican Church.
   C   One of its colonies offered a safe haven for debtors from England.
   D   Tobacco and rice were early staple crops of the region.

3. Which of the following MOST resembles the form of government adopted by the US Founding Fathers?   1.2

   A   Every adult citizen of an ancient Greek city gathers together to vote on whether or not a new law should be adopted.
   B   Only a small group of upper-class leaders have any say in appointing a new leader.
   C   The Roman Senate meets to decide what actions it should take on behalf of the people.
   D   The king orders his nobles to help him fight against his enemies or he will take away their land.

4. Which of the following documents helped establish the principle that even a monarch should be under the rule of law?   6.1

   A   the Code of Hammurabi
   B   the Justinian Code
   C   the Ten Commandments
   D   the Magna Carta

5. Of the following, which statement BEST describes the model of government established by the NC Constitution?   3.2

   A   It establishes an executive branch consisting only of the governor and a legislative branch called the "North Carolina Congress."
   B   It consists of three branches of government to ensure a separation of powers, as well as a system of checks and balances so that no branch exercises too much power.
   C   It establishes a council of State to be appointed by the governor.
   D   It establishes the governor and state legislators as elected representatives, but gives the governor the power to appoint all judges.

6. Which of the following BEST describes the difference between civil and criminal law?   4.5

   A   Criminal law has to do with federal laws, while civil law tends to deal more with state and local ordinances.
   B   Criminal law deals with federal crimes and state penal codes, while civil law deals with relationships between private individuals, organizations, businesses, etc.
   C   Someone accused of a criminal offense is called a "defendant", while someone accused in a civil case is called a "plaintiff."
   D   Criminal complaints are brought by private individuals, while civil cases are normally brought by the state.

7. Someone who believes in "natural rights" would be MOST supportive of which of the following?   1.2

   A   the Declaration of Independence
   B   autocracy
   C   writs of assistance
   D   taxation without representation

2

8. Christine has just been hired by a council to be the city manager for a mid-sized city. There will be a mayor as well, but he will serve primarily as a ceremonial representative. Christine is the one who will be primarily responsible for overseeing city government. Christine's city operates on which model of government? 3.2

A   mayor-council plan

B   council-manager plan

C   manager-mayor plan

D   city-township plan

"This is more that an outrage; it is immoral! I say again, no taxation without representation!"

---

9. Which of the following would have most likely made the above quote? 1.3

A   James Otis, in response to the Stamp Act

B   King George III, in response to the Boston Tea Party

C   Thomas Jefferson, in response to the Intolerable Acts

D   Patrick Henry, in response to the Boston Massacre

10. On which of the following principles was the *Declaration of Independence* based? 1.4

A   separation of church and state

B   autocracy

C   ethnic diversity

D   egalitarianism

11. Ted is a politician who believes that the government should be very active. He favors more government spending to provide social programs like welfare, government paid education, and national health care. He tends to oppose tax cuts unless they are for the extremely poor. Ted can BEST be described as what? 4.1

A   a liberal

B   a conservative

C   a moderate

D   an independent

12. The role of Christianity in the colonies can BEST be described how? 1.4

A   It played a limited role because the colonies believed in separation of church and state.

B   It played a major role because it ensured that the British government maintained a tight control on the colonies through the Anglican church.

C   It played a religious role, but had little affect on government, education, or social order.

D   It played a major role because it influenced colonial governments, strengthened the principle of separation of church and state, and led to the establishment of the colonies' first public schools and colleges.

13. Which of the following represents the correct chronological order of events during a presidential election year? 4.2

A   general election, primary election, national convention, caucus, votes cast in the electoral college

B   initiative, caucus, run-off election, votes cast in the electoral college, general election

C   primary election and caucuses, national convention, general election, votes cast in the electoral college

D   general election, votes cast in the electoral college, national convention

14. Which of the following was an attempt by delegates to the Constitutional Convention to resolve the question of whether or not to count slaves amongst the population? 1.5

A Great Compromise

B Missouri Compromise

C Three-fifths Compromise

D Two-thirds Compromise

15. Which of the following statements is true regarding the model of government adopted under the Constitution? 1.5

A It is an autocracy ruled by a president that must get Congress' approval on certain matters.

B It is based on federalism with the federal government consisting of a legislative, executive, and judicial branch.

C Officials who serve in each branch of government are elected directly by the people so as to be sure that the people have a say in each branch.

D It established two houses within the legislative branch, with each state being granted a certain number of representatives in each house based on population.

16. A Federalist would most likely AGREE with which of the following statements? 1.6

A "We must not give too much power to a national government, or else we could find ourselves once more under a hand of tyranny."

B "Protect the sovereignty of the states! If we do nothing else, we must make sure that the rights of the states are not sacrificed for the sake of a national government."

C "We must allow the president to assert authority and we must give the federal government the freedom to exercise powers not specifically stated in the Constitution. Otherwise, we keep the government from ruling effectively."

D "Jefferson's ideas about government, rather than Hamilton's, are the best one's for the nation to follow."

17. A period lasting more than 6 months in which prices fall, production decreases, and unemployment rises is called what? 9.1

A retraction   C recession

B recovery   D downslope

18. Before North Carolina and several other states would accept the Constitution, they insisted that what be considered for ratification? 1.7

A the death penalty

B the *Bill of Rights*

C a preamble stating the document's purpose

D a judicial branch of government

19. Which of the following is TRUE regarding the president of the United States? 2.1

A He/She represents the legislative branch of the federal government.

B His/Her office is established by Article I of the Constitution.

C He/She is elected to a term of four years.

D His/Her role is to make the laws.

20. Which of the following is a role granted to the House of Representatives by the Constitution? 2.2

A the role of confirming presidential appointments

B the role of ratifying treaties with foreign nations

C the role of impeaching the president, if necessary

D the role of declaring laws unconstitutional.

21. Which of the following is a responsibility of the US Senate? 2.2

A It nominates judges to the Supreme Court.

B It must approve presidential appointments.

C It is responsible for introducing spending bills.

D It decides whether or not a public official may be impeached.

22. Which of the following is not a recurring problem in US society?   10.5

    A   discrimination

    B   unemployment

    C   immigration issues

    D   polling data

23. In order for the president to be removed from office as a result of *impeachment*, which of the following must occur?   2.3

    A   The Senate must first vote to impeach the president. The House of Representatives then must agree with the Senate by a majority vote. Once this occurs, the president must then appear before the Supreme Court which will decide whether or not to remove the president from office.

    B   The House must present articles of impeachment to the chief justice. If the chief justice finds just cause for the charges, then the Senate votes on whether or not to remove the president from office.

    C   The Supreme Court must hear allegations against the president. If it believes he/she is guilty of wrongdoing, then the president is impeached. Congress then votes on whether or not the president is removed from office.

    D   The House must first vote to impeach the president. The case is then tried in the Senate with the chief justice presiding over the proceedings. The president is removed if two-thirds of the Senate votes he/she is guilty of wrongdoing.

24. The United States Constitution does not give the federal government the direct authority to open a national bank. Yet, in 1819, the Supreme Court ruled that the US government does, indeed, have the right to establish a bank under the "necessary and proper clause." The act of the government establishing a bank is an example of what?   2.5

    A   the federal government exercising its implied powers

    B   the federal government exercising its enumerated powers

    C   the federal government exercising checks and balances

    D   the Supreme Court overruling the Constitution

25. The First Great Awakening is an example of which of the following?   1.4

    A   impact of passionate political speeches in colonial America

    B   impact of nationalism in colonial America

    C   impact of Christianity in colonial America

    D   Egalitarian philosophy

26. What do the court cases of *Mapp v. Ohio* (1961), *Miranda v Arizona* (1961), *Gregg v. Georgia* (1976), and *Furman v. Georgia* (1972) all have in common?   2.6

    A   They all have to do with freedom of speech.

    B   They all have to do with freedom to practice one's own religion.

    C   They all have to do with equal rights for women.

    D   They all have to do with the rights of those accused or convicted of a crime.

27. Which of the following is a form of active citizenship?   4.9

    A   legal action

    B   negotiation

    C   pre-hearing settlement

    D   volunteerism

28. George is a producer of red pens. George's goal in a free enterprise system is to what? 8.2

A to make as many red pens as possible

B to make as much profit as possible

C to buy red pens at the lowest cost possible

D to do what the government dictates is best for the country

29. In North Carolina, the highest court in the state is known as what? 5.2

A Chief Court of North Carolina

B NC Supreme Court

C NC Court of Appeals

D NC Superior Court

30. The plight of African-Americans before the American Revolution can BEST be described as what? 1.1

A pleasant compared to Europe because the colonies were more open-minded

B easier than in Africa because the colonies were more advanced

C harsh because most African-Americans were slaves

D most difficult in the North because African-Americans fared better in the warmer climate of the Deep South

31. What is the main difference between common law and statutory law? 6.2

A Statutory law is written law, whereas common law is based on tradition and/or past court decisions.

B Common law is law that the public is generally aware of, whereas statutory law is usually less publicized and only known by lawyers, judges, and government leaders.

C Statutory law applies to matters of government, whereas common law applies to society as a whole.

D Common law has to do with criminal offenses, whereas statutory law has to do with civil disputes.

32. Which of the following is protected under the Sixth Amendment? 4.7

A the right to free speech

B the right to an attorney

C the right to trial by jury in a civil case

D the right to due process of law

33. George is a political activist who is opposed to certain US policies. In protest, George grabs the US flag he has in his house, takes it downtown, and burns it in public. What will likely happen to George based on the 1984 case of *Texas v. Johnson*? 2.6

A George will be arrested because it is against federal law to burn a flag.

B Other than a few mean words from some people he has offended, nothing will likely happen to George because flag burning is protected under the *First Amendment*.

C It depends on where George lives because flag burning laws differ from state to state.

D George will not get in any trouble because his actions are protected under the *Fourth Amendment*.

34. Phil's job pays him $3000 a month. However, when Phil actually gets his check, he sees that he is only taking home $2100. What happened to the rest of Phil's money? 2.8

A It was stolen by his employer.

B It was taken out to pay excise and estate taxes.

C It was taken out to pay income and social security taxes.

D It was taken out to pay fines and user fees.

35. Which of the following statements is true regarding the NC Constitution? **3.1**

   A There has only been one constitution, but it has been changed many times.

   B Unlike the federal government, the NC Constitution says nothing about the individual rights of citizens.

   C The document rejects the idea of limited government in favor of popular sovereignty.

   D The NC Constitution can be amended either by a constitutional convention or legislative initiative.

36. It is safe to say that the Enlightenment had which of the following effects on the development of political thought in the colonies? **1.2**

   A It taught colonial Americans that their leaders, in particularly the king/queen, were not to be questioned because they had a divine right to rule.

   B It taught them that individual rights mean little when compared with what is best for the state.

   C It led colonists to believe that even bad governments should be respected because, without government, chaos would rule.

   D It molded colonial views by suggesting that all humans have certain rights and that governments are accountable to the people.

37. The city of Anderaville has just opened a new school. While it teaches all subjects, its particular focus is on the arts. It receives public funds, but it is independent of the local school board. Instead, it answers to a local university and arts council that have joined forces to sponsor the school. The new school is MOST LIKELY what? **3.7**

   A a private school

   B a charter school

   C a constitution school

   D a sponsorship school

38. Which of the following is an area where the federal government alone has authority? **3.8**

   A raising taxes

   B establishing user fees

   C assessing fines

   D regulating trade

"We cannot simply lock people up and throw away the key. True, they may have committed crimes—perhaps even violent crimes— but even convicted felons are human beings. Who's to say how you and I would have behaved had we been born into poverty, or with a different skin color. We must help those who have fallen into criminal behavior to change and become successful members of society."

39. The above quote was most likely made by whom? **6.8**

   A someone who favors rehabilitation

   B someone who favors retribution

   C someone who favors recidivism

   D someone who favors capital punishment

40. The *Articles of Confederation* proved ineffective as a national body of laws for which of the following reasons? **1.5**

   A It gave too much power to the Congress and the president.

   B It did not give the federal government enough power to effectively lead.

   C It imposed taxes that citizens found offensive.

   D It prevented Congress from passing legislation regarding the Northwest Territory.

41. Which of the following describes how goods pass from producers to consumers in a free enterprise system? **8.2**

   A capital investment

   B voluntary exchange

   C consumer sovereignty

   D taxes and subsidies

42. The country of Nebo has just held its elections. 40% of the vote went to the Conservative Party, 20% to the Moderate Party, 20% to the Liberal Party, 10% to the Indifferent Party, with 10 smaller parties all getting 1%. If 100 seats in the Parliament are available and Nebo uses a multi-party system based on proportional representation, then which of the following is true?

4.1

A   The Conservative candidate goes to Parliament and the rest stay home.

B   The Conservative, Moderate, and Liberal candidates must face one another in a run-off election.

C   The Conservative, Liberal, and Moderate candidates all get the same number of seats.

D   The Conservative gets 40 seats in Parliament, the Moderates and Liberals each get 20 seats, the Indifferents get 10 seats, and the remaining 10 seats are divided among the 10 smaller parties.

43. Doug is the campaign manager for Sophia's run for the Senate. He advises her that since she is relatively unknown outside her own district, they need to launch a series of ads pointing out her accomplishments, highlighting her patriotism, and depicting her as someone who relates to the "common man." Doug is advocating which of the following?

4.2

A   negative campaigning

B   the use of "glittering generalities"

C   positive image molding

D   canvassing

44. After 2 months of advertising Sophia's qualities, Doug now switches gears. He unleashes a series of ads portraying Sophia's opponent as dishonest and incompetent. Doug's new strategy can BEST be described as what?

4.2

A   negative campaigning

B   the use of "glittering generalities"

C   polling

D   political endorsements

45. A well informed citizen would be MOST LIKELY to do which of the following?

10.3

A   refrain from voting

B   pick a political candidate who best represents his/her own views and actively campaign for him/her

C   avoid debates that could lead to conflict

D   rarely question the decisions made by government officials

46. Amy is excited because she just opened her own consulting firm. Amy loves being her own boss and not having to consult with anyone else before she makes decisions. Eventually, she even hopes to incorporate and enjoy some additional tax advantages. The only downside is that she has invested all the money herself. If the business fails, she could go bankrupt. What kind of business does Amy own?

8.7

A   sole proprietorship

B   partnership

C   cooperative

D   corporation

47. If someone wanted to understand the purpose and intent of the US Constitution, it would be BEST to read what?

2.1

A   the *First Amendment*

B   the *Declaration of Independence*

C   the *Bill of Rights*

D   the Preamble

48. Which of the following is considered a BENEFIT of freedom?

10.6

A   the need to compromise one's own position in order to accommodate those with different beliefs

B   the right of self-determination

C   guaranteed economic equality

D   guaranteed success

8

49. Candice opposes big government. She believes that the government should simply provide law and order, structure for society, national defense, and economic policies that allow the market to function as freely as possible. Candice can BEST be described as what?   4.1

   A   a liberal
   B   a conservative
   C   a moderate
   D   an independent

50. Laura has been arrested and charged with a federal crime. Which of the following statements is true regarding Laura's case?   5.2

   A   State superior court will exercise original jurisdiction over the case, however, if Laura appeals, the case will go to federal court.
   B   The US Court of Appeals will have original jurisdiction, but if Laura appeals, it will then go to the US Supreme Court.
   C   There is no way the US Supreme Court could ever hear Laura's case because it does not involve a matter of constitutional law.
   D   The US District Court has original jurisdiction over the case with the US Court of Appeals and possibly the Supreme Court exercising appellate jurisdiction.

51. The authority of the Supreme Court to declare acts of Congress unconstitutional was established in which court case?   2.5

   A   *Marbury v. Madison* (1803)
   B   *McCullough v. Maryland* (1819)
   C   *Korematsu v. United States* (1944)
   D   *Brown v. Board of Education* (1954)

52. The authority of the courts to declare acts of Congress and/or state legislatures unconstitutional is referred to as what?   2.5

   A   judicial authority
   B   legislative overrule
   C   judicial review
   D   court nullification

53. In order to make an arrest, law enforcement officials need what?   5.3

   A   either an indictment or a legal summons
   B   either an arrest warrant or probable cause
   C   either an arrest warrant or a search warrant
   D   either a bond or court docket

54. Brian wants to buy a soda and a box of popcorn at the movies. However, he only has enough money for one or the other. If Brian buys the soda, which of the following is his "opportunity cost"?   7.2

   A   the price of the soda
   B   the price of the popcorn
   C   hunger
   D   his thirst

55. The process by which existing cities incorporate previously outlying areas of the county is called what?   3.7

   A   geographic draft
   B   bill of acquisition
   C   land grabbing
   D   annexation

56. GDP, CPI, per capita gross national product, and the national debt are all what?   9.1

   A   signs that the economy is peaking
   B   signs that the economy is in contraction
   C   economic indicators used to determine the state and direction of the economy
   D   the result of economic expansion

57. In the school cafeteria there are servers, grill cooks, dishwashers, and cash register attendants. Each of these does his/her own specific task. This is a good example of what?   7.4

A   full employment

B   mass production

C   arbitration

D   division of labor

58. The idea that producers will produce whatever there is sufficient demand for, so long as they can continue to make a sufficient profit, is referred to as what?   8.4

A   supply

B   the law of supply and demand

C   economic equilibrium

D   the theory of free enterprise exchange

59. Mimi and Charlene are both from the same town. Charlene finished high school and went on to get a two-year degree in nursing. Mimi, on the other hand, graduated high school and decided to take a job in the local factory. Based on statistics and general trends, which of the following will MOST LIKELY happen?   10.3

A   Charlene will earn more money in her lifetime than Mimi will in hers.

B   Charlene will end up paying less in taxes than Mimi.

C   Charlene will get married before Mimi.

D   Charlene and Mimi will end up earning about the same.

60. Which of the following MOST accurately depicts the process for creating a law?   5.4

A   The president first signs a bill, and then presents it to Congress. Congress then sends it to a committee in each house. If the committee approves the bill, it then goes to a subcommittee. If the subcommittee votes in favor of the bill, both houses of Congress then vote on it. If both houses vote in favor of the bill, it becomes law.

B   If one house of Congress votes in favor of a bill, it then goes to a committee within that same house. If the committee recommends the bill, it then goes to the other house of Congress for a vote. If that house also votes in favor of the bill, it then presents the bill to one of its own committees. If that committee recommends the bill, the bill then goes to the president who will either sign or veto the bill.

C   Once a senator or representative introduces a bill, it goes to a committee. The committee then assigns it to a subcommittee that will study and make recommendations to the committee as a whole. If the committee decides to send it to the house of Congress of which the committee is a part, the entire body then votes on the bill. If it passes by a majority vote, it then goes to the other house. Once a bill passes both houses, it goes to the president, who will either sign or veto it.

D   All bills must originate in the House of Representatives. Once this occurs, they go to the House Rules Committee, which then assigns them to subcommittees. Once a subcommittee recommends a bill, it then goes to the whole House for a vote. Once the House passes it, it then goes to the Senate. If the Senate passes it as well, the bill then goes to the president, who will either veto or sign it.

61. Which of the following represents a non-European influence on the development of US ideas about government? 6.1

A the Enlightenment

B the Magna Carta

C common law

D the Iroquois League

62. Which of the following represents a way that private citizens can stay informed about laws and important issues? 6.4

A attend public hearings

B issue press releases

C take advantage of their franking privilege

D take part in special task forces

63. What do voting, signing a petition, taking part in protests, and volunteering to help with a campaign all have in common? 4.4

A They are each guaranteed under the *Second Amendment*.

B They each require a license before one can legally engage in them in North Carolina.

C They are all forms of political activism.

D They demonstrate citizen apathy.

64. The lieutenant governor, the NC secretary of state, and the attorney general of North Carolina all have which of the following in common? 3.2

A They are each appointed by the governor.

B Together, they comprise the entire executive branch of state government.

C They are all part of the Council of State.

D None of them have any role in the General Assembly.

65. The *Free Exercise Clause* and the *Establishment Clause* are associated with protecting which right? 1.7

A the right to free speech

B the right to peaceful assembly

C the right to freedom of religion

D the right to bear arms

66. Tanya has just been hired by a group called *Americans by Choice*. It is a group that fights for the rights of immigrants and works to lessen restrictions on immigration. Tanya's job is to use her connections and political clout to persuade representatives in the House and US senators to vote in favor of the bills *Americans by Choice* supports. Which of the following is true? 6.6

A Tanya will have to deal secretly with members of Congress because it is illegal for any group to hire someone to influence legislation.

B Tanya is a political activist and *Americans by Choice* is a lobbying firm.

C *Americans by Choice* is an independent government agency that has hired Tanya to represent their economic interests.

D Tanya is a lobbyist and *Americans by Choice* is an interest group.

67. The US Chambers of Commerce is an example of which of the following? 6.6

A an interest group representing laborers

B an interest group representing economic interest

C a think tank

D a public interest group

68. Which of the following gives the correct chronological order of events in the judicial process? 5.3

   A arrest, arrest warrant, trial, arraignment, appeal, conviction

   B complaint, preliminary hearing, plea bargaining, sentence

   C pre-trial motion, arrest, arraignment, sentencing, plea bargaining

   D preliminary hearing, trial, indictment, sentence

69. Which of the following would be an example of *self-motivation*? 10.3

   A A young man decides to get a degree in the hopes of one day starting his own business.

   B A person drops out of high school with no plan for the future.

   C A young lady is in no hurry to find a job because she gets a welfare check each month from the government.

   D A citizen constantly criticizes his state's political leaders and decides not to vote because he feels that neither candidate is trustworthy.

70. What can one assume from the following headline: "President and Congress Feud Over Fiscal Policy"? 9.7

   A The president and congress cannot agree on a tax plan and a budget.

   B The president favors higher taxes but Congress opposes them.

   C Congress and the president cannot agree on defense spending.

   D Congress and the president cannot agree on interest rates.

71. Which of the following people is MOST likely to be placed on probation? 6.8

   A someone who is convicted of speeding

   B someone who has just been convicted on misdemeanor drug charges for a third time

   C someone who has just been convicted of a capital offense

   D a "model prisoner" who has behaved well in prison and who is being considered for early release.

72. Davidson, Inc. has just built a new factory to produce the tractors that it manufactures. Which of the following factors of production would this new facility be considered a part of? 7.1

   A capital   C labor

   B land   D entrepreneurship

73. The following headline appears in a local paper: "New Product Aims to Attract Teen Girls". Which of the following economic questions does this headline answer? 8.1

   A What should be produced?

   B How will it be produced?

   C When will it be produced?

   D For whom will it be produced?

74. Julie is upset because she has just received a document notifying her that she is being sued for $5000 by one of her former clients. Which of the following is an accurate statement? 5.3

   A The document is a subpoena and Julie will be the plaintiff in a criminal case.

   B The document is a subpoena and Julie will be the defendant in a criminal case.

   C The document is a summons and Julie will be the plaintiff in a civil case.

   D The document is a summons and Julie will be the defendant in a civil case.

75. Due to inflation, the Federal Reserve decides to decrease the money supply. Which one of the following will the Federal Reserve most likely do? 9.7

A   lower the discount rate

B   implement a "easy money" policy

C   buy bonds

D   raise the reserve requirement for banks

76. Tony is about to travel to England on business. While he is there, he hopes to see some of the sites and dine at some fine restaurants. In order to know how much money he should budget, Tony needs to know how many British pounds his US dollars are worth. Tony needs to be aware of what? 9.5

A   the exchange rate

B   any current embargoes

C   international tariffs

D   whether or not the US dollar currently enjoys a comparative advantage in trade

77. Lawyers, doctors, electricians, carpenters, engineers, and stock brokers are all classified as which of the following? 7.4

A   white collar workers

B   blue collar workers

C   skilled workers

D   unskilled workers

78. In Nick's neighborhood, there are Hispanic, African-American, and white families. Some of the residents practice Christianity, some Judaism, some Islam, and still others Hinduism. Nick's neighborhood MOST reflects what? 10.2

A   equality

B   discrimination

C   multiculturalism

D   affirmative action

79. Below is a "supply & demand" schedule that shows the number of pairs of socks that producers are willing to make at various prices, as well as the number of pairs that consumers are willing to purchase at each price. Using this chart, what would happen if the price of the socks was set at $2.50/pair? 8.5

Price	Produced	Demanded
$0.50	0	1,000
$1.00	100	900
$1.50	200	800
$2.00	300	700
$2.50	400	600
$3.00	500	500
$3.50	600	400
$4.00	700	300
$4.50	800	200
$5.00	900	100
$5.50	1,000	0

A   all socks would sell because it would be the equilibrium price

B   a shortage

C   a surplus

D   no socks would be produced because it would be the equilibrium price

80. Using the same chart, what would happen if producers raised the price to $3.50/pair? 8.5

A   The socks would be priced at the equilibrium price.

B   No one would buy socks because they are priced too high.

C   a surplus

D   a shortage

81. Which of the following is an example of investment in capital? 7.4

A providing a medical plan to help employees avoid getting sick and missing work

B providing discount gym memberships to employees to help them stay in shape

C reinvesting company profits in updated technology

D paying for employees to get a graduate degree

I assure you, the most efficient market is one that understands it is the consumer and his, or her, desires that determine what businesses produce."

---

82. The above quote is promoting the principle of what? 7.6

A consumer sovereignty

B consumerism

C command economic systems

D mixed economies

83. Black Titan Steel, Inc. has just bought out its former competitor, Alligator Steel. Which of the following BEST describes this business practice? 8.6

A a horizontal merger

B a vertical merger

C forming a cooperative

D a partnership

84. Union employees at Taylor Lumber are fed up with management's refusal to give them a raise and better benefits. In addition, they are also angry that management won't even sit down to negotiate or meet with a third party. Which of the following is an option the union can still use to try and convince management to agree to its demands? 8.7

A a lockout

B arbitration

C a strike

D a layoff

85. Which of the following statements is true regarding households, businesses, and government in the US economic system? 8.3

A Households pay taxes to the government, but businesses don't.

B Households act as consumers while government and businesses act only as producers.

C The three are economically interdependent on one another.

D Government regulates what businesses can produce, but not what consumers can buy.

86. Olivia earns $4000 per month on her job. After taxes, she actually takes home $2800. Once she pays for necessities like her rent, groceries, utilities, etc. Olivia has $500 left over. Which of the following statements is accurate? 8.4

A Olivia has a personal income of $4000, a disposable income of $2800, and a discretionary income of $500.

B Olivia has a disposable income of $4000, a discretionary income of $2800, and a personal income of $500.

C Olivia's discretionary income is greater than her personal income.

D Olivia has a total income of $7300.

87. A pair of shoes that costs $80 last month, costs $100 this month. Which of the following BEST describes this economic condition? 9.7

   A   inflation

   B   recession

   C   stagflation

   D   competition

88. Economic statistics show that the nation of Klaskow produced 10 million dollars in goods and services last year. Meanwhile, the nation's census shows that it has 100,000 people living in the country. Which of the following statements is true? 9.1

   A   Klaskow has a GDP of $1,000,000.00.

   B   Klaskow has a per capita GDP of $100.00.

   C   Klaskow has a national debt of $9,900,000.00.

   D   Klaskow has a per capita GDP of $1,000,000.00.

89. Which of the following is an example of how the US government regulates and/or affects the economy? 9.2

   A   migration

   B   federalism

   C   civil lawsuits

   D   consumer protection policies

90. The country of Chanover has experienced mass migration from its northern provinces to its southern provinces over the last ten years. Given this fact, which of the following statements is true? 9.3

   A   The northern provinces have experienced industrial growth over the last decade.

   B   The economy of the South is likely shrinking.

   C   Service industries in the South have likely grown over the last decade.

   D   The population of the North is likely growing faster than that of the South.

91. Which of the following is a positive occurrence in the US economy? 9.1/9.4

   A   recession   C   expansion

   B   downsizing   D   "bear markets"

92. Which of the following has the LEAST effect on the US economy? 9.4

   A   a terrorist attack

   B   government decisions to regulate US businesses

   C   outsourcing by corporations

   D   the closing of a sole proprietorship

93. Which of the following countries would be considered "developing" rather than "developed"? 9.6

   A   Japan   C   United States

   B   Haiti   D   Canada

94. In an effort to bring down the government of Fidel Castro, the United States adopted a policy of refusing to trade with Cuba. More than 40 years later, this policy remains in effect. Which of the following is an attempt to punish another country by refusing to trade with it? 9.8

   A   a tariff

   B   a negative trade balance

   C   an embargo

   D   a trade treaty

95. Which of the following describes a key difference between personal and civic responsibilities? 10.1

   A   Personal responsibilities are not to society as a whole, but to oneself and/or only a select few.

   B   Only civic responsibilities are important.

   C   Failure to fulfill personal responsibilities never affects others in society.

   D   Personal responsibilities tend to cause tension and require sacrifice, whereas civic responsibilities rarely do.

96. The United States economy is one in which producers are generally free to produce what they want and consumers are free to purchase what they desire, so long as no laws are broken. At the same time, however, the government does regulate some aspects of the economy. The US can BEST be described as which of the following. 7.6

   A   a market economy

   B   command economy

   C   liberated economy

   D   mixed economy

97. Patricia is an elected official in the federal government. She is one of 20 people representing her home state in the house of Congress in which she serves. She hopes that in time she will have enough popularity and influence among her colleagues to be elected to the position of Speaker. Patricia is a member of what body of government? 2.2

   A   the US Senate

   B   the US Supreme Court

   C   the US House of Representatives

   D   the US Executive Branch

98. Which of the following statements most accurately defines the term "interest rate"? 8.5

   A   the level of attention that economists pay to economic activity at any one time

   B   money paid by banks and financial institutions to the US government

   C   money paid by a borrower to a lender in exchange for the use of money

   D   discounts on purchases made with a credit card

99. Someone who believes in the "tossed salad" theory would most likely support which one of the following statements? 10.2

   A   "Assimilation on the part of American citizens is crucial to our survival as a nation."

   B   "The increasing number of minorities living in our community serves to enrich our neighborhood in a great way."

   C   "It is good for our nation to have people of all backgrounds, so long as we are all willing to sacrifice our cultural differences in order to maintain the status quo."

   D   "mulitculturalism is a dangerous trend in America."

100. Which of the following is associated with a command economy? 8.2

   A   full employment

   B   private property

   C   inventions

   D   innovations

EVALUATION CHART FOR NORTH CAROLINA CIVICS AND ECONOMICS END OF COURSE TEST

Directions: On the following chart, circle the question numbers that you answered incorrectly and evaluate the results. These questions are based on the North Carolina Competency Standards. Then turn to the appropriate topics (listed by chapters), read the explanations, and complete the exercises. Review other chapters as needed. Finally, complete the practice test(s) to assess your progress and further prepare you for the *North Carolina Civics and Economics End of Course Test*.

*Note: Some question numbers may appear under multiple chapters because those questions require demonstration of multiple skills.

Chapter	Diagnostic Test Question
1. Foundations of the United States Political System	1, 2, 3, 7, 9, 10, 12, 14, 15, 16, 18, 25, 30, 36, 40, 65
2. The Government of the United States of America	19, 20, 21, 23, 24, 26, 33, 34, 47, 51, 52, 97
3. State and Local Governments Under the North Carolina Constitution	5, 8, 35, 37, 38, 55, 64
4. Active Citizenship	6, 11, 13, 27, 32, 42, 43, 44, 49, 63
5. Conflict in the United States' Political and Judicial Systems	29, 50, 53, 60, 68, 74
6. Purpose, Development, and Implementation of Laws	4, 31, 39, 61, 62, 66, 67, 71
7. Making Economic Decisions	54, 57, 72, 77, 81, 82, 96
8. The US Economy	28, 41, 46, 58, 73, 79, 80, 83, 84, 85, 86, 98, 100
9. Factors Influencing the US Economy	17, 56, 70, 75, 76, 87, 88, 89, 90, 91, 92, 93, 94
10. Issues and Responsibilities in US Society	22, 45, 48, 59, 69, 78, 95, 99

Chapter 1
Foundations of the United States Political System

This chapter addresses the following competency goal and objective(s):

Competency goal 1	The learner will investigate the foundations of the American political system and explore basic values and principles of American democracy.
Objective 1.01 1.02, 1.03, 1.04, 1.05, 1.06, 1.07, 1.08	

1.1 LIFE AND DIVERSITY IN COLONIAL NORTH AMERICA

During the 17th century, many people left England and journeyed to North America for a variety of reasons. Some wanted to gain wealth. Others hoped to find a place where they could freely practice their own religion. Together, these settlers established colonies along the Atlantic coast from Georgia to Maine. Their different motivations, as well as the geographic diversity of the land, contributed to a great deal of economic, political, and social diversity within the English colonies.

REGIONAL DIVISIONS IN THE COLONIES

The British colonies were divided into three geographic regions. The **New England Colonies** included Massachusetts, New Hampshire, Rhode Island, and Connecticut. The **Middle Colonies** consisted of New York, New Jersey, Pennsylvania, and Delaware. The **Southern Colonies** were made up of Maryland, Virginia, North Carolina, South Carolina, and Georgia. Some colonies were established as **royal colonies**. These colonies were governed directly by the king through an appointed royal governor. Other colonies (like North Carolina) were established as **proprietary colonies** because they were founded by individuals or groups to which

Original 13 Colonies

the king had granted ownership of the land. Still others were considered **charter colonies** because they were established by charters granted by the king. These charters granted colonies the right to govern themselves to a great extent.

REASONS FOR COMING TO THE NEW WORLD

After two failed attempts to settle in what is today North Carolina, the first successful English settlement was **Jamestown**, Virginia in 1607. It was founded by a **joint-stock company** (a company owned by a group of investors) called the Virginia Company. The Virginia Company hoped to make money off of the products and raw materials the colony would provide. The first few years, however, were hard. Bitter cold winters, disease, and starvation killed many of the settlers. Fortunately, the local Native Americans helped, allowing Jamestown to survive and grow. Many new settlers came to the colony hoping to get rich and obtain land.

In addition to wealth, there were other reasons people came to America. **Religious dissent** was one of the most common. The Anglican Church had long been England's official church. Since Europeans strongly identified religion with nationality, any protest or refusal to follow church teachings was seen as a betrayal. As a result, those with different religious views saw America as a place to escape persecution. One such group was the **Puritans**. They wanted to establish a community built solely on "pure biblical teaching" rather than Anglican traditions. In 1620, a group of Puritans established a colony at Plymouth, Massachusetts. These Puritans became known as the "**Pilgrims**" and celebrated the first Thanksgiving in 1621. Later, another group of Puritans established the Massachusetts Bay Colony; making New England a region strongly influenced by the Puritan faith.

Puritans

William Penn

Other colonies were founded for religious freedom as well. People like Roger Williams and Anne Hutchinson helped form Rhode Island after they left Massachusetts over disagreements with Puritan leaders. Under the leadership of William Penn, Pennsylvania became a homeland for **Quakers**. This religious group did not recognize class differences, promoted equality of the sexes, practiced pacifism (non-violence), and sought to deal fairly with Native Americans. They also made Pennsylvania a place of religious tolerance. In the early 1630s, Lord Baltimore started Maryland as a colony for **Catholics**. Although the colony actually boasted more Protestants than Catholics, it provided a place where Catholics could live and practice their faith free from persecution.

Georgia was unique among the colonies because it was established as a haven for English debtors (those imprisoned because they could not pay their debts). It also served as a buffer between the British colonies and Spanish Florida to the south.

Chapter 1

COLONIAL ECONOMY

In 1612, a man named John Rolfe discovered a new crop that was unknown in England—tobacco! Tobacco became incredibly popular in Europe and ended up being an important cash crop for Virginia, Maryland, and North Carolina. Settlers in North Carolina also produced tar, pitch, and turpentine. As a result, they came to be called "Tar Heels." Because of their hot and wet climates, rice and eventually indigo became just as important for South Carolina and Georgia as tobacco was for other southern colonies. The South's reliance on these staple crops (crops that are in large demand and provide the bulk of a

region's income) led to the rise of the **plantation system**. Plantations were huge farms owned by wealthy landowners who raised cash crops. Because these plantations required lots of manual labor, indentured servants and slavery became important parts of the southern economy. **Indentured servants** were people who could not afford to come to North America on their own. They agreed to work for a landowner for up to seven years in exchange for the landowner paying for their trip. This system eventually gave way to **slavery** (a system in which people are "owned" like property). By the mid 1600s, slavery was firmly rooted throughout the colonies, especially in the South. In South Carolina, African-American slaves actually outnumbered free Europeans throughout the 1700s. These slaves normally arrived by way of the **Middle Passage** (the route taken by ships carrying slaves from Africa to North America). The trip was called the "Middle Passage" because it was the middle leg of the **triangular trade route** (trade between 3 points: England, Africa, and the Americas). So brutal and inhumane was the treatment that these slaves endured during the Middle Passage that many of them died along the way.

In the Middle Colonies, farmers raised wheat, barley, and rye. Unlike the Southern Colonies, however, the Middle Colonies also relied on commerce. Large cities like New York and Philadelphia were home to diverse groups of people and a variety of businesses. In addition, they were important ports for shipping products overseas. Because of the nature of the economy, slaves in the Middle Colonies were not as numerous and they often worked in shops and cities, as well as on farms.

Rather than raising cash crops, the New England Colonies relied heavily on the Atlantic Ocean. Shipbuilding and fishing became leading industries in the region. New Englanders transported goods from England to other regions. From these regions they acquired products that could be traded for African slaves, etc. Although New Englanders farmed as well, their farms tended to be smaller and for the primary purpose of allowing families to be self-sufficient.

Because the British colonies all bordered the Atlantic, water travel and shipping became very important parts of the colonial economy. Since much of the territory was still rough and undeveloped, transporting goods over land was difficult. As a result, the major cities of the North and the few towns of the South tended to grow up along the coast and major waterways. The sea also provided a living for many colonists. Although some of the fish, clams, oysters, etc. they caught were for self-consumption, much of it was salted and traded overseas.

The colonial economy was also important to England. During the second half of the 1600s, many western European countries adopted the idea of **mercantilism**. They believed that a nation could best grow wealthy and secure if it exported more products than it imported. The British colonies were important because they provided both resources for England's use and additional markets for English products.

COLONIAL SOCIETY

Most colonial Americans accepted class distinctions. As a result, a small group of wealthy landowners exercised most of the power in each colony. In northern colonies, one found both farmers and merchants. In the South, society tended to be divided between rich plantation owners, poor farmers, and slaves. In 1676, this system actually resulted in an armed conflict known as **Bacon's Rebellion**. Nathaniel Bacon, a Virginia planter, rallied forces to fight Native Americans on the Virginia frontier. When the colony's governor condemned his actions, Bacon turned his army on Jamestown. Those supporting Bacon demanded more representation in government for the "common man." Bacon's Rebellion showed that colonists expected a government that served more than just the wealthy few. They wanted a government where even "ordinary" citizens have a voice.

Colonial Woman

In most cases, **colonial women** were considered to be second class citizens.   Although they tended to enjoy greater freedom and more expanded roles than women in England, they still could not vote, nor could they attend school. By law, they were normally considered to be under their husband's control. Their main responsibilities were bearing and raising children, as well as taking care of the home. In some cases, when a husband was unavailable or had died, women owned property or took on roles traditionally held by men.

COLONIAL GOVERNMENT

Due to the colonies' great distance from England, the British adopted a policy known as **salutary neglect**. In other words, they basically let the colonists govern themselves. While colonial governors were technically in charge, colonial legislatures came to possess most of the power because of their control over colonial funds. These legislatures typically consisted of two houses (much like the British Parliament). One was an advisory council appointed by the governor. The other was a body elected by voters. The freedom these colonial governments enjoyed eventually helped lead to the start of the American Revolution.

Chapter 1

ETHNIC AND RELIGIOUS DIVERSITY

While many religious groups came to America to escape persecution, not all of them believed in religious tolerance. In the Massachusetts Bay Colony, for instance, every settler had to attend and support the Puritan church. Dissenters were often banished from the colony. In 1692, this commitment to protect the Puritan faith resulted in one of the darkest episodes in American history—the **Salem Witch Trials**. Claiming that they had been possessed by the devil, several young girls in Salem, Massachusetts accused various townspeople of being witches. Before it was over, colonial authorities actually brought the accused to trial and condemned a number of them to death.

Salem Witch Trial

Religious tolerance did exist in some colonies, however. Following his banishment from Massachusetts, Roger Williams founded Providence, Rhode Island as a colony guaranteeing religious freedom. In the Middle Colonies, Pennsylvania attracted not only the English Quakers, but German Lutherans, Scotch-Irish Presbyterians, and Swiss Mennonites as well. Because New York was originally a Dutch colony, it exhibited linguistic and cultural diversity, as well as religious differences. It even boasted the colonies' first synagogue (place of Jewish worship). In Maryland, the Toleration Act protected religious freedom (at least for Christians) throughout the colony.

Although most Europeans tended to fare well once the colonies were firmly established, Native Americans and blacks were not so fortunate. While some **African-Americans** were free, most were slaves. Meanwhile, **Native Americans** were continually pushed off of land they had occupied for generations by white settlers moving west.

Practice 1: Life and Diversity in Colonial America

1. Historians traditionally divide the original thirteen colonies into which of the following categories?

   A. North, West, East, and South
   B. North, Middle, South
   C. New England, Middle, Southern
   D. New England, Middle, Plantation

2. The King has a good friend whom he wants to reward. For this reason, he gives his friend a charter to establish and govern his own territory in the Americas. This colony will be which of the following?

   A. a royal colony
   B. a proprietary colony
   C. a charter/self-governing colony
   D. a joint-stock colony

3. How did money and religion play a role in settlers choosing to come to North America from England? Give one example of a colony founded for economic reasons and one of a colony founded for religious reasons.

   James town

4.   Describe England's approach to governing its colonies.

1.2 SELF-GOVERNMENT IN THE COLONIES

ANCIENT GREECE TO THE RENAISSANCE

Earlier governments laid a foundation for the representative governments that developed in the colonies. Thousands of years before the British Empire, the ancient Greeks practiced **democracy** (a form of government in which the people rule by voting or voicing their opinions). Later the ancient Romans modified this concept by forming a **republic**. Unlike a direct democracy in which all qualified citizens vote on laws, whether or not to go to war, what taxes to impose, etc., a republic is a form of government in which the people elect representatives to vote on such matters for them.

Debate in the Roman Senate

During the Middle Ages (period of history stretching from the 5th until the 15th and 16th centuries AD) republican forms of government faded from the scene in favor of autocracies (governments ruled by a single sovereign, such as a king, queen, or emperor). As a result, most Europeans believed that those in authority were not to be questioned and that the people were to serve their leaders, rather than vice versa. Then, in the 15th century, Europe experienced a period known as the **Renaissance**. The word means "rebirth" and refers to a time in which many Europeans emphasized a reconnection with the classical ideas of ancient Greece and Rome. This led to **classical republicanism**, which took the ideas of the ancient Roman republic and revised them to fit modern Europe.

MAGNA CARTA AND PARLIAMENT

Even before the end of the Middle Ages, the first rumblings of limited government were already felt in England. **Limited government** is government that must obey a set of laws. These laws are usually in the form of a written document. In 1215, a group of English nobles forced King John I to sign such a document. Known as the **Magna Carta** or **"Great Charter"**, this document granted the nobles various legal rights and prevented the King from imposing taxes without the consent of a council. This idea of a council eventually gave birth to the British **Parliament**. Originally formed in the 13th century, Parliament came to be comprised of two houses. The upper house, known as the House of Lords, consists of appointed noblemen. The lower house, known as the House of Commons,

is made up of elected officials and provided English citizens a voice in their national government. In 1689, Parliament gained additional power as a result of the **English Bill of Rights**. Under the English Bill of Rights, the monarch could not interfere with Parliamentary elections, nor could he/she impose taxes without Parliament's consent. It also granted citizens the right to a speedy trial, forbade cruel and unusual punishment, and granted citizens the right to petition the government. Both Parliament and the English Bill of Rights became models for the US Constitution and the government it established. English government was also limited by **common law**. First established during the Middle Ages, common law is law based on tradition or past court decisions, rather than on a written statute. Today, the idea of relying on past legal decisions where no formal statute (written law) exists is an important aspect of the US legal system.

IMPACT OF THE ENLIGHTENMENT

Beginning in the late 1600s, Europe experienced the **Enlightenment**. The Enlightenment was a time that featured revolutionary ideas in philosophy and political thought. During this time, a number of philosophers introduced concepts that later helped form American ideas about government. **Thomas Hobbes** (1588-1679) wrote that all people are born with certain rights; the greatest of which is the right to protect one's own life. Since each person seeking to preserve his/her own life can lead to chaos, Hobbes believed that strong government was necessary to maintain order. He believed that the people should defer to the will of the sovereign (i.e., king). Any abuses by government are to be accepted as the price of maintaining order and peace. **John Locke** (1632 – 1704) later built on Hobbes' ideas. Locke's thoughts on government challenged the old view that monarchs possess a God-given right to rule with citizens

Thomas Hobbes

obligated to obey. Locke believed that people were born with certain **"natural rights"** that no government could morally take away. These rights include life, liberty, and property. He also advocated what is often referred to as *social contract theory*. According to this philosophy, there is an implied contract between government and citizens. Citizens are born with freedom and rights. However, for the good of society, people agree to give up certain freedoms and empower governments to maintain order. In other words, citizens submit themselves to laws and governments in order to serve the **common good** and cultivate **civic virtue** (behavior geared towards the betterment of society rather than simply one's own interests). Unlike Hobbes, however, Locke believed that if a government failed to fulfill this role, then that government should be replaced. His views were eventually used by many to justify the American Revolution.

Montesquieu (1689 –1755) was a French political philosopher who believed that the best form of government was one that featured a separation of powers. He advocated three branches of government, each with some degree of power over the others (checks and balances). **Voltaire** (1694 –1778) was another French philosopher who supported free speech, freedom of expression, and freedom of religion. **Jean Jacque Rousseau** (1712 –1778) promoted equality, a principle on which the Declaration of Independence was based.

Foundations of the United States Political System

SELF-GOVERNMENT IN THE AMERICAN COLONIES

Established in 1619, Virginia's **House of Burgesses** was the first body of elected officials in the New World. Although only white males who owned property were permitted to vote, it demonstrated a belief among colonists that citizens should have a voice in their government. In New England, the first efforts at self-government were defined in the **Mayflower Compact**. The Puritan settlers at Plymouth drafted this document while still on board the Mayflower. It established an elected legislature and asserted that the government derived its power from the people of the colony. It also implied the colonists' desire to be ruled by a local government, rather than England. This belief in representative government often took the form of **town meetings**, particularly in New England. These were times when local citizens met together to discuss and vote on issues. Once again, it gave citizens a say in their government and helped to firmly establish a belief in democratic ideals.

Signing of the Mayflower Compact

In 1636, colonists under the leadership of Thomas Hooker left the Massachusetts Bay Colony and established a new colony at Hartford, Connecticut. They wrote a body of laws for their colony called the **Fundamental Orders of Connecticut**. It stated that the government's power came only from the "free consent of the people" and set limits on what the government could do.

First Continental Congress

The influences of the Enlightenment, the idea of limited government, and the experience of over 100 years of self-government in the colonies, led to the **First Continental Congress** in 1774. The Congress was a gathering of colonial leaders that met primarily to respond to a series of laws passed by Parliament. The colonists felt that these laws violated their "natural rights." In a statement to the King, the Congress wrote that the colonists had a right to be represented in their government. Since the colonies were not represented in Parliament, they were entitled to govern themselves. When their appeal fell on deaf ears in England, the delegates met again for the **Second Continental Congress**. This time, it was for the purpose of throwing off British rule altogether.

Practice 2: Self-Government in the Colonies

1. Which of the following describes the idea that a government cannot do whatever it wants, but rather is constrained by a set of laws?

    A. Limited government   C. Democracy

    B. Classical republicanism   D. Fundamental government

2. Which of the following BEST describes John Locke's philosophy of government?

    A. Because each citizen has certain "natural rights" it is the duty of government to impose its will regardless of what citizens think.

    B. Social contract theory is an outdated philosophy and should be replaced with the idea of classical republicanism.

    C. It is the privilege of citizens to replace any government that fails to protect "natural rights" and uphold the common good.

    D. Subjects to the Crown are there to serve their king without question.

3. How did the history of British government and the ideas of the Enlightenment affect colonial government?

1.3 CAUSES OF THE AMERICAN REVOLUTION

The roots of the American Revolution went all the way back to the late 1600s. Because of mercantilism, nations tried to maintain a **favorable balance of trade**. In other words, they wanted to sell more than they bought from other countries. To maintain such a balance, nations needed colonies for additional resources and markets. In 1660, England passed the **Navigation Acts**. These laws required the British colonies to sell certain goods only to England. The few products the colonies could sell to other countries were charged a British duty (tax). Strict enforcement of the Navigation Acts ultimately contributed to the call for revolution.

Benjamin Franklin

The desire for territory produced by mercantilism also meant that nations ended up fighting over land. As British colonists moved west, they found themselves fighting French settlers and Native Americans. In 1754, this tension between French and British colonials resulted in the **French and Indian War**. It was so named because it was fought against the French and their Native American allies. After nine years of fighting, France finally surrendered and gave up its claims in Canada and all lands east of the Mississippi River. Great Britain now stood alone as the one, true colonial power in North America. In addition, a political foundation was laid that later served an important purpose. Shortly after the fighting began, British colonial leaders recognized the need for more unity. In 1754, a group of them met in Albany New York. It was there that one of the delegates, Benjamin Franklin, proposed the **Albany Plan of Union**. Franklin's plan called for a permanent union of the colonies under one representative government. Although the colonies rejected the plan, it eventually served as a model for the government that formed after the revolution.

TENSIONS RISE BETWEEN GREAT BRITAIN AND THE COLONIES

King George III

Soon after the French and Indian War, relations between England and its colonies deteriorated. The colonists had lost respect for Britain's military, viewing it as ill-prepared and unsuited for fighting on the American terrain. Meanwhile, Great Britain was heavily in debt after fighting to defend its colonies and felt that the Americans should help pay for the expense. As a result, it took a number of steps the colonists found offensive. In 1760, England began issuing *writs of assistance*. These were general search warrants that allowed British authorities to search whatever they wanted and for whatever reason. The British used these writs to board and search colonial ships as a way of enforcing the Navigation Acts. So offensive were these searches to the colonists, that when they drafted the US *Bill of Rights* years later, they included an amendment placing restrictions on the government's right to search and seizure.

Three years later, in response to Native American attacks in territories won from the French, King George III issued the **Proclamation of 1763**. It forbade colonists from settling west of the Appalachian Mountains and put the territory under British military control. Colonists resented the King's restrictions and many ignored the proclamation.

Foundations of the United States Political System

Beginning in the mid 1760s, Parliament passed a series of laws and taxes that infuriated the Americans. The **Quartering Act** required colonists to house and supply British soldiers stationed in North America. The **Stamp Act** taxed nearly all printed material by requiring that it bear a government stamp. Many printers protested the new law. In 1734, a printer named **John Peter Zenger** had won an important case in which he claimed that he could not be sued for libel if what he printed was true. The court agreed, and Zenger's victory helped affirm freedom of the press in the colonies. Now, through the Stamp Act, many saw the British government as interfering with this freedom. In response, a delegation of colonists met in what came to be known as the **Stamp Act Congress**. One of its leaders, James Otis, protested the tax proclaiming, "No taxation without representation!"

Boston Massacre

Remember, under British law, no tax could be imposed except one approved by Parliament. Since the colonies had no representation in Parliament, Otis and others believed that they should not be subject to new taxes. In protest, the colonies imposed a boycott of British goods. A boycott simply means that they refused to buy them, thereby withholding money that would otherwise go to English businesses. A group called the **Sons of Liberty** took it upon themselves to enforce the boycotts and used violence and intimidation to prevent the implementation of British laws. The boycotts, along with violent responses to the Stamp Act, eventually led England to repeal (cancel) the law. However, on the same day that it repealed the Stamp Act, Parliament passed the **Declaratory Act**. This act stated that Parliament had the authority to impose laws on the colonies. In effect, England was telling the colonies that it expected them to comply with British laws whether they felt represented or not.

In 1767, Parliament passed the **Townshend Acts**, which taxed imported goods like glass and tea. So violent was colonial reaction to these laws that England sent troops to Boston. On March 5, 1770, British soldiers who felt threatened by a mob of angry protesters fired shots that left several colonists dead or dying. The event became known as the **Boston Massacre** and was depicted as a brutal slaying of innocent civilians. As a result, colonial resentment increased.

THE REVOLUTIONARY CAUSE

Shortly after the "massacre", the Townshend Acts were repealed (except for the duty on tea) and tensions subsided. They did not, however, go away. Years of **salutary neglect** would not allow Americans to accept England's firm control over them. Many colonies organized **Committees of Correspondence**. These were groups dedicated to organizing colonial resistance against the Crown. One such committee took bold action in December 1773 when its members dressed as Mohawk Indians and marched to Boston Harbor. There, in what became known as the **Boston Tea Party**, they raided ships hauling British tea and threw the crates overboard. In response, Parliament passed the **Coercive Acts** (because of their harshness, the colonists labeled them the **Intolerable Acts**).

Boston Tea Party

These acts closed Boston Harbor and placed a military governor over Massachusetts. In addition, England expanded the Canadian border, thereby taking land away from certain colonies.

Chapter 1

Thomas Paine

Then, in 1775, all hope of a peaceful resolution was lost when fighting broke out at Lexington and Concord. As British troops were on their way to seize arms and ammunition stored by colonists at Concord, Massachusetts, they were met at Lexington by colonial militia (voluntary, local military units consisting of private citizens rather than full-time soldiers). It was there that someone (to this day no one is sure who) fired the **"shot heard 'round the world"** that started the American Revolution. In January 1776, Thomas Paine published his famous pamphlet, *Common Sense*. In it, he made a compelling case for independence that won many to the cause. Later that same year, the principles on which the revolution was based were powerfully summarized by Thomas Jefferson in the **Declaration of Independence**. It echoed many of the beliefs put forth by John Locke and others. Appealing to the "natural rights" of men and the belief that governments have a responsibility to the people, the Declaration of Independence proclaimed that the United States of America was forevermore a free nation.

Practice 3: Causes of the American Revolution

1. What were some of the reasons why relations between the colonies and England deteriorated after the French and Indian War? loss respect for British military resented the British military

2. "No taxation without representation!" refers to which of the following ideas?

    A. The French had no reason to tax Native Americans.

    B. The Continental Congress had no right to impose taxes on independent colonies.

    C. Taxes could not be imposed on territories won from the French.

    D. The colonies should not be subject to taxes from a government in which they have no voice.

3. How did the Albany Plan of Union and Great Britain's *writs of assistance* later impact the new United States government? led to the idea of Constitution

1.4 EMERGENCE OF AN AMERICAN IDENTITY

PUBLIC EDUCATION

Although most children in the colonies received little formal education, there were exceptions. New England was the first region to begin developing **public education**. Puritans believed that everyone should be able to read the Bible. Therefore, they put a high priority on literacy. This emphasis on education eventually spread to other fields as well. In 1647, Massachusetts passed laws requiring public schools for towns of 50 families or more. In addition, towns of 100 or more families were required to establish grammar schools to prepare young boys for college. Generally, only boys attended these schools, while girls were trained for "womanly duties" at home. In the Middle and Southern Colonies, public education did not come about as quickly. Parents tended to instruct their children at home. In the South, rich plantation owners often hired private tutors or sent their children to Europe to be educated.

Colonial School

Colonists also founded colleges. Initially, these colleges were primarily for the purpose of training ministers. Harvard and Yale in New England and William and Mary in Virginia were among the first colleges established.

THE IMPACT OF CHRISTIANITY

The impact of Christianity was evident throughout the colonies. In New England, nearly every aspect of life revolved around the Puritan church or some branch of Puritan religion. In the Middle Colonies, there was an unprecedented amount of **religious pluralism** (variety of religious beliefs). Most were Protestants, but they came from a variety of church traditions. Quakers, Lutherans, and Mennonites were but a few of the Christian groups that occupied the Middle Colonies. Catholics enjoyed protection in Maryland. Meanwhile, further south, most rich landowners remained members of the Anglican Church. Over time, Methodist and Baptist congregations became common among poorer Southerners and settlers along the frontier because they were willing to adopt new methods for reaching rural areas.

Beginning in the 1730s, the colonies experienced what was known as the **First Great Awakening**. The "Awakening" was a religious movement that featured passionate preaching from evangelists like Jonathan Edwards and George Whitefield. These ministers believed that many in the colonies had forsaken God for "dead religion" and called people back to "sincere Christian commitment". While many embraced their revivals (services where traveling preachers would speak), some traditional church leaders rejected such preaching as too emotional and offensive. The Great Awakening served to encourage colonists to think for themselves on religious matters. As a result, **freedom of religion** and the idea of **separation of church and state** (the government not imposing a particular religion or church membership on its citizens, but rather allowing citizens to practice their own faith) became valued colonial principles.

THE PRINCIPLE OF EGALITARIANISM

Thanks to Locke, Rousseau, and others, many people embraced **egalitarianism** in the 1700s. Egalitarianism is the idea that all men are created equal and possess "natural rights" simply because they are human beings. In the colonies, this led to representative governments and the conviction that governments derive their power from the **consent of the governed**. In other words, the government is responsible to its people. The people, therefore, are entitled to a voice and have the right to replace any unjust government. Such beliefs also contributed to a sense of American **nationalism** (pride in one's country). The more the colonies felt persecuted by England, the more they banded together. Patrick Henry electrified the delegates to the First Continental Congress when he passionately proclaimed, "I am no longer a Virginian; I am an American!" It was the first time a notable leader publicly identified himself with the "nation," rather than a single colony.

John Locke

LIMITED "EQUALITY"

Although egalitarianism was popular in principle, in practice, colonial society did not exhibit equality for all. Generally, only white males who owned land were granted **suffrage** (the right to vote). African-Americans, Native Americans, and women were not given this right. This was ironic since colonial leaders themselves claimed that no person should be subject to the laws of a government in which they have no voice.

Colonial Slavery

As mentioned earlier, **slavery** was an established part of life throughout the colonies. In South Carolina and Georgia, where rice was the predominant crop, slaves tended to be used mostly in the fields and remained somewhat segregated from white society. Since cultivating tobacco took less time than rice, slaves in Virginia, North Carolina, and Maryland also served in other capacities and had more direct contact with whites. As a result, they tended to adopt more European customs and behavior. In the Middle Colonies and New England, slaves were often trained in a craft and then put to work in shops and cities. Some were even permitted to make money provided they paid a share of their earnings to their master. In this way, some blacks were able to buy their own freedom.

Practice 4: Emergence of an American Identity

1. In which of the following colonies would one have most likely found a public school?
   A. North Carolina   B. Maryland   C. Massachusetts   D. Michigan

2. The First Great Awakening is an example of which of the following?
   A. The impact of passionate political speeches in colonial America
   B. The impact of nationalism in colonial America
   C. The impact of Christianity on colonial America
   D. The impact of belief in egalitarianism on America

3. What does it mean to say that governments derive their power from the "consent of the governed," and how did belief in this principle help justify the American Revolution?

1.5 ARTICLES OF CONFEDERATION AND THE UNITED STATES CONSTITUTION

Once the colonies declared independence, they became individual states. As such, they quickly drew up their own state **constitutions** (documents that lay out the laws and principles of a government). However, they also needed a national body of laws. Cautious about giving too much power to a central government, Congress drafted the **Articles of Confederation**. Finally ratified in 1781, this document did not give enough power to the federal (national) government for it to lead effectively. In order for any law passed by Congress to be final, at least nine of the 13 states had to agree. Since the states often had different interests, such agreement was rare. Also, the

Treaty of Paris

Articles did not grant Congress the power to impose taxes. The federal government had to *ask* the states for money. As you might imagine, this was not very effective and made it practically impossible to administer the government or provide for a national defense. In 1783, the **Treaty of Paris** officially ended the American Revolution and Great Britain acknowledged the United States as a free nation. Foreign countries quickly realized, however, the glaring weaknesses in the Articles of Confederation. As a result, Britain refused to withdraw troops from the Ohio Valley and Spain closed its port at New Orleans, cutting off the Mississippi River. Unable to raise a formidable army, the United States was in no position to oppose such actions.

Change finally came as a result of **Shay's Rebellion** in 1786. After the war, the United States experienced an economic depression, in which farm prices dropped and many farmers could not repay outstanding loans. At the same time, in order to pay war debts, the state of Massachusetts raised taxes (the national government could not impose taxes, but state governments could). Outraged, a Massachusetts farmer and Revolutionary War veteran named Daniel Shay led a number of farmers in rebellion. Without an adequate national government, Massachusetts was forced to deal with the revolt on its own. The event made it evident that a stronger central government was needed, and leaders called a convention to revise the Articles of Confederation.

THE NORTHWEST TERRITORY

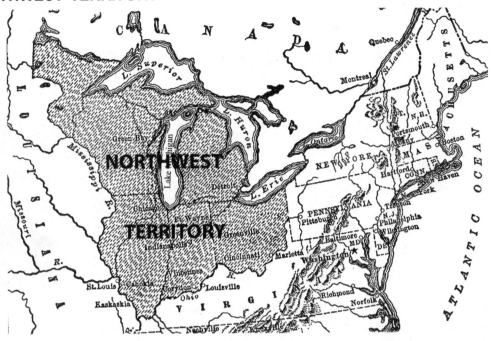

Congress did pass two important acts under the Articles. Both concerned the Northwest Territory (the region lying north of the Ohio and east of the Mississippi rivers). The **Land Ordinance of 1785** divided the land into townships and allowed Congress to raise money by selling the land to settlers. Two years later, Congress passed the **Northwest Ordinance**. This law divided the area into even smaller territories and provided guidelines under which new states could be admitted to the union. It eventually resulted in the formation of five states: Ohio, Indiana, Illinois, Michigan, and Wisconsin.

THE UNITED STATES CONSTITUTION

In 1787, a delegation met in Philadelphia to revise the Articles of Confederation. Soon after the convention began, however, the delegates decided to do away with the document altogether and write a new set of laws. The result was the **United States Constitution**. All the delegates in attendance (only Rhode Island did not send representatives) agreed that change was necessary. However, how the national government should be reorganized was a matter of much debate. Edmund Randolph and James Madison of Virginia introduced the **Virginia Plan**. They proposed a federal government made up of three branches: a legislative branch to make the laws, an executive branch to enforce the laws, and a judicial branch to make sure that the laws were administered fairly. For the legislative branch, the Virginia Plan called for two houses with representatives from each state. In each house, the number of representatives per state would be determined by population. The greater a state's population, the more representatives it would have. Larger states loved the idea; but smaller states hated it because they would be left with less representation. As a result, one of New Jersey's delegates proposed the **New Jersey Plan**. Like the Virginia Plan, it also called for three branches of government, but it wanted the legislative branch to consist of only one house with each state getting a single vote. In the end, the delegates decided on a compromise. It became known as the **Great Compromise**, or the **Connecticut Plan**, because it was proposed by Roger Sherman of Connecticut. It established a legislative branch with two houses. One house, called the *House of Representatives*, would be elected directly by the people and each state granted a certain number of seats based on population. The other house, called the *Senate*, would be elected by state legislatures with each state having two senators, regardless of population. Together the two houses would comprise Congress.

Slavery also proved to be a point of contention. Northern states had fewer slaves and argued that, since slaves were not voting citizens, they should not be counted as part of the population. Southern states, however, had far more slaves and wanted to count them. The answer to this question was important because it affected how many representatives each state would have in Congress. Again, a compromise was reached. It was known as the **Three-Fifths Compromise** because it stated that each slave would count as "three-fifths of a person." In other words, for every five slaves, a state would be credited for having three people. Meanwhile, debate about the slave trade resulted in a **slave trade compromise**. Under this agreement, Northerners who opposed the slave trade agreed to allow it to continue for twenty years, after which time Congress could impose regulations. This was important to Southerners who insisted that their economy could not survive without the slave trade.

Constitutional Convention

The Constitution also established the office of the president of the United States as head of the Executive Branch of government. However, in 1787, it was not practical to have every citizen vote for this national office. Therefore, the decision was made that the president would be chosen by electors to the **Electoral College**. This body's sole purpose is to elect the president every four years. If no majority can be reached in the Electoral College, then the election is decided by the House of Representatives (this has happened twice: 1800 and 1824).

Despite the fact that the new document was an amazing improvement from the Articles of Confederation, a number of states (including North Carolina) refused to ratify it, claiming it did not do enough to guarantee the rights of citizens. Finally, in late 1788, the last of the nine sttes needed approved the Constitution once Congress agreed to consider a number of amendments protecting civil liberties. Only North Carolina and Rhode Island held off until after these amendments had actually been submitted to Congress. When Congress met in 1789, one of its first orders of business was to pass these amendments. It consists of the first ten amendments (additions) to the Constitution and stems from many of the principles for which the American Revolution was fought.

Practice 5: Articles of Confederation and the United States Constitution

1. The Articles of Confederation proved ineffective as a national body of laws for which of the following reasons?

   A. It gave too much power to the Congress without providing for a commander of the nation's armed forces.
   B. It did not give the federal government enough power to effectively lead.
   C. It imposed taxes that led to a rebellion of farmers in New England.
   D. It prevented Congress from passing legislation regarding the Northwest Territory.

2. Why did smaller states oppose the Virginia Plan and how did the Great Compromise set their fears at ease?

  A. They opposed the Virginia Plan because it wanted to include slaves in the population count, thereby giving southern states even more power in Congress. The Great Compromise eased their fears by stating that after twenty years, Congress could decide not to include slaves in such a count.

  B. They opposed the Virginia Plan because it wanted to leave slaves out of the population count and smaller states needed their slaves counted if they were going to compete with the larger states. The Great Compromise eased their fears because it stated that slaves would be counted as three-fifths of a person in the population.

  C. They opposed the Virginia Plan because it advocated only one house in Congress that would be based on population. The Great Compromise eased their fears because it said that each state would be represented equally.

  D. They opposed the Virginia Plan because it advocated a legislative branch in which both houses of Congress would be based on population. The Great Compromise eased their fears because it called for one house to be based on population but the second to provide equal representation for each state.

3. What is the *Bill of Rights* and what purpose does it serve?

1.6 US GOVERNMENT AND THE FEDERALIST/ANTI-FEDERALIST DEBATE

Once delegates approved the new Constitution, the document went to the states for **ratification** (acceptance). Although only nine states were necessary for ratification, everyone knew it was important for *every* state to accept and support the new laws.

THE GOVERNMENT ESTABLISHED BY THE CONSTITUTION

The government established by the Constitution is a **republic**, because laws and government decisions are made by a body of elected officials. In order to prevent any one leader from becoming too powerful, the framers made sure that the new government featured a **separation of powers**. This was accomplished by dividing power between three branches of government (Legislative, Executive, and Judicial). To make sure that no one branch tried to use their authority to overpower the others, the Constitution also included a system of **checks and balances**. In other words, although one branch might enjoy a certain power, another branch can still "check" or "balance" its power if need be. For example: Congress has the power to propose and pass bills that become laws. The president, however, has the authority to "check" this power by vetoing (rejecting) the bill Congress passes, thereby preventing it from becoming a law. In turn, if Congress has enough votes, it can "balance" the president's power by overriding the veto (voting to ignore the president's rejection) in which case, the bill becomes law anyway. This is just one example of how checks and balances work.

Foundations of the United States Political System

One branch of government we have not talked much about is the **judiciary**, or **Judicial Branch**. In order to make sure that the laws passed by Congress and enforced by the president are applied appropriately, the Constitution called for a federal court system. The Judiciary Act of 1789 established both this court system and the authority of the Supreme Court. Justices (judges) are appointed by the president. However, before they can assume their duties, they must first be approved by the Senate. Once on the bench, these justices can then rule on whether or not laws passed by Congress or actions taken by the president are lawful. This is another example of checks and balances.

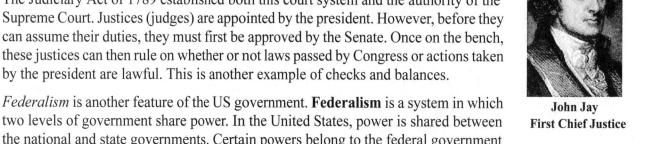

John Jay
First Chief Justice

Federalism is another feature of the US government. **Federalism** is a system in which two levels of government share power. In the United States, power is shared between the national and state governments. Certain powers belong to the federal government (negotiating treaties, declaring war, etc.) and some are given to the states (regulating public schools and local governments, deciding how elections will be run, etc.). A few are shared by both (i.e., the authority to build roads or impose taxes). Powers that are shared are called *concurrent powers*.

FEDERALISTS VS. ANTI-FEDERALISTS

Alexander Hamilton   Thomas Jefferson

The power of the central government became a major issue of debate during ratification of the Constitution. Many favored the Constitution because they believed that the United States needed a strong federal government with a powerful president at its head. Others opposed the Constitution because they feared that a powerful federal government would trample on their rights. Because of the debate, political leaders split into opposing **factions**. A faction is a group of people who are bound by a common belief or in a common cause, usually against another group bound by an opposing belief/cause. The faction that favored a strong central government and supported the Constitution was called the **Federalists**. Among their leaders were Alexander Hamilton, James Madison, and John Jay (first chief justice of the Supreme Court). The faction that opposed them and wanted to see stronger state governments was called the **Anti-federalists** (author of the *Declaration of Independence*, Thomas Jefferson, was an Anti-federalist). Federalists had a **loose interpretation** of the Constitution. They believed that the Constitution allowed the federal government to take certain actions not specifically stated (i.e., founding a national bank). By contrast, Anti-federalists held to a **strict interpretation**. They believed the federal government could only do what the Constitution specifically said. Eventually, with the support of men like George Washington, Alexander Hamilton, and John Adams, the Federalist view won. Anti-federalists did succeed, however, in securing the *Bill of Rights*.

Practice 6: The US Government and the Federalist/Anti-Federalist Debate

1. A system that ensures power is divided among several branches of government, each with the ability to limit the others' power to some degree is known as which of the following?

    A. A republican form of government
    B. Separation of powers and checks and balances
    C. Federalism
    D. Constitutional democracy

2. Which of the following describes the belief that the federal government can only do that which is specifically stated in the Constitution?

    A. A loose interpretation of the Constitution   C. Federalism
    B. A strict interpretation of the Constitution   D. Checks and balances

3. How did Federalists and Anti-federalists view the role of the federal government differently, and how did they feel about the Constitution as a result?

1.7 THE *BILL OF RIGHTS*

Of the twelve amendments that Congress passed in 1789, ten were ratified by the states. These ten amendments are known as the US *Bill of Rights*.

The *First Amendment* guarantees citizens' freedom of speech, freedom of the press (remember the case of John Peter Zenger), freedom to petition the government, and freedom to assemble. It also protects freedom of religion and establishes the principle of separation of church and state through the **Free Exercise Clause** (which forbids Congress from making any law prohibiting the free exercise of one's religious beliefs) and the **Establishment Clause** (which forbids Congress from establishing a religion).

The *Second Amendment* guarantees the **right to bear arms.** Although there is much debate today about the extent to which firearms should be available to private citizens, in the early days of the nation this right was considered crucial for maintaining armed local militias (remember, the first shots of the revolution were fired because the British attempted to take arms stored by private citizens in Concord).

The *Third Amendment* restricts **quartering** (housing) of federal troops in the homes of US citizens. Prior to the revolution, colonists were angered that they were forced to house British soldiers.

The *Fourth Amendment* protects citizens against unreasonable **searches and seizures**. The memory of Britain's *writs of assistance* inspired this amendment.

Foundations of the United States Political System

The *Fifth Amendment* clearly defines criminal proceedings by which a person may be arrested and charged with a crime. It ensures that no person shall be imprisoned or deprived of their property without **due process**. In other words, the government must obey the laws governing criminal and civil proceedings before it can put someone in jail or strip them of their property. In addition, this amendment protects citizens from the possibility of **double jeopardy**. A person cannot be tried for the same crime more than once. Neither can defendants be forced to testify against themselves in court. This is called protection from **self-incrimination.** Finally, this amendment also places limits on **eminent domain**. Eminent domain is the government's power to take private property for public use. Under the Constitution, the government cannot take a citizens property without paying "just compensation" (i.e., if the government takes someone's house, then they must pay that person what the house is worth).

Cruel Punishment

The *Sixth Amendment* protects the **rights of the accused**. This includes the right to a **public and speedy trial by jury**. A trial by jury simply means that a group of an accused person's peers decide his or her guilt or innocence, rather than a single government official. This amendment also guarantees the right to an attorney and to confront and call witnesses. The *Seventh Amendment* extends this right to a trial by jury to civil cases as well (i.e., when one person sues another for money).

The *Eighth Amendment* protects those arrested or found guilty of a crime. It prohibits the government from imposing **excessive bail/fines**. Bail is money an arrested person must pay to get out of jail until the date of his/her trial, while fines are amounts of money imposed as punishment for a crime one has been found guilty of. It also forbids **cruel and unusual punishment** of those convicted of a crime. Of course, what constitutes "cruel and unusual punishment" is often an issue of debate.

The *Ninth Amendment* simply says that the rights specifically mentioned in the *Bill of Rights* are not necessarily the only ones enjoyed by the people. Meanwhile, the *Tenth Amendment* says that those powers not restricted by the Constitution, nor delegated to the US government, are **reserved for the states**. In other words, the Constitution grants the states the authority to decide certain matters of law.

Practice 7: Bill of Rights

1. The *Free Exercise Clause* and the *Establishment Clause* are associated with protecting which of the following rights?

    A. the right to free speech
    C. the right to religious freedom
    B. the right to peaceful assembly
    D. the right to bear arms

2. Due process of law, protection from double jeopardy, and protection from self-incrimination are all guaranteed under which amendment?
    A. First
    B. Fourth
    C. Fifth
    D. Seventh

3. Which of the following statements is NOT true regarding the *Bill of Rights*?

    A. It clearly states that the rights listed in the first ten amendments are the only rights that citizens enjoy.
    B. It is comprised of the first ten amendments to the US Constitution
    C. It was not originally part of the Constitution, but rather was added later.
    D. It proclaims that certain powers are reserved for the states.

1.8 DIFFERENT MODELS OF GOVERNMENT

As mentioned before, the US government is a republic. Although similar, **republicanism** differs somewhat from democracy. While the people have a voice in their government under both models, a republic is a model of government where the people elect representatives to govern and make laws on their behalf. Meanwhile, in a direct **democracy**, the people themselves vote on such issues. In the case of the United States, it is a republic that practices federalism. **Federalism**, once again, simply means that power is shared between the federal and the state governments.

There are many other forms of government as well. An **autocracy** is a government in which power is rested in the hands of a single individual, such as an emperor or king. An **absolute monarchy** is ruled by a king or queen whose power is not limited by any laws or other bodies of government. In a **limited monarchy** (often called a **constitutional monarchy**) the king or queen must behave according to certain laws and usually shares power with other branches of government. England's government at the time of the American Revolution was just such a government, in which the king and Parliament shared power. A **dictatorship** is a model of government in which the ruling party has no restrictions. Their word is law. Many times, a dictatorship is an autocracy, because the dictator is a single individual. However, a collective body can also form a dictatorship as well. In **totalitarianism**, the state is considered far more important than individuals. Therefore, nearly every

Adolf Hitler

aspect of society is controlled by the government and political opposition is not permitted (i.e., Nazi Germany under Adolf Hitler). The "natural rights" championed by the founders of the United States would mean little in a totalitarian form of government. An **oligarchy** is a government in which power is in the hands of a small group of people. By comparison, an **aristocracy** is a government in which power rests in the hands of the upper classes. Aristocracies tend to offer little chance for poorer people to break out of poverty and change their social status, because the upper classes use their power to protect the status quo (keep things the way they are). Some societies base their government on religion. This kind of government is called a **theocracy**. The Taliban government overthrown by US forces in Afghanistan in 2001 was an example of a theocracy, because it was based on an interpretation of Muslim law. Finally, there is **anarchy**. Anarchy refers to the concept of having no government at all. No society, of course, can exist very long in a state of anarchy.

Practice 8: Different Models of Government

1. Two countries are deciding whether or not to declare war on each other. The first country calls on all of its citizens to vote on whether or not they want to go to war. The second country has an elected legislature that will decide on whether or not to fight. Which of the following BEST describes the models of government in the two countries?

    A. The first country is a democracy, while the second country practices federalism.

    B. The first country is an oligarchy, while the second country is a theocracy.

    C. One of the countries must be totalitarian and the other one representative.

    D. The first country is a direct democracy, while the second country is a republic.

2. England at the time of the American Revolution can BEST be described as which of the following and for what reason?

    A. An absolute monarchy because King George III possessed most of the power in Great Britain.

    B. A limited monarchy because colonial legislatures would not support Parliament's decisions.

    C. A limited monarchy because the king was subject to British law and had to share power with Parliament.

    D. A dictatorship because the king tried to strictly control the colonies.

3. A state decides to use the Ten Commandments as its nation's laws, and appoints a Rabbi to lead its new government. What form of government is this?

    A. an oligarchy   C. an absolute monarchy

    B. a limited monarchy   D. a theocracy

CHAPTER 1 REVIEW

A. Define the following key terms.

New England Colonies	John Locke	religious pluralism
Middle Colonies	natural rights	First Great Awakening
Southern Colonies	social contract theory	freedom of religion
royal colony	common good/civic virtue	egalitarianism
separation of church and state	charter colony	Mayflower Compact
Jamestown	town meetings	consent of the governed
religious dissent	nationalism	puritans
pilgrims	suffrage	
Fundamental Orders of Connecticut	First/Second Continental Congress	Great Compromise/Connecticut Plan
constitutions	Quakers	favorable balance of trade
Catholics	Navigation Acts	plantation system
French and Indian War	Treaty of Paris	indentured servants
Albany Plan of Union	Shay's Rebellion	slavery
writs of assistance	Land Ordinance of 1785	middle passage
Proclamation of 1763	Northwest Ordinance	triangular trade route
Quartering Act	mercantilism	Stamp Act
United States Constitution	Bacon's Rebellion	Stamp Act Congress
Virginia Plan	colonial women	John Peter Zenger
New Jersey Plan	salutary neglect	Sons of Liberty
Salem witch trials	Articles of Confederation	Declaratory Act
African-Americans in colonial America	Native Americans in colonial America	Committees of Correspondence
democracy	Townshend Acts	republic/republicanism
Boston Massacre	Three Fifths Compromise	Renaissance
classical republicanism	slave trade compromise	limited government
Boston Tea Party	Magna Carta/"Great Charter"	Coercive/Intolerable Acts
electoral college	Parliament	"shot heard 'round the world"
English Bill of Rights	*Common Sense*	Bill of Rights
common law	Declaration of Independence	ratification
enlightenment	Thomas Hobbes	public education
separation of powers	Montesquieu	checks and balances
judiciary/Judicial Branch	Jean Jacque Rousseau	federalism
factions	federalists/anti-federalists	loose/strict interpretation
Free Exercise Clause	Establishment Clause	right to bear arms
quartering	searches and seizures	due process
double jeopardy	self-incrimination	eminent domain
rights of the accused	public and speedy trial by jury	excessive bail/fines
cruel and unusual punishment	reserved for the states	autocracy
absolute monarchy	limited/constitutional monarchy	dictatorship
totalitarianism	oligarchy	aristocracy
theocracy	anarchy	

Foundations of the United States Political System

B. Choose the correct answer.

1. A colony ruled directly by the king, usually through an appointed governor, would be known as which of the following?
   - A. royal colony
   - B. proprietary colony
   - C. self-governing colony
   - D. charter colony

2. If one wanted to live in colonial America in a place that featured diversity, commerce, and religious tolerance, then one would MOST LIKELY want to live in which region?
   - A. New England
   - B. The Middle Colonies
   - C. The Southern Colonies
   - D. The Northwest Territory

3. Which of the following was NOT a motivation for European settlers who founded British colonies in North America?
   - A. the hope of wealth
   - B. religious freedom
   - C. a chance to escape debtors prison in England
   - D. the desire to start an independent nation

4. The following quote is MOST LIKELY from whom?

   > "The institution of slavery is vital to our economy. Why, I bet we have as many African slaves as we do free Europeans...perhaps even more. Without them, we could not begin to produce the tobacco for which there is a market in England and elsewhere."

   - A. a Puritan leader in New England
   - B. a Quaker in Pennsylvania
   - C. a rich landowner in Massachusetts
   - D. a plantation owner in Virginia

5. A politician goes before Parliament and passionately proclaims that the American colonies are crucial to the British economy. He tells his colleagues that it is important that England export more products to other countries than it imports. Otherwise, England's wealth and security will be in jeopardy. He believes the colonies are important because they provide both resources for production and markets for English goods. This politician is advocating which of the following?
   - A. salutary neglect
   - B. protection of the triangular trade route
   - C. mercantilism
   - D. repeal of the Navigation Acts

6. Which of the following BEST explains the effect of Bacon's Rebellion on the formation of the US government?
   - A. It was the event that made it clear that the Articles of Confederation needed to be revised.
   - B. It demonstrated that colonists wanted a government in which even "ordinary" citizens have a voice.
   - C. It led directly to the Second Continental Congress declaring independence.
   - D. It showed that citizens in the new nation would not tolerate unjust taxes.

7. Which of the following describes a government that is subject to certain laws?
   - A. democracy
   - B. autocracy
   - C. limited government
   - D. salutary neglect

42

Chapter 1

8. Each of the following helped lay a foundation for the form of government that was adopted by the United States, EXCEPT:
   - A. the Magna Carta.
   - B. totalitarianism.
   - C. the Enlightenment.
   - D. the Roman republic.

9. Which of the following contributed to the start of the American Revolution?
   - A. British debt following the French and Indian War
   - B. Bacon's rebellion
   - C. Shay's rebellion
   - D. Ratification of the Constitution

10. British *writs of assistance* prior to the American Revolution, eventually led to which of the following amendments being included in the *Bill of Rights*?
    - A. First Amendment
    - B. Fourth Amendment
    - C. Sixth Amendment
    - D. Tenth Amendment

11. The following quote is MOST LIKELY from whom?

    "While I agree that power must be divided among several branches of government, I cannot agree to this plan. It proposes that both houses of the legislative branch be comprised of representatives from each state. That is fine and good. But it also proposes that, in each house, the number of representatives per state is to be based on population. Should we, the smaller states, have less of a voice in our own government because we are fewer in number? Did not our citizens spill blood to make this nation free as well. No! To approve this plan would be to impose a form of tyranny on us again. What good is representation if it is destined to mean nothing."

    - A. a delegate to the First Continental Congress from a small colony
    - B. a delegate to the Constitutional Convention who is protesting the New Jersey Plan
    - C. a delegate to the Second Continental Congress who is opposing the Constitution
    - D. a delegate to the Constitutional Convention who is opposing the Virginia Plan

12. Which of the following is not true regarding the government established by the US Constitution?
    - A. It is a direct democracy.
    - B. It is a republic.
    - C. It features federalism.
    - D. It depends on a system of separation of powers and checks and balances.

13. Someone who supported ratification of the Constitution, believed that the president should have a lot of power, and held a loose interpretation of the Constitution, was MOST LIKELY a member of which faction?
    - A. Federalists
    - B. Anti-federalists
    - C. Sons of Liberty
    - D. Albany Plan of Union

14. Under the *Bill of Rights*, the Free Exercise Clause and the Establishment Clause are included in the First Amendment for the purpose of doing what?

    A. protecting citizens' freedom of speech

    B. ensuring that *writs of assistance* will not be used by the US government

    C. maintaining the "natural right" to practice one's own religion

    D. making sure that states can maintain ready militias

15. The difference between a republic and a democracy is BEST described by which of the following statements?

    A. A democracy allows each citizen to have a voice in government, whereas a republic only allows a select few.

    B. A democracy usually features elected officials while a republic features leaders appointed by a monarch.

    C. A democracy is a system in which each eligible citizen votes on nearly every issue (laws, declarations of war, etc.) while a republic is a system in which citizens elect officials who then vote on such matters on their behalf.

    D. A democracy promotes freedom and "natural rights" while a republic usually promotes the welfare of the state above the rights of individuals.

Chapter 2
The Government of the
United States of America

This chapter addresses the following competency goal and objective(s):

Competency goal 2	The learner will analyze how the government established by the United States Constitution embodies the purposes, values and principles of American Democracy.
Objective 2.01, 2.02, 2.03, 2.04, 2.05, 2.06, 2.07, 2.08, 2.09	

2.1 PRINCIPLES OF THE UNITED STATES CONSTITUTION

The Founding Fathers of the United States based the US Constitution on the principles of popular sovereignty and limited government. **Popular sovereignty** is the belief that governments are created by, and are subject to, the will of the people. **Limited government** means that the government must obey a body of laws; it is not free to do whatever it wants. In the United States, the government must abide by the Constitution.

ASPECTS OF THE US CONSTITUTION

The first sentence of the US Constitution is known as the **preamble**. It serves to explain the purpose and intent of the document. The preamble is followed by three articles that establish the three branches of US government. Article I establishes the **legislative branch**, known as Congress. It consists of two houses: the House of Representatives and the Senate. It is the role of the legislative branch to make the laws. Article II establishes the **executive branch**. The president of the United States serves as the head of this branch, and he/she is responsible for enforcing federal laws. Article III creates the **judicial branch**. This branch consists of the federal court system with the Supreme Court acting as the highest court in the land. The role of the judicial branch is to make sure that laws are applied appropriately.

The Government of the United States of America

3 BRANCHES OF GOVERNMENT

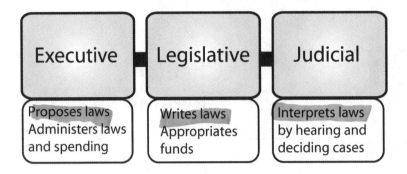

Executive	Legislative	Judicial
Proposes laws Administers laws and spending	Writes laws Appropriates funds	Interprets laws by hearing and deciding cases

FEDERAL AND STATE POWERS

Several clauses in the Constitution clarify the authority of the federal government. The *Elastic / "Necessary and Proper" Clause* authorizes Congress to "make all laws which shall be *necessary and proper*" for carrying out its duties under the Constitution. For example, because the Constitution gives Congress the power and responsibility to coin and regulate money, Federalists successfully argued that the US government had the right to establish a national bank. In other words, they passed a law they deemed "necessary and proper" for carrying out a constitutional responsibility. As you can see, this clause serves to expand Congress' authority beyond what is specifically stated in the Constitution. That's why it is called the *Elastic Clause*. Powers that are assumed under this clause are referred to as **implied powers**. By contrast, **enumerated / expressed powers** are those powers of

US Capitol

government which are specifically spelled out. Whenever Congress claims certain implied powers under the Elastic Clause, it is for the purpose of carrying out its enumerated powers within the Constitution.

White House

The Constitution also establishes the relationship between the national and state governments. The *Supremacy Clause* establishes the Constitution as the supreme law of the land. This means that if any state law contradicts the Constitution, then the state law is overruled. Those powers which are granted to the federal government are called **delegated powers**. Powers that are reserved for the states (*Tenth Amendment)* are called **reserved powers**. Meanwhile, **concurrent powers** are powers that are shared between the national and state governments. For example, both the federal government and the state of North Carolina can impose taxes (and wouldn't you know it; they both do). Finally, the *Full Faith and Credit Clause* requires the states to respect each other's laws. This means that the courts in one state must uphold the laws, civil claims, and court orders of another state. Therefore, if Bill is ordered by a court in North Carolina to pay $5,000 in damages, he can't move to Montana to get out of it.

Amazingly, the United States Constitution has only been amended (added to or changed) 27 times. The longevity of the document and its ability to remain relevant is in large part due to its **flexibility**. Because it tends to focus on principles rather than dealing in specifics, it often leaves its meaning open to debate, thereby allowing it to adapt to changes over time.

Practice 1: Principles of the Constitution

1. The belief that governments are created by, and are subject to, the will of the people is known as what?

    A. limited government
    B. popular sovereignty
    C. federalism
    D. reserved power

2. The office of president of the United States is part of which branch of government?

    A. judicial
    B. Article II
    C. executive
    D. legislative

3. What is the *Elastic Clause* and why is it so named?

2.2 STRUCTURE, POWERS, AND LIMITATIONS OF THE FEDERAL GOVERNMENT

As a limited government, the United States makes sure that its public officials abide by the **rule of law**. There are legal guidelines that the Congress, the courts, and even the president must obey. These guidelines are laid out in the Constitution.

THE LEGISLATIVE BRANCH (CONGRESS)

Article I of the Constitution establishes the two houses of Congress as the legislative branch of government. The **House of Representatives** is determined by population. The greater a states population, the more representatives that state has. Members of the House of Representatives serve two year terms. The second house is the **Senate**. Two senators who serve six year terms represent each state in this house. Originally, the state legislatures rather than the people elected senators. However, in 1913, the *Seventeenth Amendment* changed this. Now, senators are elected directly by citizens just like representatives to the House.

Each house of Congress is granted certain powers and responsibilities. Some powers are shared by both. For instance, both houses must approve a **bill** (a proposed law) before it can become a **law** (a rule which society is legally bound to uphold and abide by). Other powers are possessed by one house, but not the other. Only the House of Representatives may introduce tax bills. By comparison, only the Senate has the power to block or confirm presidential appointments (people the president

House of Representatives in Session

nominates to fill cabinet positions, seats on the federal courts, or other public offices).

To guard against corruption in the legislative branch, the framers of the Constitution granted to Congress the ability to punish members if necessary (Article I / Section 5). In case of serious wrongdoing, both houses have the option of either *censure* or *expulsion*. **Censure** is when a senator or representative is publicly reprimanded by his/her colleagues for inappropriate behavior. **Expulsion** is when a senator or representative has done something so offensive that he/she is actually removed from Congress. Before a member of either house can be expelled, two-thirds of its membership must concur (agree with the decision).

Congressional Committee

As mentioned earlier, both houses of Congress play an important role in passing laws. To help in this process, both the House and the Senate rely on the **committee system**. Before a bill goes before the entire House or Senate for a vote, smaller groups (committees) within each house take time to consider it. The committee will then examine, debate, and perhaps even question outside individuals concerning any bill. Then, it will either recommend or decline to recommend the bill for approval to the whole body. Committee chairpersons are chosen and committee seats allotted according to a **seniority system**.

Traditionally, the longer one has served and faithfully represented the interest of his/her political party, the more consideration he/she receives. Senators and representatives desire these positions because they give them greater influence in Congress. Senators who are opposed to a bill have the option of using a *filibuster*. According to Senate rules, debate on a bill cannot end so long as a senator is still speaking. A **filibuster** is a tactic in which a senator delays a vote on a bill he/she fears will pass by continuing to talk. Senators have been known to read books out loud and tell jokes (both of which are allowed) just to avoid shutting up. Usually, while this is happening, other senators who agree with him/her are attempting to sway as many votes as they can. To prevent a handful of senators from using a filibuster to halt the passage of an otherwise popular bill, the Senate adopted **cloture**. Under this procedure, if at least three fifths of the present senators (60 if all 100 are present) are in favor of ending a debate, then the filibuster is ended and a vote can occur.

For their services as senators and representatives, members of Congress receive a salary. In addition, they also enjoy **immunity**. No member of Congress can be arrested while attending congressional sessions. The only exceptions are if they are accused of treason, a felony, or "breach of the peace."

CONGRESSIONAL LEADERSHIP

Robert Byrd
Current President Pro Tempore

Nancy Pelosi
Current Speaker of the House

The top post in the House of Representatives is the **speaker of the House**. He/she is elected by the members of the House and is therefore usually a member of the majority party. The **vice president** presides over the Senate.   However, the vice president only votes if his/her vote is needed to break a tie. When the vice president is not present, the **president pro tempore**, also known as the **president of the Senate**, presides. He/she is the highest ranking senator in the body and is elected by fellow senators. He/she is typically the most senior member of the majority party.

The two major parties (Republican and Democrat) within the Senate and House of Representatives also have leaders. The **majority leader** is the elected leader of the majority party. Conversely, the **minority leader** leads the minority party. There is also a majority and minority **whip**. The whip's job is to make sure that members of the party vote the way the party leadership wants them to.

LIMITATIONS OF CONGRESS

Article I / Section 9 places specific restrictions on Congress. For one, Congress cannot suspend *Writ of Habeas Corpus*. A writ is a means by which a detained person can request that a judge review their case to make sure that their detention is legal. In other words, if you get thrown in jail, you have the right to go before a judge within a reasonable amount of time. Congress may not suspend this right except in cases of rebellion, invasion, or to ensure public safety. Neither can Congress pass bills of attainder or *ex post facto* laws. **Bills of attainder** are legislative acts which convict people of a crime without a trial. *Ex post facto* **laws** make some past activity illegal, even though it was not illegal at the time. For instance, if the government established a law making profanity on television illegal, it could not prosecute people for using profanity on TV prior to the law being passed. In addition, the legislative branch may not grant **titles of nobility** (Sorry, but no matter what you do, Congress cannot name you the *Duke or Duchess of North Carolina*).

THE EXECUTIVE BRANCH

Article II establishes the offices of president and vice president as the executive branch of government. The president serves as the nation's **head of state** (leader) and is elected to a term of four years. Originally, there was no limit on how many terms a president could serve (Franklin Roosevelt was elected 4 times). In 1951, however, the *Twenty-Second Amendment* limited presidents to two terms.

The president fulfills a number of roles. He/she is the **commander-in-chief** of the nation's armed forces and the country's **chief diplomat**. It is the president, or one of his/her representatives, who meets and negotiates with leaders and representatives of other countries. The president has the power to negotiate and present to Congress treaties. A **treaty** is a formal agreement between two or more countries. However, the Senate must ratify a treaty before it is final. In some situations, the president has the authority to enter into **executive agreements** with other nations. These agreements do not require Senate ratification. As the nation's **chief executive**, the president also has the power to appoint officials, such as members of his/her cabinet and judges to preside over federal courts. The Senate must confirm these appointments for them to be final. The president acts as a **legislative leader** who proposes programs, budgets, and legislation for

Current President George W. Bush

congressional consideration. He/she is an **economic leader** because many of the policies and programs he/she implements (i.e., cutting taxes or imposing tariffs) have impact on the US economy. The president fulfills the role of **party leader.** He/she is the acknowledged head of whatever political party he/she is a part of and has great influence over policies, how members of the party vote, and who runs for office. The more popular a president is with voters, the more influence that president has. Candidates for office want to be identified closely with him/her if it will help them gain popularity. Therefore, they will be much more likely to vote for bills and back policies that the president supports if he/she is viewed positively by the public.

The Government of the United States of America

The president is also granted certain powers. One of the most notable is the power to **veto** (reject by refusing to sign) bills passed by Congress. However, if both houses of Congress have two-thirds who still favor the bill, then they can override the president's veto and the bill becomes a law anyway. At times, the president may issue **executive orders** directing government agencies to take certain actions. Executive orders carry the force of law. The president possesses the power to grant **pardons**. Pardons excuse a person from being punished for a criminal offense (such as when President Jimmy

Carter pardoned those who had evaded the draft during Vietnam). He/she can also **commute sentences** (shorten the time someone must spend in prison for a crime) and offer **reprieves** (delay the implementation of a sentence; for instance, if there is new evidence that needs to be considered).

The Constitution requires the president to report to Congress "from time to time" on the state of the Union. In modern times, this has been done in the form of the president's annual *State of the Union Address*. This is a speech that the president gives before both houses of Congress every January, in which he/she reports on the state of the union and proposes what he/she would like to see Congress do in the coming year. Although the Constitution does not require the president to report on the state of the Union in person, most modern-day presidents do so because it affords them the opportunity to speak directly to the US public.

What if the president cannot fulfill his/her term? For example, what if the president dies or becomes too ill to continue in office? In order to ensure that the nation is never without a leader, the Constitution provides guidelines for **presidential succession** (who becomes president if the current president can't continue). Article II, Section 1 states that, if the president is unable to continue in office, the vice president will then assume his/her powers. Originally, the wording of this section did not make it clear whether or not this meant the vice president became president; or if it only meant that he/she temporarily assumed the president's powers while remaining vice president. The *Twenty-fifth Amendment* removed this confusion in 1967. It clearly states that, under such circumstances, the vice president will become president. Next in line is the speaker of the House, followed by the president pro tempore.

Andrew Johnson

Finally, the Constitution allows for the removal of a president who violates the Constitution. This process is called **impeachment**. Only the House of Representatives may impeach the president, vice president, or other "civil officer of the United States" (i.e., federal judges and members of the president's cabinet). Just because an official is impeached doesn't mean they have been found guilty or that they will be removed. First, they must stand trial in the Senate. The Senate serves as a jury that hears the evidence, while either the chief justice of the United States, the vice president, or the president pro tempore presides over the proceedings. Who presides is determined by who is being impeached. If two-thirds of the Senate finds that the official is guilty, then he/she is removed from office. Only two presidents in US history have ever been impeached: Andrew Johnson in 1868 and Bill Clinton in 1998. Neither was convicted by the Senate.

THE JUDICIAL BRANCH

Article III of the Constitution establishes the Judicial Branch of government. This branch consists of the federal courts with the United States Supreme Court acting as the highest court in the land. The Supreme Court has the final say on whether or not an action or piece of legislation violates the Constitution. As such, it can overturn (reverse) decisions made by lower federal courts and even state courts if the Court believes the case deals with an issue of federal law. The US Supreme Court consists of nine justices. The lead justice is referred to as the **chief justice of the United States**. The other eight justices are called **associate justices**. All federal judges, even those on lower courts, must be appointed by the president and confirmed by the Senate. Unless they are impeached and removed from office, these justices serve for life or until they retire.

John Roberts
Current Chief Justice

Federal courts can hold both appellate and original jurisdiction. **Original jurisdiction** refers to a court's authority to hear cases that have not yet been heard. **Appellate jurisdiction** refers to a court's authority to review the decisions of lower courts. For example, when someone who is condemned to die for a crime appeals to the Supreme Court to have their execution stopped, they are asking the Court to use its *appellate jurisdiction* to overturn the decision of a lower court that used its *original jurisdiction* to sentence them to death. **Concurrent jurisdiction** refers to cases in which more than one court has jurisdiction. For instance, in some cases, both federal and state courts have equal authority to hear a case. By contrast, **exclusive jurisdiction** means only one court system has the authority to rule. Bankruptcy, copyright and patent cases, and suits brought against the US government are all cases in which the federal courts have exclusive jurisdiction.

One of the most important powers of the judicial branch is *judicial review.* This is not a power specifically granted by the Constitution. However, it was established by precedence in 1803. **Precedence** is when past court decisions are used to make legal rulings because the law is open to interpretation or there is no written statute. (Review Chapter 1, Section 1 regarding common law.) *Judicial review* refers to the authority of the Judicial Branch to declare certain acts of Congress unconstitutional. In other words, Congress could pass a bill and have it signed by the president, only to have the courts rule that it violates the Constitution.

Practice 2: Structure, Power and Limitations of the Federal Government

1. Patricia is an elected official in the federal government. She has served 3 terms in office; each two years in length. She is one of 20 people representing her home state in the house of Congress in which she serves. She hopes that in time she will have enough popularity and influence among her colleagues to be elected to the position of Speaker. Patricia is a member of what body of government?

    A. the US Senate
    B. the US Supreme Court
    C. the US House of Representatives
    D. the US Executive Branch

2. Which of the following is NOT a role granted to the US Senate by the Constitution?

    A. the role of confirming presidential appointments
    B. the role of ratifying treaties with foreign nations
    C. the role of impeaching the president if necessary
    D. the role of voting on proposed bills

3. Which of the following is NOT a role delegated to the president by the Constitution?
    A. He/she is commander of the nation's military forces.
    B. He/she acts as the party's Majority Leader.
    C. He/she is the nation's chief diplomat.
    D. He/she can propose legislation to Congress for consideration.

4. What is impeachment and what else must take place for it to result in an official being removed from office?

2.3 HOW THE CONSTITUTION ADAPTS AND CHANGES

Knowing that changes to the Constitution would likely need to be made, the framers included two means by which the document could be amended. The first is initiated by Congress. If both houses of Congress pass a proposed amendment, that amendment then goes to the states. If three-fourths of the states approve the amendment, it then becomes part of the Constitution. This is how the *Bill of Rights* came into being. The other means by which a change can occur is through a **constitutional convention**. This occurs when two-thirds of the states call for a special meeting to consider proposing amendments to the Constitution. If they are proposed, then they must be approved by three-fourths of the states. **Amendments 1–10** comprise the *Bill of Rights*. (Review Chapter 1.7) Since their adoption, however, there have been an additional 17 amendments (27 overall).

Eleventh Amendment (1798)	places limits on an individual's right to sue states.
Twelfth Amendment (1804)	requires electors to the Electoral College to cast separate ballots for president and vice president.
Thirteenth Amendment (1865)	outlaws slavery throughout the United States.
Fourteenth Amendment (1868)	defines **citizenship** as "all persons born or naturalized in the United States", thereby extending citizenship to freed blacks. It also guarantees equal protection for all citizens under the law and states that no citizen will be deprived of life, liberty, or property without **due process** (*Fifth Amendment*).
Fifteenth Amendment (1870)	extends the right to vote to all citizens, regardless of race.
Sixteenth Amendment (1913)	gives Congress the power to impose an income tax (your parents aren't very happy about this one).
Seventeenth Amendment (1913)	establishes that US senators will be elected directly by the people rather than by the state legislatures.

Eighteenth Amendment (1919) known as "Prohibition", it made the manufacture, sale, and transport of alcoholic beverages illegal.

Nineteenth Amendment (1920) grants women **suffrage** (the right to vote).

Twentieth Amendment (1933) establishes when presidential and congressional terms are to begin and end. It also requires Congress to assemble each year and states that, should the president-elect (the person elected president but not yet sworn into office) die before taking office, the vice president-elect shall assume the presidency.

Twenty-first Amendment (1933) repealed Prohibition (cancelled the 18th Amendment).

Twenty-second Amendment (1951) sets **presidential term limits** by limiting the president to just two terms in office.

Twenty-third Amendment (1961) grants the District of Columbia electors in the Electoral College.

Twenty-fourth Amendment (1964) ensures the rights of citizens to vote by banning poll taxes (poll taxes were a method used in many southern states to keep blacks from voting).

Twenty-fifth Amendment (1967) clearly establishes **presidential succession** by stating that the vice president is to be sworn in as president if the president leaves office before his/her term is up. The amendment also states that, should the office of vice president become vacant, the president will appoint someone to that office who must then be approved by both houses of Congress.

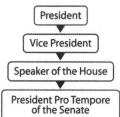

Twenty-sixth Amendment (1971) establishes the legal voting age for national elections to be 18 years

Twenty-seventh Amendment (1992) establishes that Congress cannot grant itself a pay raise unless it comes after the next congressional election. This amendment was actually first proposed by representatives from North Carolina in 1788, but the states refused to ratify it. It was resurrected in 1982 and became part of the Constitution ten years later.

The Government of the United States of America

While the Founding Fathers were very wise to allow for an amendment process, they were perhaps even more masterful in how they allowed the Constitution room to adapt. By leaving certain areas vague, the framers left aspects of the document open to debate and interpretation. As a result, the meaning and implementation of the Constitution has evolved over time, even though the wording has changed very little.

One area in which the flexibility of the Constitution is evident is in **judicial decisions and review**. Where the meaning of the law is open to interpretation or no written specifics are outlined in the Constitution, the decisions of the courts have been accepted as authoritative. The Constitution has also been determined to allow for certain **presidential actions**. For instance, the Constitution does not specifically outline how to handle land acquisitions. Yet the government recognized Thomas Jefferson's ability to assume power not specifically given to the president when he approved the Louisiana Purchase. **Congressional action** is also evidence of the Constitution's flexibility. For example, Congress can pass laws limiting how the president conducts foreign policy; a power not specifically granted to

Presidential Cabinet

Congress under the Constitution. Finally, the Constitution adapts over time because it allows for certain **customs and traditions**. There is nothing in the Constitution about a presidential cabinet. However, in order to effectively govern and represent the United States in today's world, the president relies heavily on his various advisors and cabinet heads. The Cabinet is an example of a custom allowed, though not directly stated in, the Constitution.

Practice 3: How the Constitution Adapts and Changes

1. A special meeting called by at least two-thirds of the states for the purpose of proposing amendments to the Constitution is called what?

    A.   congressional action   C.   a constitutional convention

    B.   a judicial review   D.   ratification

2. The president is limited to just two terms under which amendment?

    A.   First   C.   Twenty-second

    B.   Thirteenth   D.   Twenty-fifth

3. When President George W. Bush chose certain individuals to serve on his cabinet, this was an example of what kind of authority allowed by the Constitution?

    A.   presidential action   C.   enumerated

    B.   custom and tradition   D.   congressional

2.4 IMPORTANT COURT CASES AND THE UNITED STATES CONSTITUTION

When the Constitution was written more than two centuries ago, it did not go into as much detail regarding the powers of the judicial branch as it did the legislative and executive. It provided no set structure other than to define the boundaries of jurisdiction and to say that there would be a Supreme Court. Ironically, despite its vague beginnings, the Judicial Branch has arguably done more to shape the meaning of the Constitution than either of the other two branches.

CASES ESTABLISHING THE AUTHORITY OF THE FEDERAL GOVERNMENT

One of the most important powers the judicial branch has is the power of *judicial review*. As mentioned earlier, this is the authority to declare certain laws passed by Congress, or even state legislatures, unconstitutional (in violation of the Constitution). This power is not specifically delegated to the courts by the Constitution. Rather, it was established in a landmark court case known as *Marbury v. Madison (1803)*. Just before leaving office, President John Adams (a Federalist) appointed a number of Federalist judges. However, he did not get a chance to deliver their commissions (documents officially appointing them) before his presidency ended. When Thomas Jefferson (an Anti-federalist) succeeded him as president in 1801, he refused to deliver the commissions because he did not want these Federalists to serve. In response, some of the judges sued. The Supreme Court agreed that the judges were entitled to their commissions. *However*, the Court also ruled that the Supreme Court did not have

**John Marshall
Chief Justice, 1803**

authority to force the president to deliver the commissions under the Constitution. In so doing, the Supreme Court declared part of the Judiciary Act unconstitutional and established the Court's power of *judicial review*.

Franklin D. Roosevelt

Two other cases that defined the powers of the federal government also occurred during the first half of the 19th century. In *McCullough v. Maryland (1819)*, the court dealt with the question of whether or not Congress had the right to establish a national bank. In addition, if Congress did, could the state of Maryland impose taxes on it? The Court ruled that the *Elastic Clause* allowed Congress to establish a national bank because it was an action "necessary and proper" for carrying out its constitutional duties. It also ruled that Maryland did not have the authority to impose taxes on a federal institution. The case both reinforced the principle of "implied powers" within the Constitution and the *Supremacy Clause* which states that federal powers exceed those of the states. A few years later, in *Gibbons v. Ogden (1824)*, the Supreme Court established that only the federal government could regulate interstate commerce. Again, the Court affirmed the Constitution as having authority over the commerce laws of states.

The Government of the United States of America

During World War II, the US Supreme Court heard a landmark case dealing with the implied powers of the president. Specifically, it dealt with an executive order issued by President Franklin D. Roosevelt. In his order, the president authorized the internment of thousands of Japanese Americans. Japanese American citizens were rounded up, taken from their homes, and forced to live in government camps. That might sound shocking today, but at the time, many supported the move because the US was at war with Japan. One Japanese American challenged the order as a violation of his civil rights. However, in *Korematsu v. United States (1944)*, the Supreme Court ruled that the internment was not unlawful because of the "military urgency of the situation." The case reinforced the power of presidential executive orders.

Manzanar Japanese Internment Camp

CASES DEALING WITH RACE AND SEGREGATION

Segregation is a term that refers to the separation of groups (i.e., blacks and whites). There are two types of segregation. *De jure* segregation is segregation sanctioned by law. For instance, when buses in the South use to require blacks to sit separately from whites, this was de jure segregation. *De facto* segregation is segregation that is brought about by social or economic circumstances rather than written law. When blacks and whites tend to live in separate neighborhoods because, on average, one community is financially better off than the other, this is an example of de facto segregation. The Supreme Court has made landmark decisions affecting both.

The Court originally sanctioned de jure segregation in *Plessy v. Ferguson (1896)*. Homer Plessy, a man who was one-eighth black, was arrested for riding in a "whites only" railway car in Louisiana. With only one justice dissenting (disagreeing with the final decision of the Court) the Supreme Court ruled that segregation is lawful, so long as the facilities provided for both races are equal. In 1954, the NAACP (National Association for the Advancement of Colored People) argued a case before the Supreme Court that challenged the *Plessy* decision. The case revolved around a young, African-American girl named Linda Brown. Brown had been denied enrollment at a school close to her home because it was all white. In *Brown v. Board of Education of Topeka (1954)*, the Supreme Court struck down segregation in public schools on the grounds that separate facilities were inherently "unequal" because they did not present minority

NAACP Lawyer Thurgood Marshall

students with the same opportunities that were offered in white schools. Later, in *Heart of Atlanta Motel, Inc. v. United States (1964)*, the Court ruled that the US Congress could use its power to regulate interstate commerce to strike down racial segregation within states because it potentially hinders interstate business.

Closely related to the issue of desegregation (also called *integration*) is the topic of busing. First implemented in the early 70s, busing is a method of integration in which students are required to attend schools outside the boundaries of what would normally be their school district. It is meant to deal with the de facto segregation that occurs in education because blacks and whites often live in different school districts. The practice was challenged in the courts and reached the Supreme Court on appeal. In ***Swann v. Charlotte-Mecklenburg Board of Education (1971)***, the Court agreed with a lower court decision allowing busing as a means for integrating public schools.

In 1965, President Lyndon Johnson coined the phrase "affirmative action." It refers to a policy designed to help minorities who have traditionally been discriminated against. Under this policy, such minorities are given special consideration and/or are actively recruited for jobs, admittance to universities, etc. Eventually, affirmative action was challenged in federal courts. In 1973 and 1974, a white applicant to medical school in California was denied admittance after twice applying. He sued, claiming that his constitutional rights had been violated because the school reserved 16 spots for minority candidates. In ***Regents of UC v. Bakke***, the Supreme Court agreed that such quotas violated the *Fourteenth Amendment*. However, the Court did affirm that race could be used by the school as a consideration in admission.

Lyndon B. Johnson

CASES DEALING WITH THE BILL OF RIGHTS

The *Bill of Rights* was added to the US Constitution for the purpose of protecting civil liberties. However, how these amendments and others are applied is often a matter of debate. What constitutes "cruel and unusual punishment?" What is included in "free speech?" Am I allowed to scream "fire!" in a public building just to watch people trample themselves as they rush to get out? Does "freedom of the press" mean I can print whatever I want, whenever I want? Do I have to forfeit my right to counsel (a lawyer) if I can't afford to hire one? The courts have taken on the crucial role of dealing with these kinds of questions.

There have been a number of key court decisions regarding the rights of those convicted and/or accused of a crime. In 1972, the Supreme Court struck down the death penalty as a method of punishment. It ruled in ***Furman v. Georgia (1972)*** that the death penalty was not constitutional in the way that it was applied. In some cases, those committing serious crimes (murder, rape, etc.) were sentenced to death, but in similar cases, others received life in prison. Four years later in ***Gregg v. Georgia (1976)***, the Court upheld the death penalty so long as proper and consistent guidelines were provided to juries in deciding whether or not to sentence someone to death. Together, the two cases established that the death penalty does not constitute cruel and unusual punishment, so long as it is applied in a fair and consistent manner. In 1961 and 1966, the Supreme Court ruled on landmark criminal cases involving the *Fourth* and *Fifth Amendments*. In ***Mapp v. Ohio (1961)***, the Court ruled that evidence seized from a person's residence without a search warrant constitutes an "illegal search" and cannot be used at trial. Two years later, the Court ruled in ***Gideon v. Wainwright (1963)*** that states are required under the *Sixth* and *Fourteenth* Amendments to provide attorneys for criminal defendants who cannot afford them. That same year, a Mexican immigrant named Ernesto Miranda was arrested and interrogated by police without the presence of a lawyer. During the interrogation, he confessed to the crimes of kidnapping and rape. After his conviction, the case was appealed all the way to the Supreme Court. In ***Miranda v. Arizona (1966)***, the Court ruled that both Miranda's *Fifth Amendment* protection against "self-incrimination" and his *Sixth Amendment* right to counsel had been violated. The case established the *Miranda Rule*, which states that law enforcement agencies must inform anyone they arrest that they have these rights. Often called *"Miranda Rights"*, you hear them recited whenever you watch your favorite cop show and hear the words, "You have the right to remain silent… you have the right to an attorney…"

The Government of the United States of America

Few settings have provided as many notable court cases as US public schools (i.e., *Brown v. Board of Education* and *Swann v. Charlotte-Mecklenburg Board of Education*). Again and again, the courts have been called to rule on the extent to which the *Bill of Rights* applies in an educational setting. In **New Jersey v. TLO (1985)**, the Court ruled that *Fourth Amendment* rights apply to students. The case involved the searching of a student's purse at a New Jersey high school. The search revealed that the student both used and sold marijuana. The Court ruled that, in order for school officials to conduct such a search, they must first have "reasonable suspicion" that a student is guilty of wrongdoing. In this case, the Court upheld the search because the student had been caught smoking. Many of the most notable public school cases have involved the *First Amendment*. One such case involved the state of New York's decision to authorize the reading of an official school prayer. Although the prayer was non-denominational and students were free to excuse themselves from reciting it, the state's decision was challenged as a violation of the United States Constitution. The Supreme Court agreed in **Engel v. Vitale (1962)**, and ruled that any prayer instituted by the state — even one that is voluntary — is a violation of the *First Amendment*. In **Tinker v. Des Moines (1969)**, the Court ruled that student behavior not disruptive to the learning environment (in this case, the wearing of armbands to protest the Vietnam War) is protected by the *First Amendment* as freedom of speech. In another case, the Supreme Court ruled in **Bethel School District v. Frasier (1986)** that schools can prohibit speech that violates the values of public education (in this case, the use of profanity at a school assembly). In **Hazelwood v. Kuhlmeier (1988)**, the Court addressed *First Amendment* rights in schools as it relates to freedom of the press. A high school newspaper printed articles dealing with pregnancy and divorce which the principal found inappropriate and therefore censored. The Supreme Court agreed with the principal stating that schools may censor any material that is not consistent with the school's mission. Over time, the courts have made it clear that constitutional rights do extend to schools. However, their rulings also demonstrate that the nature of the school setting sometimes allows for certain restrictions on these rights.

One landmark *First Amendment* case that did not involve public schools was **Texas v. Johnson (1984)**. It involved the arrest of a man who was caught burning a US flag in protest. The Supreme Court ruled that state laws forbidding the burning of a US flag are unconstitutional because they violate freedom of speech. Interestingly, in June 2006, a proposed amendment to the Constitution to ban flag burning failed to pass in the Senate by just one vote.

Practice 4: Important Court Cases and the United States Constitution

"This ruling means that before the death penalty can be reinstated, state governments must show that it will not be applied arbitrarily. As long as the Court feels that states randomly execute some criminals while sentencing others who have committed similar crimes to life in prison, it will continue to view the death penalty as unconstitutional."

1. The above quote is referring to which landmark court case?

   A. *Furman v. Georgia*   C. *Texas v. Johnson*

   B. *Gregg v. Georgia*   D. *Engel v. Vitale*

2. *Bethel School District v. Frasier, Texas v. Johnson, Hazelwood v. Kuhlmeier,* and *Engel v. Vitale* all involved questions about which of the following?

   A. freedom of speech   C. the *First Amendment*

   B. freedom of the press   D. the *Fourteenth Amendment*

3. *Marbury v. Madison* was a key court case in US history because it established what?
   A. implied powers of Congress
   B. implied powers of the president
   C. judicial review
   D. the federal court system and the authority of the Supreme Court

4. How did the cases of *McCullough v. Maryland, Gibbons v. Ogden,* and *Korematsu v. United States* help reinforce powers of the federal government?

2.5 CONFLICTS AND CONTROVERSIES SURROUNDING CONSTITUTIONAL ISSUES

Many of the issues that divided Federalists and Anti-federalists regarding the Constitution still inspire debate today. Federalists believed in a strong federal government. They felt that the national government's powers needed to be broadly defined in order to function effectively. For this reason, they favored a **loose interpretation** of the Constitution which would allow the three branches of government to take actions not specifically delegated to them in the document. By contrast, the Anti-federalists wanted stronger state governments. They were strong believers in *states rights*. **States rights** refers to the extent to which states are free to make and live by their own laws. For this reason, Anti-federalists had a **strict interpretation** of the Constitution.

STATES RIGHTS VERSUS FEDERAL POWER

The *Supremacy Clause* makes it clear that federal powers exceed those of the states. However, the *Tenth Amendment* clearly says that certain powers are reserved for the states. Finding the balance between states rights and federal authority is often a point of controversy. For instance, every ten years (although recent court decisions could lead to it happening more often) states redraw state and congressional districts in a process called **redistricting**. Although this process is usually a matter of state authority, the federal government has gotten involved from time to time. For instance, in 1965, Congress passed the Voting Rights Act. This law made it illegal for states to engage in redistricting designed to limit the political power of minorities. Later federal court decisions served to make all forms of racially based redistricting illegal (i.e., states cannot use redistricting as a form of affirmative action).

The Government of the United States of America

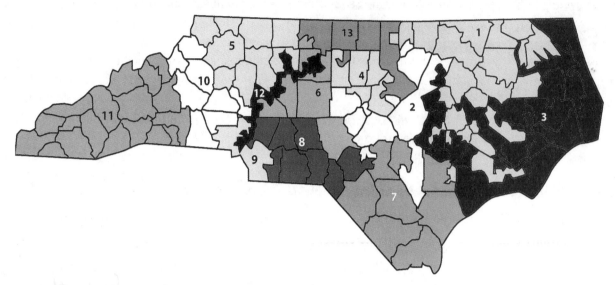

North Carolina Congressional Districts

Another issue that currently shines light on the debate between state and federal powers is that of same-sex marriages/civil unions. Many people claim that it should be left to the individual states to decide if they will recognize same-sex unions or not. Others believe that the federal government should get involved. Those who encourage federal involvement range from those who want the courts to protect such relationships as a "civil right", to those who advocate ratifying a constitutional amendment to prevent the practice. In the near future, other controversies appear likely to also become heated issues. Should states be able to pass their own illegal immigration laws, or is that strictly an issue for the federal government? Will the Supreme Court's 1973 decision guaranteeing a woman's right to unrestricted abortion on demand remain in place, or will recent appointments to the Court lead to states once again being able to establish their own abortion laws? Just as they were 200 plus years ago, political leaders are often divided on the question of how much power the Constitution gives to the states versus the enumerated and implied powers of the federal government.

OTHER ISSUES AND QUESTIONS

One key issue of debate is that of **majority rule versus minority rights**. The United States is meant to be a government based on the will of the people. But what happens when what the majority wants threatens the rights of the minority? For example, consider the South before the mid 1960s. The white majority seemed perfectly happy with segregation, but the minority black population felt oppressed. Things did not change until the federal government got involved. Similarly, what if 80% of a community believes that those who desecrate the US flag should go to jail? If that's what the majority wants, then what's wrong with that? Well, plenty if you ask the 20% who believe strongly that people should be free to desecrate the flag as part of their *First Amendment* rights (i.e., *Texas v. Johnson)*. These examples serve to illustrate the conflict that sometimes exists between the idea of majority rule and the principle of minority rights.

Separation of church and state is another issue of intense debate in the United States. Many people are surprised to learn that the phrase appears nowhere in the Constitution. However, the principle is implied in the *First Amendment*'s *Free Exercise Clause* and *Establishment Clause*. Some citizens argue that the Constitution merely requires the government to refrain from establishing an official church or promoting one religion over another. Others believe that the principle of "separation of church and state" requires that the government make no acknowledgment of religious belief whatsoever. The debate has centered on such questions as: *Is it ok to have prayer in public schools? Can references to Christianity be made during school holiday programs? Can religious symbols (i.e., crosses, menorahs, or the Ten Commandments) be displayed in government buildings? Is it right for the federal government to provide aid to charities with a religious affiliation?* Because people's personal faith and convictions about God are so strong, this issue has produced some of the most emotional debate regarding the intent of the Constitution.

In recent decades, the issue of private citizens owning firearms has been a hot topic. Many citizens believe that private citizens' access to firearms should be strictly limited, if not prohibited altogether. They tend to point out statistics regarding violent crime and the rising number of gun-related deaths in the United States. Their opponents are quick to respond that the *Second Amendment* guarantees the **right to bear arms**. They argue that limiting access to guns is a violation of the Constitution. Gun control advocates answer this by emphasizing that the *Second Amendment* was originally intended to protect the existence of local militias.

Fed up with what they perceive as corruption and abuse of power in government, many citizens favor **term limits** for public officials. The *Twenty-second Amendment* places such a limit on the office of president, and many states limit the number of terms someone may serve as governor as well. But no such limit exist for representatives to the House or US senators. As a result, some officials have served for decades. Proponents of term limits say that this has created a system where politicians work to maintain their power rather than serve the people. They claim that officials will be more likely to focus on the job for which they've been elected rather than personal interests if they are limited to only a brief time in office. Others disagree, arguing that the Constitution imposes no such limitations and citizens should be free to elect an official as often as they want.

One final topic that has been at the forefront of debate since the terrorist attacks of 9/11 has been that of **civil liberties versus national security**. Throughout US history, in times of war or national crisis, the US government has enacted laws limiting the rights of citizens. Usually, this is done in the name of national security. Some of these limitations are granted by the Constitution. For instance, in Article I / Section 2, the Constitution says that *writ of habeas corpus* may be suspended in the event of rebellion or invasion. President Lincoln did just this during the Civil War. However, most of the time, the issue is not so clear. Early in the nation's history, Federalists passed the Alien and Sedition Acts for the purpose of discouraging any rebellion which might resemble the one that occurred in France. Anti-federalists attacked these laws as a serious denial of civil rights and even passed a resolution stating that states could ignore any federal law they felt went beyond the bounds of the Constitution. During World War I, Congress passed laws making it illegal to criticize the government. As mentioned earlier, the Court upheld Roosevelt's decision to limit the rights of Japanese Americans during WWII. Today, laws like the **PATRIOT Act** have produced similar controversies. This law relaxes some of the Constitutional restrictions placed on law enforcement to allow them to secure evidence more easily. Proponents of the law say that it is necessary if the US is to have any hope of preventing future terrorist attacks and protecting the lives of US citizens. Opponents claim that it gives US law enforcement powers which are too broad and violates the Constitution. Statistics show that most citizens are willing to sacrifice certain civil liberties in the name of **"homeland security"** (making sure that the US is not hit by another terrorist strike). Citizens often differ, however, on the extent to which they support surrendering such freedoms.

INTEREST GROUPS

Interest groups often arise out of political controversies. **Interest groups** are groups advocating a certain cause. They use the political process (supporting candidates, campaigning for their position, lobbying politicians, etc.) in an attempt to either encourage or prevent change to existing policies. Because of the controversies that arise regarding the Constitution, such groups have come to be an important force in US politics. In most important debates, there are interest groups fighting for both sides.

Practice 5: Conflicts and Controversies Surrounding constitutional Issues

1. Which political faction would have been MOST supportive of the federal government getting involved in redistricting and why?

    A. Federalists because they favored a loose interpretation of the Constitution
    B. Anti-federalists because they favored a strict interpretation of the Constitution
    C. Federalists because they felt that states should have no powers
    D. Anti-federalists because they favored a strong central government

2. 90 people out of 100 want to tear down the old houses that sit at the front of their neighborhood because they believe that they are unattractive and want to replace them with a flower garden and a new sign. The owners of the houses protest that such an action would violate their civil rights. What is this an example of?

    A. the conflict that sometimes exists between individual liberties and national security
    B. debate over what is implied in the *Free Exercise Clause*
    C. tension over the *Second Amendment*
    D. the conflict that sometimes arises between the idea of majority rule and the principle of minority rights

3. Why is the PATRIOT Act an object of debate regarding the Constitution?

2.6 SOURCES OF REVENUE FOR THE NATIONAL GOVERNMENT

One of the reasons the Articles of Confederation failed was because it provided no effective means for raising national revenue. **Revenue** is money that the government takes in. It is crucial that the government be able to raise money so that it can pay certain **expenditures**. Expenditures are those things which the federal government must pay for (i.e., national defense, government salaries, federal programs, etc.). Therefore, under the Constitution, the national government was granted the power to raise revenue. There are several ways this is done.

Chapter 2

TAXES

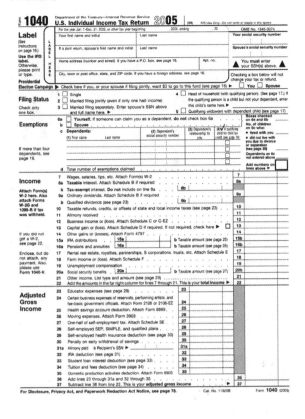

The most common way the government raises revenue is through taxes. These taxes may either be a **direct tax** paid directly to the government (i.e., income taxes paid every year), or an **indirect tax** collected through an agent other than the government (i.e., the gas station to whom you pay a tax on gas). There are several kinds of taxes. **Income tax** is a tax placed on the income citizens earn. This is usually done by "withholding income tax." Employers pay taxes directly to the government out of an employees pay *before* he/she ever gets their money. Every year, citizens file an **income tax return** showing how much they owe in taxes. If what they owe is greater than what has been withheld, then the citizen must pay the difference. If, however, what is owed is less than what was withheld, the citizen is entitled to a tax refund from the government. **Corporate taxes** are taxes placed on businesses. **Excise taxes** are taxes placed on specific products; such as a tax on cigarettes. **Estate taxes** are taxes placed on money or property inherited by an heir after somebody dies. **Tariffs** are taxes placed on products imported from a foreign country. Traditionally, they have been used in attempts to protect US manufacturers. The government also withholds taxes for **Social Security**. First implemented during the Great Depression, Social Security is a program meant to provide an income to individuals who have reached the age of legal retirement or are unable to work. Because US citizens are living longer and the program is paying out more benefits than ever before, many experts are concerned about its long-term stability. **Regressive taxes** take a larger percentage of income from those who earn less. For example, if a certain model of television costs $400 and two people each pay 6% tax when they purchase one, the person who makes less money will feel it more because the amount of the tax will be a higher percentage of his/her income. Conversely, a **progressive tax** increases in percentage as income rises. The federal income tax is designed as a progressive tax because the more one earns, the greater percentage the government requires him/her to pay. A **proportional tax** is one where everyone pays the same percentage. For instance, if a tax is passed requiring everyone to pay a flat 10% of their income, then the percentage of income taken by the government would be the same for everyone. Both the national and state governments impose taxes.

FINES AND FEES

Taxes are not the only way the government collects money. Another means is by **user fees** which the government charges people to use certain services. (i.e., fees charged to camp in a national park or money paid by trucking companies to use federal highways.) The government also collects money from **fines**. Fines are simply amounts of money that are imposed as punishment for criminal or civil offenses. Both businesses and individuals can be required to pay fines.

GOVERNMENT SPENDING

As mentioned earlier, the government must have the power to raise revenue because it has to spend money. The money which the federal government plans to spend each year is the **national budget**. The president may propose a budget, but only Congress can approve it. If the government spends more money than it has in revenue for a given year (and this is common), then the government has a **budget deficit**. This willingness by the government to spend money that it doesn't have is called **"deficit spending"** and is sometimes considered a good thing (such as when President Roosevelt engaged in deficit spending to help lift the nation out of the Great Depression). If, however, the government spends less than it has in revenue, then it is said to have a **budget surplus**. If the amount spent

by government is equal to its revenue, then the government has a **balanced budget**. Some leaders and citizens favor adding a constitutional amendment requiring a balanced budget each year. The **national debt** refers to how much money the government owes. When the government ends the year with a surplus, the debt shrinks. When it finishes with a deficit, the debt increases. To help cover itself those times that it spends more than it has, the government issues **treasury bonds**. These are certificates sold to individuals in exchange for money that they are loaning to the government. These individuals can then cash in their bonds at a later date, having earned interest on the loan.

Practice 6: Sources of Revenue for the National Government

1. What kind of tax occurs when the government takes a percentage of what you earn at work for the purpose of raising federal or state revenue?

   A. excise tax   B. tariff   C. income tax   D. regressive tax

2. Due to the government spending billions of dollars to provide disaster relief following an earth-quake in California, it actually spent three times what the national budget had allotted for this event. The government is now experiencing what?

   A. national expenditure   C. budget deficit
   B. budget surplus   D. balanced budget

3. A tax in which a person who earns less actually ends up paying a higher percentage of their income is called what?

   A. progressive tax   C. regressive tax
   B. proportional tax   D. really depressing

2.7 IMPORTANT FEDERAL AGENCIES

The federal government provides a number of services it deems necessary. These services range from collecting taxes and keeping track of the nation's population, to enforcing laws and caring for the health of citizens.

Chapter 2

FEDERAL LAW ENFORCEMENT AND ESPIONAGE

The **Federal Bureau of Investigation (FBI)** is part of the US Justice Department and is the federal government's top law enforcement agency. Its primary role is to investigate violations of federal crimes and crimes that cross state lines. One of its main objectives since 2001 has been to battle terrorism. Under the Patriot Act, the FBI has enjoyed more flexibility in how it is able to legally conduct searches and gather information. Also involved in this battle against terrorism is the **Department of Homeland Security**. Created after the 9/11 attacks, this department has the responsibility of preventing future terrorist attacks in the US, reducing the threat of such attacks, and minimizing the effects of such an attack should one occur. This department is also responsible for dealing with the effects of natural disasters such as earthquakes and hurricanes. The **Central Intelligence Agency (CIA)** was created after World War II and is the federal agency charged with conducting espionage. It is up to the CIA to spy and gather intelligence on the activities of foreign countries. Since 9/11, many of its operations have been geared towards locating terrorists and uncovering terrorist plots. The **Bureau of Alcohol, Tobacco, and Firearms (ATF)** enforces federal laws regarding firearms and explosives. It also enforces laws dealing with the manufacture, transportation, and distribution of alcohol and tobacco. The **Drug Enforcement Agency/Administration (DEA)** enforces laws against drug trafficking. Although the FBI also has jurisdiction over federal drug cases in the US, the DEA has the authority to pursue US drug investigations abroad as well. As part of the Department of Homeland Security, the **United States Citizenship and Immigration Services (CIS)** enforces laws and administers procedures for dealing with immigration and foreign visitors to the United States. The **Internal Revenue Service (IRS)** can also be classified as a law enforcement agency. Although it is most commonly recognized as the agency that collects taxes, it also has the authority to investigate and arrest those who evade paying federal income tax. The IRS is part of the Treasury Department.

DEALING WITH DISASTER

As mentioned before, the Department of Homeland Security is charged with dealing with natural disasters which occur in the US. The agency within the department that is responsible for planning for and responding to such disasters is the **Federal Emergency Management Administration (FEMA)**. This organization came under intense criticism in 2005 for its failure to adequately plan and provide relief for victims of hurricane Katrina. The **National Transportation Safety Board (NTSB)** conducts studies for improving

transportation safety. It also investigates plane crashes, train wrecks, and other accidents involving modes of transportation.

HUMAN HEALTH AND NUMBERS

The US government has also taken upon itself the role of protecting and maintaining the health of its citizens. The **Center for Disease Control (CDC)** in Atlanta, Georgia conducts research and responds to the threat of potential outbreaks of serious diseases. While much of the CDC's work goes on behind the scenes and is only occasionally noticed by citizens, millions feel the direct effects of Medicaid and Medicare everyday. **Medicare** is a federal program that provides health insurance for those over 65 and those with certain disabilities. **Medicaid** is a health insurance program funded by both the federal government and the states, and provides benefits for those with low incomes.

Finally, there is the *US Census Bureau*. The **US Census** is simply a population count that is taken every ten years. It is the duty of the **US Census Bureau** to take the census and compile important information based on it (i.e., what parts of the nation are growing the fastest, what percentage of the nation's citizens are minorities, etc.). It is the census that determines how many representatives each state has in Congress.

Practice 7: Important Federal Agencies

1. Using the PATRIOT Act to his advantage, an agent of the federal government obtains valuable information involving a terrorist plot being planned in Detroit. This agent MOST LIKELY works for which agency?

   A. FBI   B. DEA   C. IRS   D. CDC

2. A person from Russia wants to come to the US to work for three years. In order to acquire the right documents, his case will need to be processed by which agency?

   A. FBI   B. CIA   C. CIS   D. CDC

3. What roles do the FBI, CIA, and the Department of Homeland Security each play in fighting terrorism?

CHAPTER 2 REVIEW

A. Define the following key terms.

popular sovereignty	preamble	legislative branch
majority rule vs. minority rights	civil liberties vs. national security	elastic / "necessary and proper" clause
limited government	judicial branch	implied powers
enumerated/expressed powers	Federal Bureau of Investigation (FBI)	Bureau of Alcohol, Tobacco and Firearms (ATF)
Supremacy Clause	delegated powers	reserved powers
concurrent powers	Full Faith & Credit Clause	rule of law
Article 1	House of Representatives	Senate
bill	law	censure
expulsion	committee system	seniority system
filibuster	cloture	*Hazelwood v. Kuhlmeier*
New Jersey v. TLO	*Texas v. Johnson*	loose interpretation
strict interpretation	states' rights	redistricting
right to bear arms	term limits	Patriot Act
homeland security	interest groups	revenue
expenditures	direct/indirect tax	income tax
income tax return	corporate taxes	excise taxes
tariffs	Social Security	regressive taxes
progressive tax	proportional tax	user fees
fines	immunity	speaker of the House
vice president	majority leader	minority leader
separation of church and state	flexibility (of the Constitution)	president pro tempore/president of Senate
whip	*Writ of Habeas Corpus*	bills of attainer
ex post facto laws	titles of nobility	Article II
head of state	commander-in-chief	treaty
executive agreements	chief executive	legislative leader
economic leader	party leader	veto
executive orders	pardons	commute sentences
reprieves	*State of the Union Address*	presidential succession
impeachment	Article III	associate justices
judicial review	precedence	constitutional convention
judicial decisions & review	presidential action	national budget
budget deficit	deficit spending	budget surplus
balanced budget	national debt	treasure bonds
Medicare	Medicaid	US Census Bureau

The Government of the United States of America

US census	US Supreme Court	chief justice of the US
original, appellate, concurrent, and exclusive jurisdiction	constitutional amendments 1 – 27	Department of Homeland Security
Central Intelligence Agency (CIA)	Drug Enforcement Agency (DEA)	US Citizenship and Immigration Services (CIS)
Internal Revenue Service (IRS)	Federal Emergency Management Administration (FEMA)	National Transportation and Safety Board (NTSB)
Center for Disease Control (CDC)	*Heart of Atlanta Motel, Inc. v. United States*	*Swann v. Charlotte-Mecklenburg Bd. of Ed.*
congressional action	customs and traditions	*Marbury v. Madison*
McCullough v. Maryland	*Gibbons v. Ogden*	*Korematsu v. United States*
Plessy v. Ferguson	*Brown v. Bd. of Education*	*Regents of UC v. Blake*
Furman v. Georgia	*Gregg v. Georgia*	*Mapp v. Ohio*
Gideon v. Wainright	*Miranda v. Arizona*	*Engel v. Vitale*
Tinker v. Des Moines	*Bethel School District v. Frasier*	

B. Choose the correct answer.

1. Which of the following are principles on which the founding fathers based the United States government?

    A. states' rights over federal law
    B. delegation of all powers to the federal government
    C. the non-existence of concurrent powers
    D. popular sovereignty and limited government

2. Which of the following statements BEST defines what the preamble to the Constitution is and the purpose that it serves?

    A. It is the first sentence of the Constitution and serves to lay out the rights guaranteed to US citizens.
    B. It is the first sentence of the Constitution and serves to explain the purpose and intent of the document.
    C. It is the first sentence of the Bill of Rights and serves to explain the purpose of the first ten amendments to the Constitution.
    D. It is the last statement in the Bill of Rights and serves to express that citizens have more rights than just those mentioned in the first ten amendments.

Chapter 2

3. Congress choosing to establish a national bank in the early days of the nation, Congress choosing to regulate interstate commerce, and Congress deciding to pass laws limiting how hotels and public facilities in states are run are all examples of which of the following?

    A. the legislative branch's use of implied powers

    B. the legislative branch's use of expressed powers

    C. the judicial branch's use of judicial review

    D. the executive branch's use of implied powers

4. Which portion of the Constitution establishes the office of president of the United States?

    A. Article I   B. Article II   C. Article III   D. the preamble

5. The president of the United States has been accused of violating the Constitution. There is a movement in Washington, DC to remove him from office. In order for this to happen, what process will have to occur?

    A. The vice president will have to initiate a decree of impeachment. Once this occurs, if a majority of the House and the Senate agree that the president is guilty of the charges, then he is removed.

    B. The president must first be censured. If this does not convince him to step down, then the Senate must vote on whether or not to impeach the president. If two-thirds of the Senate agrees, then the president is removed from office.

    C. The House must bring formal charges against the president. The president then has the right to be heard before the Supreme Court. If the Court finds him guilty, then he will be removed from office.

    D. The House must vote to impeach the president. Once this occurs, the case is then heard in the Senate. Because it is the president, the chief justice will preside over the proceedings. If two-thirds of the Senate finds that the president is guilty, then he is removed from office.

6. Which of the following is NOT a power of Congress?

    A. initiate impeachment proceedings.   C. pass laws

    B. introduce tax bills   D. issue bills of attainder

7. Which of the following is not a role or power of the president?

    A. the power to veto legislation

    B. the power to negotiate and propose treaties to the Senate

    C. He/she may remove federal justices from the bench.

    D. He/she acts as the nation's chief diplomat.

8. A North Carolina state court convicts a criminal defendant of a felony. The defendant argues, however, that the police conducted an illegal search, violating his constitutional rights. The case has gone all the way to the Supreme Court on appeal. In ruling on this case, the Supreme Court is about to exercise what kind of jurisdiction?

    A. original jurisdiction   C. criminal jurisdiction

    B. appellate jurisdiction   D. concurrent jurisdiction

The Government of the United States of America

9. How many times has the United States Constitution been amended since 1788?
   A. 10   B. 21   C. 27   D. 100

10. What is Judicial Review and which court case established it?
    A. The power of the federal courts to overturn presidential appointments; it was established in *Marbury v. Madison.*
    B. The power of the Supreme Court to rule on interstate commerce; it was established by *Gibbons v. Ogden*
    C. The power of the Supreme Court to overturn cases establishing segregation; it was established in *Brown v. Board of Education.*
    D. The power of the Supreme Court to rule on whether or not laws passed by Congress and the states are constitutional; it was established in *Marbury v. Madison.*

11. *"Although the defendant's claim that the sentence of death imposed upon him constitutes 'cruel and unusual punishment' is noted; it is the decision of this court that the sentence is constitutional. This is because, in the eyes of this court, it appears that the lower court followed legal procedures correctly and provided the jury hearing the case with adequate guidelines of instruction. It also appears to this court that these guidelines were consistent and fair with those issued to juries in other death penalty cases. Therefore, this court finds itself in agreement with the lower court and hereby upholds the sentence."*

    What Supreme Court case does the above judge's statement MOST seem to be in agreement with?

    A. *Furman v. Georgia*   C. *Miranda v. Arizona*
    B. *Mapp v. Ohio*   D. *Gregg v. Georgia*

12. Which of the following is a controversy that has persisted since the days of the Federalists and Anti-federalists?
    A. the issue of *de jure* segregation
    B. whether or not quotas can be used to further affirmative action
    C. the question of federal power versus states rights
    D. whether or not the legislative branch should have one or two houses

13. A state passes a law requiring citizens to stand for a moment of prayer prior to the beginning of legal proceedings in state courthouses. Although the law does not require citizens to participate in the prayer so long as they stand and remain silent, the law is challenged in federal court as a violation of the Constitution. What part of the Constitution will the arguments in this case MOST LIKELY center on?
    A. the *Elastic Clause*
    B. the *Supremacy Clause*
    C. the *Free Exercise Clause* and the *Establishment Clause*
    D. the *Eleventh Amendment*

14. Federal law enforcement officers have been tracking a possible terrorist plot for months. They receive an anonymous tip that a key meeting of suspected terrorists is about to occur within the half hour. Immediately, they make arrangements to raid the meeting and confiscate evidence that indicates the group is guilty of plotting to blow up an elementary school. The defendants' lawyers challenge the arrest in federal court because the agents did not obtain a warrant first. In addition, they also argue that some of the evidence obtained beforehand was gathered illegally. The federal government claims that, under the PATRIOT Act, the agents had all the authority they needed. This conflict involves which of the following questions?

   A.   the constitutionality of anonymous tips

   B.   the relevancy of the Sixth Amendment in today's world

   C.   whether or not citizens' Second Amendment rights are always protected

   D.   the protection of civil liberties versus the importance of national security

15. Which of the following methods is the most common way the government raises revenue?

   A.   taxes   C.   treasury bonds

   B.   refunds   D.   user fees and fines

Chapter 3
State and Local Governments Under the North Carolina Constitution

This chapter addresses the following competency goal and objective(s):

Competency goal 3	The learner will analyze how state and local government is established by the North Carolina Constitution.
Objective 3.01, 3.02, 3.03, 3.04, 3.05, 3.06, 3.07, 3.08, 3.09	

3.1 THE NORTH CAROLINA CONSTITUTION

Following the *Declaration of Independence* in 1776, North Carolina drafted its first state constitution. Because it was meant to be **flexible**, provisions were included to allow it to be changed and amended over time. The North Carolina Constitution can be amended by a constitutional convention of the people, or by legislative initiative. A **constitutional convention** is a special convention called for the purpose of revising or amending the constitution. If two-thirds of each house of the General Assembly agrees, then a proposition is presented to the state's qualified voters. The public will then vote either in favor of, or

against, having a convention. If the state's qualified voters say "yes" to the proposal, then a convention of elected delegates will assemble. If this convention votes in favor of changing the constitution, then their proposed amendments are presented to the citizens of NC for yet another vote. This vote is called a **referendum**. If the majority of voters favor the change, then it is adopted. Amendments may also be introduced by **legislative initiative**. This occurs when three-fifths of both houses of the General Assembly vote in favor of submitting proposed amendments to the state's qualified voters without a convention. As in the case of a constitutional convention, the proposed amendments are then presented to the voters in the form of a referendum.

HISTORICAL BACKGROUND OF THE NORTH CAROLINA CONSTITUTION

North Carolina has had three constitutions. The first was drafted after the Declaration of Independence in 1776. However, the document rested almost all of the government's power in the legislative branch and gave no real power to the governor. Only legislators were elected by all of the people, rich landowners elected senators, and the General Assembly appointed the governor and other important officials.

In 1835, delegates held a convention and amended the constitution so that governors were popularly elected. In 1862, leaders called another convention to allow for secession (leaving the Union to join the Confederacy). After the Civil War, the state drafted a new constitution in 1868. It lengthened gubernatorial terms from two years to four, and was modeled after the ideals of Reconstruction. For this reason, it was not popular with more conservative North Carolinians. Finally, in 1971, North Carolina drafted and ratified its current constitution.

PRINCIPLES ON WHICH THE NORTH CAROLINA CONSTITUTION IS FOUNDED

Many of the principles forming the basis of the US Constitution also serve as a foundation of the North Carolina Constitution. The NC Constitution establishes a government based on **popular sovereignty** (serving the will of the people). It also establishes a **limited government**, in which even public officials are subject to the laws of the state. The North Carolina government is based on a **separation of powers** and a system of **checks and balances**. Just like the federal government, North Carolina's state government has three branches. The **General Assembly** serves as the legislative branch. The **governor** and the **Council of State** serve as the executive branch. The state courts, with the **NC Supreme Court** serving as the highest court in the state, serve as the judicial branch. As with the federal government, each one of these branches has specific roles and authority so that no one body becomes too powerful.

**Jim Hunt
First NC Governor to
win a second term in office**

STRUCTURE OF THE NORTH CAROLINA CONSTITUTION

The North Carolina Constitution begins with a **preamble** (opening sentence that defines the intent of the document) that reads as follows:

> *"We, the people of the State of North Carolina, grateful to Almighty God, the Sovereign Ruler of Nations, for the preservation of the American Union and the existence of our civil, political and religious liberties, and acknowledging our dependence upon Him for the continuance of those blessings to us and our posterity, do, for the more certain security thereof and for the better government of this State, ordain and establish this Constitution."*

Following the preamble are fourteen articles. Within Article I is the ***Declaration of Rights***. Similar to the US Constitution's *Bill of Rights*, this section of the NC Constitution outlines the rights of citizens. It has 30 sections and ensures such rights as free elections, religious liberty, freedom of speech/press, and the right to an education. Following are the different articles of the constitution and what they address.

Chapter 3

Article I	declaration of rights	**Article VIII**	corporations
Article II	legislative branch	**Article IX**	education
Article III	executive branch	**Article X**	homesteads and exemptions
Article IV	judicial branch	**Article XI**	punishments, corrections and charities
Article V	finance	**Article XII**	military forces
Article VI	suffrage and eligibility	**Article XIII**	conventions; constitutional amendment and revision
Article VII	local government	**Article XIV**	miscellaneous

One difference worth noting between the US Constitution and the NC Constitution is the manner in which changes are made. In the US Constitution, changes are always attached at the end as amendments. However, in the NC Constitution, changes are actually **incorporated** into the document. In other words, they are drafted into the document as if they were originally part of it.

Practice 1: The North Carolina Constitution

1. Which of the following statements is true regarding the NC Constitution?

    A. There has only been one constitution, but it has been changed many times.

    B. Unlike the federal government, the NC Constitution says nothing about the individual rights of citizens.

    C. The document rejects the idea of limited government in favor of popular sovereignty.

    D. The NC Constitution can be amended either by a constitutional convention or legislative initiative.

2. What is a *referendum*?

    A. a special convention called for ratifying changes to the constitution

    B. a statement of individual rights found in Article I of the NC Constitution

    C. a process by which citizens vote to accept or reject a proposed change to the state constitution

    D. a process by which changes to the constitution are drafted into the document as if they were originally part of it

3. How is the model of government set up by the NC Constitution similar to the government set up by the US Constitution? How is the manner in which changes are made to the two documents different?

3.2 NORTH CAROLINA'S STATE AND LOCAL STRUCTURE OF GOVERNMENT

STATE GOVERNMENT

Beverly Eaves Perdue
Current Lt. Governor

Mike Easley
Current Governor

The North Carolina Constitution establishes the framework for both state and local governments. As mentioned before, there are three branches of government at the state level. The legislative branch is comprised of the **General Assembly** (NC's version of Congress). It consists of two houses: the House of Representatives (120 members) and the NC Senate (50 members). Each member of the General Assembly serves two year terms. It is the role of the General Assembly to prepare bills that—with the governor's approval or an override of the governor's veto—will become **statutes** (state laws). The executive branch consists of the **governor** (the state's highest executive officer) and the Council of State. Among other duties, the governor prepares and recommends the state budget to the General Assembly, makes sure state laws are properly executed, acts as commander-in-chief of state military forces (i.e., the National Guard), and has the power to call special sessions of the legislature. The governor also has the authority to veto legislation. However, it is interesting that this power was only granted to the governor in 1996, making North Carolina the last state to give such power to its chief executive. The **Council of State** consists of several elected department heads, including the **lieutenant governor** (the state's second highest executive officer). The lieutenant governor presides over the Senate, but has no vote unless there is a tie to be broken. He/she is also the first in line to succeed the governor should he/she be unable to complete his/her term. Those elected to the office of governor or lieutenant governor serve for four years and are limited to no more than two consecutive terms (Governor Jim Hunt actually served four terms, but they were not all consecutive). The governor also has a **cabinet** consisting of the heads of various state departments. The key difference between the Cabinet and the Council of State is that one body is elected while the other is appointed by the governor.

Council of State (elected by the people)	Cabinet (appointed)
Lieutenant Governor	Secretary of Administration
Secretary of State	Secretary of Commerce
Attorney General of North Carolina	Secretary of Correction
Commissioner of Agriculture	Secretary of Crime Control and Public Safety
Commissioner of Insurance	Secretary of Cultural Resources
Commissioner of Labor	Secretary of Environment and Natural Resources
Superintendent of Public Instruction	Secretary of Health and Human Services
State Treasurer	Secretary of Revenue
State Auditor	Secretary of Juvenile Justice and Delinquency Prevention
	Secretary of Transportation

Finally, the judicial branch is made up of the state courts. It is responsible for making sure that the laws of the state are being properly applied and that legislation passed by the General Assembly is consistent with the constitution.

LOCAL GOVERNMENTS

Article VII / Section 1 of the NC Constitution states that the General Assembly shall provide for the organization and government of counties, cities, and towns. Several important government offices exist at the county level. **County commissioners** serve as elected representatives on behalf of the county. Their job is to make sure that the needs of the county are being met within the boundaries of state laws. The Board of Commissioners appoints a **county manager** who acts as the county's chief administrator and makes sure that policies are properly implemented. Article VII Section 2 mandates that each county shall have an elected **sheriff** to serve as the county's chief law enforcement official. Sheriffs have both criminal and civil authority, and they are elected to four year terms.

In addition to county governments, there are also governments that oversee cities, townships, and special districts. Cities and towns differ mainly in terms of size. Cities are larger and tend to consist of residential, industrial, and business areas. An extremely large city (for example, a population of half a million or more) is called a **metropolis**. **City governments** usually have an elected **mayor** who serves as the chief executive officer and shares power with an elected **city council**. A member of the City Council, particularly in larger cities, is often referred to as an **alderman**. It is the City Council that considers and passes city **ordinances** (laws specific to a particular city). This model is called a **mayor-council plan**. Another model of city government is called the **council-manager plan**. Under this model, citizens elect a council which then hires a city manager. The manager answers to, and can be replaced by, the council. This form of government is popular among larger cities. Many times, cities that use this model will still have a mayor. The mayor, however, usually only serves a ceremonial role or acts as the head of the City Council, while the city manager carries out the real duties of overseeing city government.   Unlike counties that rely on an elected sheriff for law enforcement, cities usually hire a **police chief** who answers to the mayor or city manager. **Townships**, or towns, are generally smaller than cities and tend to be governed by **town councils** comprised of elected officials. Finally, there are some bodies of government designed for **special districts**. These are districts set up for the implementation of a specific service. Examples include school districts, fire protection, waste management systems, etc. An example of a body of government established for a special district would be the local **Board of Education**. Comprised of elected representatives, it is in place for one specific service; to oversee public education in a given district.

Changes to the NC Constitution must be approved by voters in a referendum. Local laws can be amended through a similar process called a **local act**. A local act is put before the voters of a city, town, or community and, if approved, is adopted as law.

Practice 2: Structure of Government at State and Local Levels

1. The lieutenant governor, the secretary of state, and the attorney general all have which of the following in common?

   A. They are each appointed by the governor.

   B. Together, they comprise the entire executive branch of state government.

   C. They are all part of the Council of State.

   D. None of them have any role in the General Assembly.

2. Which of the following is NOT a power or duty of the governor?

   A. call special sessions of the legislature

   B. appoint members of the Council of State

   C. veto proposed statutes

   D. commander-in-chief of the state's military forces

3. David has just been hired to be the city manager for a mid-sized city. There will be a mayor as well, but she will serve primarily as a ceremonial representative. David is the one who will be primarily responsible for overseeing city government. David's city operates on which model of government?

   A. mayor-council plan   C. manager-mayor plan

   B. council-manager plan   D. city-township plan

3.3 AUTHORITY AND LIMITATIONS OF GOVERNMENT AGENCIES AND PUBLIC OFFICIALS

PUBLIC OFFICIALS

The North Carolina Constitution defines the powers and responsibilities of public officials. Under Article III / Section 4, the **governor** is responsible for making sure that the state's laws are faithfully executed. The **lieutenant governor**, meanwhile, presides over the NC Senate (for a list of other duties of the governor and lieutenant governor. (Review section 3.2., chapter 3.) However, the constitution also limits the powers of these executives by both its system of checks and balances and by term limits on each office. Article VII / Section 2 establishes that each county shall have a **sheriff** to act as its chief law enforcement officer, and that he/she shall be elected to a four year term. Article IV establishes state district, superior, and appellate courts. It also establishes the NC Supreme Court, which is led by a chief justice and six associate justices. This article outlines the powers, jurisdictions, and limitations on the various courts. It also defines the requirements for **judges**, as well as the procedures by which they are elected and assigned. Article IV / Section 16, states that justices to the supreme court, judges to the court of appeals, and superior court judges shall be elected to terms of eight years. Section 10 states that district court judges shall be elected to four year terms. Judicial power of the state is granted to the courts, and the General Assembly has no power or jurisdiction that rightfully pertains to the courts except in matters of impeachment.

North Carolina Courts		
Court	**Jurisdiction**	**Judges' Terms**
District	Prescribed by the general assembly. District courts hear misdemeanor criminal cases and civil cases involving smaller amounts of money.	4 years
Superior	Original general jurisdiction throughout the state. Superior courts hear appeals from district courts, as well as felony criminal and more serious civil cases.	8 years
Court of Appeals	Appellate jurisdiction over cases heard in lower state courts.	8 years
NC Supreme Court	Appellate jurisdiction over cases heard in lower state courts (including the Court of Appeals). It also has the power of judicial review over legislation passed by the General Assembly and authority to review appeals from a final order or decision of the NC Utilities Commission, when authorized by law.	8 years

GOVERNMENT AGENCIES

Article III / Section 11 requires the state of North Carolina to place all **state agencies** under one of no more than 25 departments. These agencies provide a number of services and perform various roles. For example, the **Department of Health and Human Services (DHHS)** is the largest government agency in NC. It is responsible for ensuring the health, safety, and well-being of North Carolinians. It is headed by a secretary appointed by the governor. The **Department of Transportation (DOT)** is also led by an appointed official and is charged with the responsibility of providing a safe and efficient transportation system. Article X addresses "Homesteads and Exemptions." This predominantly has to do with real estate and property rights. The responsibility for issues involving real estate falls to the **Register of Deeds**. This office acts as the custodian for all land transaction documents, deeds of trust, and other legal documents regarding real estate. These departments represent just a few examples of the many agencies that exist and operate under the North Carolina system of government.

Practice 3: Authority and Limitations of Government Agencies and Public Officials

1. The NC Constitution requires the General Assembly to approve the governor's budget before it becomes official. What is this an example of?

   A. limitations placed on the governor by term limits

   B. limitations placed on the governor by the courts

   C. limitations placed on the governor by a system of checks and balances

   D. limitations placed on the budget by the register of deeds

2. Which of the following is true regarding North Carolina judges?

   A. All judges are elected to a term of 8 years.

   B. Lower court judges are elected, but supreme court justices are appointed by the governor.

   C. Supreme court justices and judges on the Court of Appeals are elected to 8 year terms; but lower court judges are appointed by the chief justice.

   D. Unlike federal judges who are appointed for life, all state judges are elected officials who serve a set term.

3. The DHHS, DOT, and Register of Deeds, are all examples of what?

   A. departments led directly by the lieutenant governor

   B. departments led by members of the council of state

   C. state agencies carrying out a number of roles and responsibilities

   D. state agencies established under Article X of the NC Constitution

3.4 THE AUTHORITY OF STATE LAW AND THE BILL OF RIGHTS

Without question, the NC Constitution stands as the state's final authority on state law. Over the years, there have been a number of court cases that have served to reinforce this authority. One such case was that of *State v. Mann (1830)*. In 1829, a slave master named John Mann shot and wounded a female slave he had leased from another owner. Mann was then prosecuted and convicted of battery. Mann appealed the conviction, arguing that the law did not limit the measures a master might use to force obedience from a slave. The NC Supreme Court ruled in favor of Mann, stating that "the power of the master must be absolute, to render the submission of the slave perfect." Judge Thomas Ruffin made it clear that the court's sympathies rested with the wounded slave, but that its ruling must be based on the letter of NC law. The case served to demonstrate that it is the state constitution, not the sympathies of the court, which serves as the ultimate legal authority.

Female Slave

Almost a century and a half later, in what became known as the *Leandro Case (1997)*, school boards and students from several low-income counties and urban areas sued the state for failing to fulfill its constitutional obligation to provide a quality education. They claimed that the state's formula for funding schools did not provide their districts with sufficient funds for "at risk" kids and students whose first language was not English. The NC Supreme Court agreed. In their decision, the court reinforced the fact that even the North Carolina government is obligated to live up to the guidelines of the constitution. It also said that if the state fails to meet its obligation, the courts may intervene to ensure proper management and funding of the educational system.

Chapter 3

HOW THE BILL OF RIGHTS AFFECTS STATE LAW

Like all states, North Carolina is subject to the *Supremacy Clause* of the United States Constitution. This means that North Carolina law must comply and be consistent with federal laws. The ***Fourteenth Amendment***, which was ratified in 1868, defines **citizenship** (who is considered a citizen of the United States) as anyone born or naturalized in the United States. It also clearly states that anyone who is considered a citizen of the United States is also a legal citizen of the state in which they reside. The amendment goes on to ensure that no state shall abridge or deny the **civil rights** (rights guaranteed by the US Constitution) of any citizen without due process of law. Any rights guaranteed by the US Constitution cannot be denied by any provision of the NC Constitution. In effect, the *Fourteenth Amendment* serves to extend the ***Bill of Rights*** to state residents.

**Representative
Thaddeus Stevens
Championed Civil Rights
During Reconstruction**

Susan B. Anthony

The ***Fifteenth Amendment*** ensures the **voting rights** of citizens. It states that all citizens have the right to vote regardless of race, color, or "previous condition of servitude." Ratified in 1870, this amendment granted the right to vote to freed slaves. In time, many southern states used creative approaches to try and get around these amendments and prevent African-Americans from voting. Eventually, however, the federal government began to act in the 1950s and 60s, handing down court rulings and passing legislation that ensured minorities the right to vote. Interestingly, however, the *Fifteenth Amendment* did not grant the right to vote to women. That change finally came in 1920 with ratification of the ***Nineteenth Amendment***. This amendment states that the right to vote shall not be abridged or denied on account of sex. In effect, the *Nineteenth Amendment* extends protection of a **woman's right to vote** to the states.

Practice 4: State Law and the Bill of Rights

1. Which of the following is a true statement?

    A. The NC Constitution is the final authority on state law, however it can be overruled by the NC Supreme Court.

    B. The North Carolina government cannot be sued for failure to obey the constitution.

    C. The *Fourteenth Amendment* serves to guarantee the civil rights of those living in North Carolina.

    D. Women's voting rights are guaranteed to NC citizens under the *Fifteenth Amendment*.

2. The idea that state government must meet its constitutional obligations to its citizens is reinforced by which of the following?

    A. the US Supreme Court's decision in *Leandro v. US*

    B. the NC Supreme Court's decision in *State v. Mann*

    C. the NC Supreme Court's decision in the *Leandro Case*

    D. the *Nineteenth Amendment*

3. Which of the following means that women are guaranteed the right to vote in North Carolina?
    A. ratification of the *Fourteenth Amendment*
    B. the court's decision in the *Leandro Case*
    C. ratification of the state constitution
    D. the addition of the *Nineteenth Amendment* to the US Constitution

3.5 CONTROVERSIES SURROUNDING THE POWERS OF STATE GOVERNMENTS

ANNEXATION

Today, there are a number of controversies surrounding the powers of North Carolina's state government. One of these is the issue of annexation. **Annexation** is the process by which a city expands by taking over outlying and previously independent areas. Proponents of annexation point out that cities provide these areas with valuable services like trash collection, sewage services, public safety services, water, and so forth. Annexation is sometimes opposed by those living in annexed areas, however, because it usually means having to pay new city taxes, utility connection fees, and having to adhere to city zoning ordinances.

MONEY

The North Carolina Constitution requires the state to maintain a **balanced budget**. In other words, state expenditures (what the state spends) cannot exceed state revenues (money the state takes in). While this makes a lot of sense, it is not always an easy task. To help the state bring in more revenue, North Carolina instituted a state **lottery** in 2005 to assist in funding public education. The lottery is a subject of controversy in the state. Those who favor the lottery focus on the fact that it raises millions of dollars for education without imposing new taxes. If people don't want to pay for a lottery ticket, then they don't have to. Many opponents, however, attack the lottery on moral grounds. They claim it is nothing more than state sponsored gambling. Some also complain that it entices those who are poor to spend money in the hopes of getting rich on something that offers them almost no chance of winning.

EDUCATION

Other controversies relating to education include questions surrounding charter schools and school busing. **Charter schools** are public schools that are specially "chartered" by some sponsor group (such as a public agency, university, or other entity) to provide an alternative to traditional public schools. Although they are funded with state money, charter schools operate independent of district school boards. In return for greater independence from district policies, these schools make themselves accountable to their sponsoring group for how they are performing. Charter schools that fail to produce the results for which they were founded can be closed. In essence, charter schools are public schools that act similar to

private schools. Sometimes they are geared to a specific population; such as pregnant teens or kids with behavioral problems. Other times, they may focus on specific fields (math, science, the arts, etc.). Proponents of charter schools praise them for providing an alternative to traditional education. They point out statistics that suggest traditional public schools are doing an inadequate job of educating students compared to other developed nations. They claim charter schools will help turn this trend around by forcing public schools to engage in competition. Critics of charter schools claim that it is not fair for public funds to go to schools geared towards such a limited population. They claim that other schools are left depleted because gifted students often leave for these alternative programs. In response, supporters remind citizens that many charter schools are designed to serve the disadvantaged, rather than gifted students.

School busing is a method of integration in which students are required to attend schools outside the boundaries of what would normally be their school district. Beginning in the late 1960s, school systems began using busing as a means to integrate schools. Those who favor the practice say it is essential for providing racial diversity and preventing de facto segregation in schools, because whites and blacks often live in different neighborhoods. Opponents point to the inconvenience of having to bus children long distances. They also claim the practice violates civil rights because it makes race a major factor in school assignments. Although busing is not nearly the "hot button" issue it was 30 years ago, it still remains an issue of controversy in urban areas where whites, African-Americans, and other minority populations often remain socially segregated.

OTHER CONTROVERSIAL TOPICS

There are a number of other topics of controversy as well. For instance, what is the proper role of the state in providing **disaster relief**? Controversy regarding this issue received national attention in New Orleans, Louisiana in 2005 following hurricane Katrina. In the midst of all the horror and destruction, government officials applied blame and pointed fingers at one another as they argued over which level of

North Carolina Constitution

government had most failed to fulfill its role; local, state, or national. The role of state and local governments versus the role of the federal government, as well as each level's ability to work together, is an important question in times of crisis.

In addition, **political corruption** has always been an issue of concern. While many public officials serve admirably, state and local governments are also susceptible to corrupt leaders who engage in illegal activity. Bribery (accepting illegal payments or favors in exchange for votes and/or support) and graft (using a political position for financial gain) are just a couple of ways corruption can infect state and local governments. Usually, politicians engage in such activities to get rich and/or to maintain their political power. One area in which the courts have sought to limit corruption is in *redistricting*. (Review section 2.5 in chapter 2.) **Redistricting** occurs when states redraw state and congressional voting districts. Usually, this is done every ten years after the national census. At  times, politicians try to manipulate the outcomes of elections by engaging in **gerrymandering**. This is a process in which districts are drawn for the purpose of ensuring election outcomes. The name is derived from a district drawn by Massachusetts Governor Elbridge Gerry in the early 1800s. Because the district was obviously drawn to disadvantage Gerry's opponents and was shaped like a salamander, the term "gerrymander" came to mean the act of drawing districts to maintain a political advantage. As mentioned before, this kind of redistricting has been declared illegal when it is done to either disadvantage or favor a particular race. However, gerrymandering solely for the purpose of helping one political party over another is not technically illegal. Some might argue, however, that it is unethical.

Practice 5: Controversies

"We like living the way we have been. We don't need your garbage collection and your police department to keep us safe. All you want is to charge us a bunch of taxes and fees to use your water and sewage lines."

1. This person is MOST LIKELY opposing what?

    A. annexation
    B. federal disaster relief
    C. charter schools
    D. a balanced budget

2. Tommy dropped out of school because of all the trouble he was having with the law. Now, after some time in jail and drug rehab, Tommy wants to get his education. He enrolls in a school especially geared towards helping "at risk" teens. The school is funded by public money, but it is independent of the local school district. It sounds like Tommy probably attends which of the following?

    A. a private school
    B. a traditional public school
    C. an annexed school
    D. a charter school

3. What are some arguments for and against North Carolina's lottery?

3.6 HOW STATE AND LOCAL GOVERNMENTS RAISE REVENUE

Just like individuals, governments have to stay on top of their **finances** (money). As mentioned earlier, the NC Constitution requires the government to maintain a balanced budget. This requires revenue and responsible spending.

TAXES

As with the federal government, the primary way in which state and local governments raise revenue is through taxes. Citizens of North Carolina are required to pay **state income tax**. This is a tax that people pay to the state based on a percentage of their annual income. Corporations in NC pay **corporate**

income tax, which requires them to pay a percentage of their yearly profits. **Property taxes** must be paid by those who own certain types of property, such as a home or land. Property taxes are usually imposed by county or municipal governments and are determined by **assessments** (estimating the property's value). The higher the value one's property is assessed at, the higher the amount of taxes that person must pay. **Inheritance tax** is tax that must be paid on what one inherits from someone who has died. In other words, before you make plans to spend that million dollars your long, lost uncle left you, you better be aware that you have to pay taxes on that money. Closely related to inheritance tax is **estate tax**. Estate tax is also collected when a person dies. When someone passes away, the assets and property that he/she leaves behind is called an *estate*. The value of the estate is assessed and a tax must be paid before it can then be transferred to the deceased's heir. For example, if Betty's father dies and leaves his estate to her, then Betty must pay the estate tax. North Carolina also imposes **sales tax** on goods and services purchased by consumers. The tax is equal to a percentage of the price. This means that the more expensive a product is, the more money one must pay in taxes. Finally, **excise taxes** are taxes on specific "non-essential" goods; like cigarettes and alcohol.

FEES AND FINES

The state also raises money by charging fees for **permits and licenses**. You had to — or will have to — pay a fee to receive your driver's license. That money goes to the state. Fishing licenses, business licenses, building permits, and so forth, all require fees that help finance state and local governments. **User fees** are charged to people who benefit from the use of public facilities. Paying to use the picnic area at a city park, or money spent to drive on a toll road are two examples of user fees. **Disposal fees** are paid to state or local governments for the removal of waste (i.e., trash or yard debris). Land developers usually have to pay **impact fees** that are used to finance the building or expansion of government buildings; such as police and fire stations, libraries, water/sewage plants, etc. **Fines** also provide money for state and local governments. Fines are money paid as punishment for a crime or some civil offense.

OTHER MEANS OF REVENUE

Another way that governments raise revenue is through the sale of **state and municipal bonds**. State and local governments issue bonds in exchange for cash. The government body that issues the bond then pays back the bond holder (person or entity that purchased the bond) at a later date with interest. The state or city benefits from the sale of the bond because it increases revenue. The bond holder benefits from the bond because it acts as an investment that earns them money over time.

State and local governments also receive money as a result of intergovernmental revenue. **Intergovernmental revenue** is money received from federal, state, or local governments in the form of grants, shared revenues, and special payments. For example, state governments often receive **federal grants in aid**. This is federal money issued to a state to help finance things like Medicaid, highways, disaster relief, special community programs, etc. Sometimes, the federal government uses its control over grant money to persuade states to adopt certain policies. For instance, the US government convinced some states to raise their legal drinking age from 18 to 21 by threatening to withhold federal highway funding if they refused.

Practice 6: Revenue

1. Name 3 methods by which state and local governments raise revenue and define each method.

2. Donnie wants to buy a new leather coat. He has exactly $100 to spend. He finds an awesome coat that is exactly what he's been looking for that cost $95.99. However, when he goes to pay for it, he discovers that he will have to pay more than $100. Donnie forgot to allow for what?
   A. excise tax
   B. user fees
   C. property tax
   D. sales tax

3. Money paid by city residents to have their trash collected each week is an example of what?
   A. property tax
   B. disposal fee
   C. impact fee
   D. municipal bond

3.7 STATE AND LOCAL AGENCIES/SERVICES AND HOW THEY ARE FUNDED

There are a number of state and local agencies that provide various services for citizens of the state. Each agency is funded by either the local, state, or federal government; or by some combination of the three. The following are some examples of these agencies and how they are funded (F = federal, S = state, L = local):

Community College System – Provides post-secondary education. Programs range from completing high school diplomas, to certificate programs and associate degrees. These institutions also provide up to two years of credits that can transfer to regular four year colleges and universities. Through the Community College system, more citizens have an opportunity to further their education. {S, L}

Cooperative Extension Service – A service provided through a partnership between the state's land-grant universities (NC State / North Carolina A&T) and community agencies to help improve the lives of citizens through research and education. Areas of focus often include agriculture, home atmosphere, economic development of the community, and the environment. {F, S}

Court Facilities – Hold civil and criminal court proceedings, as well as housing important records dealing with civil and criminal cases. {S, L}

Jails, Prisons, and Youth Detention Centers– Jails confine those awaiting trial or transfer to a state prison. Jails also house those sentenced to shorter periods of confinement. Prisons serve the purpose of housing adults who must serve longer periods of time, while youth detention centers house juveniles convicted of serious crimes. {S}

**Central Prison
Raleigh**

Board of Elections – Most counties have a Board of Elections that is responsible for carrying out the process of elections efficiently. For instance, they set up and operate polling sites, make sure votes are properly collected, and ensure that those who vote are properly registered. {F, S}

Mental Health Services – Provide services for the treatment of mental illness, drug addiction, and emotional problems. {F, S}

Public Health Services – Provide services meant to ensure the health of citizens. {F, S}

Public Schools – Meant to ensure that every North Carolina citizen has an opportunity for a quality education. {F, S, L}

Soil and Water Conservation – Administers programs to protect and conserve the state's soil and water resources. {F, S}

Tax Assessment – Assess the value of property, etc. within a given county for the purpose of properly imposing taxes. {S, L}

Airports – Provide for air travel and shipment by providing landing and loading areas for aircraft. While many airports are large facilities that transport thousands of passengers per day, others are relatively small and serve predominantly small aircraft. Airports get some money from vendors who use their facilities, as well as government funding. {S, L}

Social Services – Provide services necessary to the community; such as placing abused children in safe homes, investigating alleged charges of abuse, helping underprivileged families, assisting those with mental illness, helping families facing crisis, etc. Its intent is to help disadvantaged citizens improve their standard of living. {F, S}

Ambulance Services – Provide emergency medical transportation to hospitals, etc. {L}

North Carolina Constitution

Museums – The state and local communities often feature museums. These are institutions open to the public which conserve and display artifacts and special exhibits. In addition, museums conduct research and provide additional resources of education. While nearly all museums receive government funding, many also take in money by charging admission or asking for private donations. {F, S, L}

Libraries – Like museums, libraries also provide materials for research and education. However, libraries tend to house books and other written reference materials. Most libraries provide a service in which citizens can "check out" (borrow) materials from the library so as to be able to read or study them at home. {L}

Public Transportation – Most larger and more densely populated areas provide public transportation (i.e. public buses). Local and state governments usually subsidize public transit, with the remaining costs being collected via user fees charged to passengers. The Federal Transit Administration (FTA) also provides funding to cities which operate mass transit systems. {F, S, L}

Emergency Management Agencies – These agencies range from agencies that are concerned with the daily public safety of local residents (i.e., police and fire departments) to agencies concerned with huge natural disasters. Funding for these agencies can come from the federal, state, or local governments, depending on the agency and its responsibilities. {F, S, or L}

Freedom Park

Department of Parks and Recreation – Responsible for maintaining local and state parks. {S, L}

Public Housing – Government owned housing for low-income families. {F}

Public Utilities – Companies that maintain the infrastructure of a public service. For example, they provide electricity, drinking water, natural gas, sewage, and other services essential to a community. They are normally subsidized by the state, with user fees being charged to customers of the utility. {S}

Practice 7: State and Local Funding

1. Which of the following is at least partially funded by the federal government?

    A. the North Carolina Cooperative Extension Service
    B. North Carolina prisons
    C. North Carolina tax assessments
    D. the North Carolina community college system

2. Which of the following agencies would MOST LIKELY be responsible for finding a safe home for an abused child?

    A. The North Carolina Detention Center
    B. NC public schools
    C. social services
    D. public health services

3. What service does the Community College System offer and how is it funded?

CHAPTER 3 REVIEW:

A. Define the following key terms

flexible (NC Constitution)

constitutional convention

referendum

legislative initiative

Fifteenth Amendment

voting rights

Nineteenth Amendment

woman's right to vote

annexation

balanced budget

lottery

preamble

Declaration of Rights

political corruption

redistricting

gerrymandering

county commissioners

county manager

property tax

metropolis

estate tax

alderman

permits and licenses

ordinances

impact fees

town councils

board of education

judges

Department of Health and Human Services

jails, prisons, youth detention centers

State v. Mann

Leandro Case

Fourteenth Amendment

citizenship

social services

ambulance services

museums

libraries

public transportation

emergency management agencies

NC Supreme Court

school busing

disaster relief

public housing

public utilities

cabinet

state income tax

corporate income tax

city governments

inheritance tax

city council

excise taxes

council-manager plan

disposal fees

townships

state and municipal bonds

federal grants in aid

Cooperative Extension Service

Department of Transportation

Register of Deeds

mental health services

public health services

soil and water conservation

tax assessment

airports

popular sovereignty

limited government

separation of powers

checks and balances

General Assembly

governor

lieutenant governor

charter schools

Dept. of Parks and Recreation

incorporation into the constitution

statutes

Council of State

state finances

county commissioners

sheriff

assessments

mayor

sales tax

mayor-council plan

user fees

police chief

fines

special districts

local act

state agencies

court facilities

board of elections

public schools

North Carolina Constitution

B. Choose the correct answer.

1. 32 NC senators and 61 members of the NC House of Representatives have voted in favor of proposing amendments to the state constitution. Is this enough to send a referendum calling for these changes to the state's qualified voters?

    A. Yes, this is more than enough members of each house to present the amendments in a referendum.

    B. No, there are not enough members of the Senate who support the proposals.

    C. No, there are not enough members of the House who support the proposal.

    D. No, because a constitutional convention must always be called first.

2. The governor, the General Assembly, and the NC courts are all subject to the laws of the state and the articles of the NC Constitution. This is an example of what?

    A. popular sovereignty   C. separation of powers

    B. limited government   D. legislative referendum

3. Which of the following MOST resembles the first ten amendments to the US Constitution?

    A. Articles II-III of the NC Constitution   C. the state preamble

    B. the *Declaration of Rights*   D. the legislative initiative

4. The US Constitution and the NC Constitution have each of the following in common EXCEPT:

    A. They were both intended to be flexible documents that could change and adapt over time.

    B. Changes to each document are added by a process called *incorporation*.

    C. Each establishes three branches of government and a system of checks and balances.

    D. Each begins with a preamble.

5. Bill wants to be part of the Council of State as the North Carolina commissioner of insurance. What will Bill have to do to attain this office?

    A. Bill will need to run for this office and win it in an election.

    B. Bill better get close to the governor so that the governor will appoint him to this office.

    C. Bill needs to submit his resume' to the governor to show him/her that he is qualified for the position.

    D. Bill will have to first be elected to the Council of State; then ask the lieutenant governor to assign him to the position of commissioner of insurance.

6. Maggie has been appointed to the office of secretary of transportation. Maggie is part of what?

    A. the council of state   C. the NC Senate

    B. the governor's cabinet   D. the NC House

7. Jody is an elected official who acts as the chief executive of a small city. She oversees city government and works closely with a group of elected officials that serve as the legislative branch of the city's government. The city Jody serves MOST LIKELY operates on what model of local government?

    A. council-manager plan   C. mayor-council plan

    B. manager-alderman plan   D. city-township plan

8. Which of the following is true regarding the judicial branch of state government?
   A. Judges are appointed by the governor for life.
   B. Judges are appointed by the governor but must be approved by the Senate.
   C. Judges are elected officials, all of which serve 8 year terms.
   D. Judges are elected officials with district court judges serving shorter terms than superior court judges.

9. The *Fourteenth Amendment* served to do which of the following?
   A. free slaves who lived in North Carolina and other southern states
   B. extend civil rights guaranteed under the US Constitution to citizens of North Carolina regardless of race
   C. guarantee freed slaves the right to vote in North Carolina
   D. guarantee women the right to vote in North Carolina

"I oppose this action on moral grounds. While it is true that we must raise the standards of education and this—undoubtedly—requires revenue, I do not believe it is right to raise money by exploiting and playing on the fears of the lower classes; who, in vain hope, will lose dollar after dollar in an attempt to beat the odds and ease all their financial woes overnight. How sad it is that the state government of North Carolina has, in effect, become a bookie."

10. The above quote is MOST LIKELY opposing what?
    A. legislative initiative
    B. the state lottery
    C. the failure to provide disaster relief
    D. charter schools

11. The majority party in Raleigh has managed to successfully redraw the state's voting districts, so as to guarantee that their candidates have an advantage in the next election. This party has just engaged in what practice?
    A. popular sovereignty
    B. limited redistricting
    C. gerrymandering
    D. graft

12. The minority party in Raleigh has protested the redistricting mentioned in question #11. They have challenged the move in the courts. In order for the minority party to win their case, they will have to prove which of the following?
    A. The redistricting was done with the intention of giving the majority party an advantage in the next election.
    B. Redistricting is unconstitutional.
    C. The redistricting was done right after the census was taken.
    D. The redistricting was done so as to favor or deny representation to a particular race.

13. Phil gets his property tax bill from Mecklenburg County and notices that he is having to pay $400 more in taxes on his house this year than he did last year, even though he hasn't moved. What has MOST LIKELY happened?

    A. Phil did not pay enough taxes the year before and is being charged the difference.

    B. Phil has earned more money this year and therefore is being charged a higher percentage of his income.

    C. Phil's house has been assessed at a higher value this year than it was the year before.

    D. Phil inherited his house and is having to pay an additional tax.

14. Frank's business is designing and building new residential neighborhoods. Although the community is glad to be growing, the new homes and increasing population will require increased public services. In order to help pay for this, the city will likely charge Frank what?

    A. construction tax

    B. user fees for the land

    C. fines for using the area

    D. an impact fee

15. Thanks to state and local funding, Mary was able to get her GED. It wasn't easy. She dropped out of high school to have a baby. She went to night school GED classes for over a year to finish. Now, she's even thinking about staying at the same school to take courses that will prepare her to transfer to a college. Mary is MOST LIKELY benefiting from which of the following?

    A. services at a youth detention center

    B. the state's community college system

    C. an emergency management agency

    D. the Cooperative Extension Service

Chapter 4
Active Citizenship

This chapter addresses the following competency goal and objective(s):

Competency goal 4	The learner will explore active roles as a citizen at the local, state, and national levels of government.
Objective 4.01, 4.02, 4.03, 4.04, 4.05, 4.06, 4.07, 4.08, 4.09	

4.1 POLITICAL PARTIES

The United States Constitution says nothing about political parties. In fact, President George Washington warned the nation that forming such parties would have harmful effects on US government. Despite Washington's pleas and the fact that they are not addressed in the Constitution, however, political parties have become an important part of US politics. From the days of the Federalists and Anti-federalists (eventually known as the Democratic-Republicans) to today's Republicans and Democrats, the United States has always had political parties.

PARTY SYSTEMS

Political parties are organizations that promote political beliefs and sponsor **candidates** (people running for political office) under the organization's name. Many of the world's democracies operate on what is called a **multi-party system**. In such a system, there are numerous political parties that hold government seats. The Netherlands, Israel, and Denmark are just a few examples of countries operating on this kind of system.

Israel Parliament

In a multi-party system, parties are usually given representation in government proportional to the number of votes they receive in an election. For example, say that there are 10 seats available in Parliament. Party A receives 40% of the vote, party B receives 30%, and parties C, D, and E each receive 10%. Proportional representation means that party A gets 4 seats, party B 3 seats, and parties C, D, and E each get 1 seat. All five parties will be represented

Active Citizenship

in Parliament, with party A having most of the influence. Under a multi-party system, parties only need to receive a *plurality vote*, rather than a *majority vote*, to remain in power. A **majority vote** is when a party must win the majority of votes cast in order to win the election. In a **plurality vote**, a party does not need to win a majority of votes; it simply needs to win more than the other parties. Think about the example we just gave featuring parties A, B, C, D, and E. Party A did not receive a majority of votes (it received only 40%) but it did win the plurality (more than any of the other parties).

By contrast, the United States operates on a **two-party system**. This is a system in which only two primary parties dominate a nation's politics. In the United States, these two parties are the Democrats and Republicans. In general, **Democrats** are identified as more **liberal**. Liberals tend to favor a more active government. They advocate government programs to provide welfare, health needs, job assistance, etc. This is because liberals view government as having a broad role. They believe government should help provide for the physical needs, education, and monetary security of its citizens. **Republicans**, however, are generally seen as more **conservative**. Conservatives believe that less government is better. They believe the role of government is simply to provide law and order, protection of its citizens' rights, and a national defense against foreign threats. Conservatives believe that it is government's job to provide citizens with the opportunity for success, not guarantee it. Of course, in reality, some Democrats are conservative and some Republicans are liberal. Both parties also have *moderates*. **Moderates** are those whose beliefs fall somewhere in the middle, between liberal and conservative.

Ross Perot (independent)

Why does the US feature a two-party system while many other nations have multi-party systems? The answer is largely due to the way the US conducts elections. Take, for example, congressional elections. In a multi-party system based on proportional representation, each party receives a number of seats based on the number of votes it receives. But in the United States, things are done differently. If a state is entitled to 15 representatives, then that state is divided into 15 individual voting districts. Each district then elects one winner to represent them. This means that if the Democratic candidate wins 51% of the vote, the Republican 42%, the Libertarian 6%, and the Reform Party 1%, then there is still just one winner—the Democrat. Only the Democratic candidate will go to Congress; the other three are flat out of luck. As a result, it is more beneficial in the United States to align oneself with one of the two major parties that actually have a chance of winning. Sometimes, however, **third parties** (parties other than the Republicans and Democrats) and **independents** (those not affiliated with a party) do play a role in US politics. In the late 1800s, the Peoples Party (also known as the Populists) initiated a number of key reforms. In 1912, Theodore Roosevelt actually won more votes for president as the Progressive Party candidate than did the incumbent Republican. In 1992, Bill Clinton (a Democrat) won the election with only 43% of the vote. This was largely due to Ross Perot's independent campaign that pulled support away from

**Mass. Senator
Ted Kennedy (liberal)**

**Former NC Senator
Jesse Helms (conservative)**

President George HW Bush. Historically, however, while third party candidates and independents have won some government offices and, at times, influenced policies, they generally do not win the White House or a majority in Congress.

Some countries use a **one-party system**, in which only one party is allowed to operate. As a result, citizens' ability to have a say in their government is greatly limited under such a system. China's Communist Party is an example of a one-party system.

US PARTY STRUCTURE AND FUNCTION

Political parties serve **several functions**. They nominate candidates for office, structure the voting choice (limit the list of candidates to those who have a real chance of winning—usually the Republican and Democratic candidates), coordinate the actions of government officials (i.e., facilitate the different branches of government working together), and establish party *platforms*. The **platform** is the party's statement of programs and policies it will pursue once its candidates are in office. It is made up of several **planks**. The term "plank" refers to an individual policy within the platform. For example, if the Republican platform states that the party opposes abortion, favors increased military spending, and supports a constitutional amendment against flag burning, then each one of these issues

represents one plank of the platform. Parties normally adopt their platform every four years at their national convention. The **national convention** consists of **delegates** (representatives) from each state and US territories that meet to **nominate** (choose) candidates for president and vice president.

Since third parties rarely win elections in the US, most interest groups choose to align themselves with one of the two major parties, rather than branching out on their own. This leads to interesting coalitions. **Coalitions** are the banding together of different groups for the purpose of achieving political success. For instance, auto workers in Michigan and civil rights activists in the South may, on the surface, not seem to have much in common. However, they may band together for the purpose of supporting candidates that will back both their interests. Some groups within a party might be seen as **radical** because they hold extreme opinions. For instance, those advocating massive government reforms and/or government control over certain institutions are often tagged as "radicals" (i.e., those favoring government control of businesses or health care). Other groups are seen as **reactionary** because they "react" to what they view as radical changes or movements. Reactionary groups tend to value the status quo or want to see a return to more traditional ways. Since both groups tend to be seen as "too extreme" by many citizens, they find it advantageous to be part of a larger coalition within one of the major parties.

"Boss" William Tweed of early N.Y. Political Machine

At the state and local levels, **political machines** still play an active role in certain areas. Originally, political machines were state and local party organizations that chose party candidates and greatly influenced the outcome of elections. Often corrupt, they played a major role in politics during the late nineteenth and early twentieth centuries. These machines often "bought" votes through **patronage** (promising a certain position to individuals in exchange for their support). Today, however, these machines have less direct say over the outcome of elections and focus mainly on mobilizing voters who will support their candidates. Patronage still takes place to a certain extent, but the process is not as corrupt as it use to be, and those appointed to positions usually have to meet certain qualifications.

Active Citizenship

To get their supporters to the polls, parties often rely on **"grassroots"** efforts. Like the roots that lie unseen below the surface, yet are necessary for grass to grow, grassroots campaign efforts are those efforts made by volunteer and local party members who actively educate, campaign, and encourage citizens to get out and vote for the party's candidates. Although their labor is "unseen", it is crucial for effective campaigns.

Practice 1: Political Parties

1. Party leaders gather at the national convention to nominate their candidates for president and vice president. While there, they draft a list of policies and programs the party will support. What is this list of policies and programs called?

    A. the party plank   C. the party machine

    B. the party platform   D. the party system

2. In the United States, only the Republican and Democratic parties truly dominate the political scene. This demonstrates that the US operates on which kind of political system?

    A. multi-party   B. a republic   C. two-party   D. coalition

3. How does the manner in which the United States conducts elections contribute to its two-party system?

4. How do *liberals* and *conservatives* view the role of government differently?

4.2 ELECTIONS AND VOTING

ELECTIONS

Local, state, and federal officials are voted into office by means of a **general election**. These elections are held in November of an election year (usually even numbered). This is the time in which voters choose between the Republican, Democratic, and any third party/independent candidates for public office. However, before the general election is held, each party must first decide which candidate will represent them. After all, there may be ten Democrats who want to be the party's nominee for president, or six Republicans who want to run for governor. To decide on a single nominee, each major party holds primary elections a few months prior to the general election. In **primary elections**, voters choose between candidates within the same party. The candidate who wins the most votes receives the party's nomination. However, as is the case in general elections, if there are several candidates running and no one wins a clear majority, then there will be a **run-off election** between the

Victory Speech

top vote getters (usually the top two). In this case, the top vote getter in the run-off election wins. It is important to note, however, that run-off elections do not occur in presidential elections since they involve the Electoral College. If a presidential candidate fails to win a majority of electoral votes, then the winner is decided by the House of Representatives. Some states (i.e., Iowa) choose their party's nominee for president by means of a **caucus** rather than a primary. In the caucus system, party members hold local meetings to choose delegates. These **delegates**, in turn, choose other delegates to vote in favor of nominating a certain candidate at the **national convention**. While national elections and most state elections are **partisan** (it is clearly stated what party a candidate belongs to), local elections and some state positions are sometimes *non-partisan*. In a **non-partisan election**, a candidate's party affiliation is not made known on the ballot. This encourages voters to focus on the candidates' credentials rather than what party they belong to.

There are also "special elections." A **recall election** is an election that is called to determine if voters want to remove a sitting official from office before his/her elected term is up. This occurred in California in 2003, when Governor Gray Davis was recalled and defeated by Arnold Schwarzenegger. An **initiative** is when citizens force a vote on a particular issue by getting enough citizens to sign a petition. Citizens may also vote on **propositions**, such as whether or not they support a certain policy or changes in the law.

California Governor Arnold Schwarzenegger

THE ELECTORAL COLLEGE

In presidential elections, the winner is not directly chosen by the people but by **electors** to the **Electoral College** (review section 1.5 in chapter 1). Each state possesses a certain number of electoral votes (1 for each of its senators and representatives in Congress). Whoever wins the majority of votes in a given state is awarded *all* of that state's electoral votes. For example, North Carolina has 15 electoral votes. Say that Republican Pete wins 51% of the votes in NC compared to Democrat Nancy's 49%. Even though the vote was close, Pete gets all 15 of NC's votes in the Electoral College. Whichever candidate wins the majority of electoral votes wins the election. Normally, whoever wins the most individual votes also wins in the Electoral College. However, as recently as 2000, this was not the case. Although Al Gore won more of the popular vote, George W. Bush actually won the needed majority of electoral votes. Under our current system, it was Bush rather than Gore who was elected president.

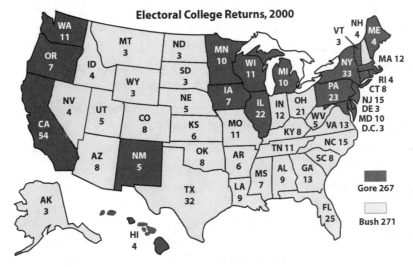

Electoral College Returns, 2000

CAMPAIGNS

In order to win an election, a candidate must have an effective **campaign** (strategy for winning / process of running for office). If the candidate is his/her party's nominee, then he/she can count on the support of the party. In addition, campaigns are often supported by **political action committees (PACS)**. These are groups organized to ensure that the candidates who will back issues most important to the PAC get elected and remain in office. PACs primarily contribute money to the campaigns of candidates they support. Most funding for campaigns come from **private resources**, such as PACs or private donors. However, since 1976, presidential candidates also have access to **public funding**. Candidates must demonstrate that they have broad support and raise a certain amount of money privately first. Once these conditions are met, candidates in both the primary and general elections may accept public funds; but to do so, they must agree to limit their campaign spending.

Money is just one aspect of a successful campaign. They also require wise strategy and lots of hard work. **Canvassing** is when volunteers go door-to-door in neighborhoods or station themselves in public places for the purpose of encouraging citizens to vote for their candidate. **Political endorsements** (statements of support) from influential leaders and/or organizations are also valued, because they often lead to large numbers of votes. For instance, when a conservative group formally endorses a Republican candidate or a union endorses a Democrat, people who respect or are affiliated with these organizations are more likely to vote for the candidate as well.

To win votes, campaigns also produce a great deal of propaganda. **Propaganda** is information meant to influence voters to support a specific candidate over another. The information may, or may not, be true; but it is always biased (meant to favor one candidate). Such propaganda is often called **"stacking cards"**. This is because, just like a magician using a "stacked deck" to perform a card trick, propaganda is often misleading. "Stacking cards" can take the form of television, radio, or printed ads. It can be geared towards either positive or negative **image molding**. It can focus on molding a positive public perception of the candidate it supports, or a negative public perception of the candidate it is aimed at defeating. **Positive campaigning** often tries to appeal to mainstream voters by portraying the candidate as **"just plain folk"**. This is because the candidate wants to be seen as relatable, and "just like" the voters themselves. By contrast, **negative campaigning** often takes the form of **name calling**, in which candidates accuse one another of terrible offenses, incompetence, and/or past betrayals of public trust. In order to avoid alienating voters, candidates often speak in **"glittering generalities"** during election campaigns. In other words, they say things that appeal to emotions or are consistent with popularly held values without getting so specific as to offend voters. For example, a candidate may say something like, "We must protect Social Security at all costs," but he/she will not say that they intend to raise taxes to do so. This is because they realize that most citizens support Social Security but hate paying taxes.

THE VOTING PROCESS

On Election Day, voters report to **polling places** to cast their votes. Schools, churches, community centers, and public facilities are all commonly used as polling places. Which polling place a voter reports to is determined by the **voting district** and **precinct** in which they live. A voting district determines which candidates a person may vote for. A citizen may vote only for candidates that are running to represent his/her district. By comparison, a precinct is that area to which one has been assigned to vote. There are normally several voting precincts within a given district. In order to vote, one must make sure that they are properly registered. The purpose of **voter registration** is to make sure that only qualified citizens vote, and that they only vote once. In most states, voters must register prior to election day. In a few, however, voters may register at their polling place.

Chapter 4

Precincts often differ in the type of ballot that they use. A **ballot** simply lists the candidates for office from which the voter may choose. Some use *punch card ballots* that require a voter to punch a small hole next to the name of the candidate they are voting for (Florida used these types of ballots during the 2000 presidential election in which there was so much controversy). An *optical scanning ballot* is one in which voters mark their choice directly on the ballot. *Voting machines* feature levers that correspond to each candidate, and voters need only flip the lever of the candidate they choose. Finally, *computer touch screen ballots* have become more common in recent years. As the name suggests, voters simply touch the name of the candidate they choose on a computer screen and their vote is recorded. A local **board of elections** is usually responsible for facilitating and overseeing the voting process.

One phenomenon that can occur during elections is referred to as **"jumping on the bandwagon"**. The term can actually be used in two ways. Candidates are often said to "bandwagon" when they adopt currently popular issues and causes simply because they know to do so will win votes. However, voters are also said to "bandwagon" on election day. This occurs when voters begin to vote for candidates who it appears will win. One reason that this sometimes occurs is due to **exit polls**. These are surveys taken by either campaign workers or news media, in which voters are asked who they voted for as they leave the polls. News media use exit polls to try to predict the outcome of elections prior to all the votes being counted. If such data suggests that a candidate is assured of victory, it can affect how those still yet to vote cast their ballots—or whether they cast them at all.

Practice 2: Elections and Voting

1. The Democratic and Republican candidates for lieutenant governor have just squared off in a tough election. After all the votes were counted, the Democratic candidate pulled out a narrow victory. He will be the state's next lieutenant governor. This describes what?

    A. the results of a general election
    B. the results of a primary election
    C. the results of the state caucus
    D. the results of the Electoral College

2. Miriam's congressional campaign has just launched a series of ads. Half of the ads feature her past accomplishments and talk about her patriotism. The other half criticize her opponent and point out that he was investigated by the IRS. ALL of Miriam's ads are examples of what?

    A. negative campaigning
    B. positive campaigning
    C. canvassing
    D. propaganda

3. Describe how the president of the United States is elected.

4. Why do candidates often speak in "glittering generalities"?

5. What are exit polls and how can they affect voting?

4.3 ISSUES, OPINIONS, AND ACTIVISM

INFLUENCE OF THE MASS MEDIA

US culture is greatly influenced by its mass media. Nowhere is this more evident than in politics and public opinion. The term *mass media* refers to the impact journalists, celebrity personalities, writers, etc. have on society via television, radio, and printed materials. Through news reports and other forms of communication, the mass media plays a major role in forging the nation's **public agenda** (what issues are most important to US citizens). As a result, it also has great impact on US politics. Issues like US military actions, concerns about the environment, unemployment, health care, and minority rights are all examples of issues that have impacted politics, in part due to their coverage in the media.

While most agree that the mass media helps define the important issues of the day, citizens are often divided on whether or not they believe the mass media is guilty of **bias** (favoring one stance or political position over another). Since journalists are expected to accurately report facts rather than support political agendas, any news agency or publication thought guilty of bias tends to lose credibility. News agencies and networks accused of bias claim that they simply report the facts they uncover. Accusers say that reporters often go in search of what they *want* to find, rather than objectively reporting all sides of a story.

PUBLIC OPINION

In order to determine **public opinion** (what citizens think), both politicians and news agencies often conduct polls. **Polls** are surveys that are taken using some form of **random sample** (small group of people that hopefully represents some larger group as a whole). Political candidates often use these polls to help them campaign effectively. Public opinion polls also serve to impact **party platforms**. If the media consistently highlights a certain issue (i.e., abortion, stem cell research, the War on Terror, health care, etc.) and/or if polls show that people feel strongly about it, then political parties are likely to feel compelled to express a position on it in their platform.

POLITICAL ACTIVISM

Political activism refers to the act of being politically involved. It is the means by which private citizens can make their opinions known and their voices heard. Activism can take simple forms like **voting** for the candidate of one's choice or signing a petition. A **petition** is a form signed by citizens in support of a certain change or government action. If enough people sign a petition, it can force a special vote or at least influence the decisions of public officials. A more radical **activist** (those who engage in political activism) might take part in political **protests**. These protests can take a number of forms (marches, sit-ins, hunger strikes, etc.) and are usually carried out in opposition to a government policy. Most radical activists are very passionate about their beliefs. While it is admirable to be involved in political causes, both politicians and activists must be careful not to commit libel or slander. **Slander** is any false statement made about someone for the intent of harming their public image (i.e., a political opponent). Similarly, **libel** is any published lie that has the same intent (i.e., printing a false story in the newspaper).

Voting, petitions, and protests are all methods by which citizens try to impact public policy. Sadly, some citizens have no interest in taking part in the political process. Although they have the right to vote, they rarely exercise it. Although they enjoy freedom of speech, they have no interest in making their voice heard. Such an attitude of "not caring" is referred to as citizen **apathy**.

LOBBYISTS

Political **lobbyists** are a kind of "professional activist". Lobbyists are hired by interest groups to influence legislation in Congress and/or state legislatures. Some have expressed concern that lobbyists have too much influence on the political process, thereby encouraging elected officials to serve the needs of lobbyists' clients rather than the public good. In 2006, scandals surrounding lobbying practices on Capitol Hill led to the introduction of new legislation aimed at preventing improper activity between lobbyists and lawmakers.

Practice 3: Issues, Opinions, and Activism

1. Which one of the following would NOT be considered part of the mass media?

   A. NBC's nightly news broadcast
   B. *The New York Times* newspaper
   C. The president's *State of the Union Address*
   D. *Newsweek* magazine

2. Why would political bias be a negative thing for journalists?

3. Which of the following is NOT a form of political activism?

   A. voting
   B. marching in protest of current immigration laws
   C. starting a petition drive against a new city ordinance
   D. sitting around the table with friends complaining about the government

4.4 INSURING "DOMESTIC TRANQUILITY"

The Preamble to the US Constitution states that one purpose of the document is to "insure **domestic tranquility**." In other words, the laws of the land are meant to maintain an orderly and beneficial society. Domestic tranquility thrives when citizens decide to both embrace their civic responsibilities and obey the laws of the land.

COMPLIANCE WITH THE LAWS OF SOCIETY

US society is governed by both criminal and civil laws. **Criminal laws** deal with crime and define the punishments for criminal offenses (i.e., theft and murder are criminal offenses). Collectively, those acts defined as criminal in a particular state, along with the penalties for committing them, are referred to as the state's **penal code**. The punishment for most criminal offenses is determined by **mandatory sentencing**. This means that the law itself states the minimum/maximum punishment that can be imposed on someone convicted of a certain crime. This prevents judges and/or juries from sentencing people inconsistently or unfairly. If the government chooses to charge someone with a crime, then that person must face  criminal **prosecution**. This is when the state—or, in some cases, the federal government—brings formal charges against the accused in court and argues for his/her conviction. If the accused is found guilty of the crime, then he/she may be sentenced to either **incarceration** (time in jail, prison, or a youth detention center) or probation. **Probation** is when a convicted person is ordered to behave in a certain manner (i.e., stay away from a certain place/person, get drug treatment, perform community service, etc.) in exchange for a *suspended sentence*. In other words, so long as the individual does what the court orders him/her to do, the sentence will not have to be served. However, if he/she does not, then the court can activate the suspended sentence (usually jail time) and revoke the probation. There are two types of probation: **supervised and unsupervised**. If probation is *unsupervised*, then the convicted person need only show up at court on the designated day and show proof that they have complied with the conditions of their probation. If it is *supervised*, then the convicted person must periodically report to a probation officer who will monitor them and make sure they are doing as the court ordered. If the probationer (person on probation) does not, then the probation officer has the authority to arrest him/her and take him/her back to court. In less serious criminal cases, the convicted person may have to only pay a **fine** rather than going to jail or being placed on probation. Criminal laws are meant to maintain **public safety**.

Civil laws are those laws that govern relationships between private individuals and/or entities. For example, say a landlord and a tenant are arguing over who is responsible for an insect problem. Since no crime has been committed, this kind of case would be settled in **civil court**. Unlike criminal trials that are initiated by the government, civil trials must be initiated by individuals, organizations, or businesses. Civil cases begin when one side brings a **lawsuit** (claim that a person, business, etc. has been wronged) against another side with which they have a dispute. The side that initiates the lawsuit is called the **plaintiff**. The side against whom the lawsuit is filed is called the **defendant**. Unlike criminal cases, where the accused can face incarceration or some other form of criminal punishment, defendants who lose civil cases normally have to pay **damages** (money) to the plaintiff. If defendants *win* a civil case, then they don't have to pay anything other than their attorney's fees. In some cases, the defendant **counter sues** the plaintiff. If the defendant wins, then the plaintiff has to pay damages to the defendant; even though the defendant is not the one who filed the suit in court. Business disputes, property disputes, charges of medical malpractice, and divorce proceedings are all examples of cases that are handled in civil courts.

CIVIC RESPONSIBILITY

The United States Constitution protects the rights of citizens and gives them a direct say in how their government operates. With freedom and a voice in government, however, also come certain **civic responsibilities.** These are responsibilities that citizens must be willing to take on in order for US society to function properly. Voting, paying taxes, and obeying laws are all examples of civic responsibilities. In addition, there are also acts of **public service.** Serving on juries, running for public office, and taking part in community projects (i.e., cleaning up the neighborhood) are just a few examples of public service. Some citizens become **volunteers.** They sacrifice their time and energy to serve the community, even though they don't get paid anything for it. Volunteerism is both a valuable way people serve, and a great way for citizens to obtain *"real world experience"*. Take, for example, a young person who wants to be a nurse who decides to volunteer at a children's hospital. Not only does that person perform a great service by helping children, but he/she also gets practical experience in the medical profession as well. Suppose someone who wants to be a teacher volunteers to tutor special needs kids. Once again, that person is helping to make their community a better place while also gaining valuable experience.

For many active citizens, accepting and living up to their civic responsibilities is a matter of **patriotism** (devotion to one's country). They view living in the United States and the freedoms it affords as a great privilege. They feel it is their patriotic duty to do all they can to participate and serve their community, state, and nation.

A Few Examples of Organizations Through Which Citizens Serve	
• **Peace Corps**	Sends US volunteers to developing foreign nations to serve as teachers, engineers, technicians, health workers, etc. It was established by President John F. Kennedy in 1961.
• **AmeriCorps**	Network of non-profit organizations, public agencies, and faith-based organizations that serve citizens in a number of ways — including public education and environmental services. It was established by President Bill Clinton in 1993.
• **Job Corps**	Program designed to give "at risk" youth and young adults the skills they need to succeed in the workforce. It provides both educational services and training for employment. It was established in 1964 under President Lyndon B. Johnson.
• **Senior Corps**	Group consisting of older citizens who volunteer their time to help others. Some assist fellow senior citizens who need help with their daily needs. Others act as "foster grandparents" to young people in need of love and attention. Senior Corps demonstrates that citizens are never too old to actively serve their community.

Practice 4: Domestic Tranquility

1. Which of the following statements BEST describes "domestic tranquility" as it is used in the preamble to the Constitution?

    A. good relations between the US and a foreign country
    B. an orderly and properly functioning society
    C. a place where everybody is happy all the time
    D. a place where no laws are needed because people are honest and caring

2. Patty borrowed Francine's car and wrecked it. Patty refuses to pay for the damages because she claims that the wreck was caused by Francine failing to service the car properly. Furious, Francine is going to sue Patty for the $5000 needed to fix the car. This case will be heard in which of the following?

    A. civil court
    B. criminal court

    C. civic court
    D. suspended court

3. Give 3 examples of how a citizen can carry out his/her civic responsibilities?

4. What is "patriotism" and how does it motivate some citizens to serve?

4.5 BENEFITS AND COSTS OF PUBLIC SERVICE

US citizens are given the right to elect their own officials, express their political opinions, and have influence over legislative and judicial procedures. However, for every benefit there is a cost. In order for US society to function, citizens must be willing to make sacrifices in order to maintain a government empowered by the people.

PARTICIPATION IN THE JUDICIAL PROCESS

The *Sixth Amendment* guarantees those accused of a criminal offense the right to a trial by an **impartial jury**. In other words, a panel of unbiased citizens, rather than a single government official, decides whether or not the accused is guilty of a crime. The *Seventh Amendment* extends this right to civil cases as well. Citizens usually learn that they have been selected for **jury duty** (serving on a jury) by receiving a notice in the mail. In most cases, jury duty is mandatory unless one is released from duty by the court. Citizens can be released from jury duty

either by showing that they are not qualified to serve, proving that they have a just cause for being dismissed from service, or as part of the *voir dire*. The **voir dire** is a process that occurs prior to the actual trial, in which attorneys for both sides ask potential jurors questions. If one of the attorneys feel that a certain citizen might be biased against his/her side, then that attorney may dismiss, or ask the judge to dismiss, that potential juror from service. Jurors in North Carolina must be 18 years old, able to speak English, and have no felony convictions. Juries usually consist of 12 members.

The jury system is intended to prevent unfair verdicts by biased or corrupt judges. However, in order for this system to operate, citizens must be willing to pay the **costs of serving on a jury**. For instance, jury duty takes *time*. In some cases, a juror might only sacrifice a day. However, in many cases, jurors might have to spend days or even months serving. In more serious cases, such as a murder trial or a civil case worth millions of dollars, a jury might have to be **"sequestered"**. In other words, the jury may have to be isolated from society for a while, in order to assure that their decision will not be influenced by factors outside of the courtroom (i.e., media coverage, public opinions about a high-profile case, etc.). As a result, jurors often have to spend long periods of time away from family, work, and other pursuits. For jurors whose jobs pay an hourly wage, jury duty often means *financial sacrifice*. While jury duty usually pays a set amount of money for each day a juror serves, it is normally less than an average salary. Even for those whose pay is not affected, the inconvenience and problems created by missing days of work often leads to additional stress and tension. There is also the *emotional cost* of jury duty. For some, deciding whether or not another human being goes to prison creates great anxiety. In some cases, such as extremely violent crimes, jurors may have to hear testimony and view evidence that is emotionally disturbing as well. Time, money, and emotional strain can all be costs of participating in the judicial process.

PARTICIPATION IN THE POLITICAL PROCESS

Freedom of the press helps ensure that US citizens remain an **informed electorate** (people who vote in an election). US citizens have a right to know what is going on in their government, judicial system, and the world in general. They have the privilege of deciding who their leaders will be and participating in the political process. Citizens take part in the political process in a number of ways. By **voting**, they are able to influence who serves in a particular public office. Through **volunteering**, citizens can take a more active part in the campaigns of candidates they support. Some volunteers pass out pamphlets. Some canvass neighborhoods trying to inform residents about their candidate. Still others answer phones at campaign headquarters. Volunteers play a key role in effective campaigns. Some citizens join **PACS** or **interest groups** in an effort to influence elections and political policies. A few even participate in **political protests**. These protests usually take the form of a group of people gathering to make known their disapproval of some aspect of the government. Finally, some citizens actually run for and **serve in public office**.

Yet, for all the great benefits of participating in the political process, there are also costs. Voting, volunteering, and serving all take time. Time that could be spent with family, earning money, or engaging in some leisure activity is sacrificed for the sake of participating in the political process. In many cases, citizens donate money to campaigns and PACs that could have been saved or spent on something else. In the case of those who choose to run for political office, there is the **loss of privacy** and the likelihood of **political attacks**. News media often makes public nearly every aspect of a candidate's past, and political opponents are likely to publicly attack a candidate's motives, character, and/or past record of service. In addition, campaigns require lots of time and energy. In some cases, candidates may have to make appearances all over the state, or even the country, within a few hours. As a result, many qualified people choose not to seek office due to the high cost it requires of both themselves and their families.

PUBLIC SERVICE

Public service can take a number of forms. Some citizens volunteer to mentor struggling students or "at risk" youth. Some spend time with elderly citizens who otherwise may be forgotten. Others deliver meals to "shut-ins" or act as counselors at community centers. From volunteering at non-profit organizations, to building houses for those in need, to volunteering to clean up garbage along the interstate, citizens engage in public service every day. Such service requires sacrifices. However, most citizens who serve consider the sense of satisfaction they get from helping to better their society as being well worth any cost they may have to pay.

Practice 5: Public Service

1. The right to a trial by jury for a criminal defendant is guaranteed under which amendment to the Constitution?

    A. First   B. Sixth   C. Seventh   D. Ninth

2. Losing time from work, being away from one's family, and having to deal with the emotional stress of hearing about a violent crime are all examples of what?
    A. benefits of public service   C. costs of volunteering
    B. costs of serving in public office   D. costs of jury duty

3. Voting, volunteering to help with a campaign, and running for county commissioner are all examples of what?
    A. participation in the judicial system   C. participation in political protests
    B. participation in the political process   D. costs of public service

4. How do money, time, and energy all become costs of public service?

4.6 PARTICIPATING IN CIVIC LIFE, POLITICS, AND GOVERNMENT

It is never too early for citizens to become involved in public service. Even students who are too young to officially vote, run for office, or serve on juries can become familiar with these processes in a number of ways.

- **Mock elections** – pretend elections that allow students to plan campaigns, debate political issues, conduct polls, analyze polling data, and go to the polls to cast their vote.

- **Moot Courts** – pretend courts where students are able to research and investigate criminal/civil cases, prepare evidence, try cases as attorneys, hear cases as judges, and rule on cases as mock jurors.

- **Community service** – allows students to learn the value and sense of satisfaction that comes from civic involvement by actually serving others. It gets students involved in helping the community through volunteering their time and energy, either individually, or as a group. Students may serve meals at a homeless shelter, mentor a younger child, take meals to the elderly, or volunteer in any number of ways. Community service combined with classroom instruction serves as an effective means of *service learning*.

Service learning is a method in which students learn the value of **civic involvement** (the involvement of citizens in government and the community) by combining classroom curriculum with actual, hands-on service to the community.

Practice 6: Participating

1. Mock elections, moot courts, and community service all serve to do what?

   A. reach out to those in need in a community

   B. teach students about the judicial process

   C. educate students by exposing them to what public service/civic involvement feels like

   D. encourage students to become involved in politics

2. Which of the following is the BEST example of *service learning*?

   A. Students take a course in civics that involves lectures, reading, and two written papers on the importance of community service.

   B. Students spend a Saturday cleaning up the city park because they want to use the park for a school function.

   C. A teacher takes her students to the state capital to sit in on a legislative session and see first-hand how laws are created.

   D. Brian takes a class in civics in which he is required to serve as a volunteer at a local community center, as well as complete classroom assignments and write a paper on his experiences.

4.7 CIVIL CONFLICT

With millions of citizens living in the United States, conflicts inevitably arise. Most of the time, these conflicts are relatively simple and easily resolved between individuals. Sometimes, however, conflicts require more involved methods of conflict resolution. Often they may result in **legal action** in which one individual, group, or organization, claims to have been wronged by another individual, group, or organization. Legal action results when the "wronged" party (plaintiff) decides to take the other party (defendant) to civil court and sue them for damages. If the amount of money they are asking for is relatively small, then the case may be heard before a magistrate in **small claims court**. However, if the amount is higher it will go before a judge and, quite possibly, a jury. Many cases never reach court, however. They are resolved by a **pre-hearing settlement**. In a "settlement", the two parties agree to a set amount of damages without going to court. Usually, the amount is less than what the plaintiff originally asked for, but more than what the defendant was originally willing to pay. Although it is not what either originally wanted, both sides find it acceptable and are willing to settle rather than invest the time and money necessary to go to court.

Active Citizenship

There are other forms of conflict resolution as well. Many times, conflicts are resolved through negotiation. **Negotiation** is when interested parties **collaborate** (work together) to come to conclusions that are acceptable to both sides. Effective negotiation requires **compromise**, because both sides usually have to give up something in order to reach an agreement. Sometimes disputing parties need the intervention of a third, objective party. **Mediation** is when the two disputing sides invite a third party to help them find a solution. In some cases, the two sides may even agree to make the decision of a neutral third party legally binding. This process is called **arbitration**, and it is often used by parties who feel that the judicial process is too slow or expensive.

Negotiation

Practice 7: Civil Conflict

1. Bill builds a fence around his backyard. His neighbor, Tony, informs him that he has built part of the fence on his property. Since both plan on living next to each other for some time, they decide to talk and agree that Bill's fence can stay, provided Bill allows Tony to store both of his motorcycles in Bill's garage. This is an example of which of the following?

   A. mediation   B. arbitration   C. negotiation   D. legal action

2. Zenmark Technologies has filed a civil suit against Megabuzz, claiming that they violated trademark laws. In the end, the case did not go to court after all. After a meeting of both sides' lawyers, Megabuzz agreed to pay Zenmark half of what they were asking in damages, in exchange for Zenmark dropping the case. This case appears to have been settled how?

   A. in small claims court   C. through mediation

   B. through arbitration   D. through a pre-hearing settlement

3. What is arbitration and why do some parties choose to use it instead of the judicial system?

CHAPTER 4 REVIEW

A. Define the following key terms.

political parties
candidates
multi-party system
majority vote
plurality vote
two-party system
Democrats
means of participating in the political process
liberal
ballot
public service
mock elections
moot courts
community service
service learning
platform
plank
national convention
delegates
nomination of candidates
coalitions
protest
slander/libel
apathy
patronage
criminal laws
primary election
prosecution
partisan election
suspended sentence
proposition
civil laws
campaign
plaintiff/defendent
counter-sue
canvassing

"just plain folk"
name calling
"glittering generalities"
polling places
voting district
precinct
voter registration
costs of participating in the political process
conservative
board of elections
third parties
independents
one-party system
functions of political parties
public opinion
polls
random sample
political activism
voting
petition
activist
mediation
arbitration
political machines
domestic tranquility
general election
mandatory sentencing
caucus
non-partisan election
initiative
public safety
Electoral College
lawsuit
damages
public funding
public service

impartial jury
jury duty
voir dire
costs of serving on a jury
sequestered
informed electorate
Republicans
probation (supervised, unsupervised)
moderate
"jumping on the bandwagon"
exit polls
mass media
public agenda
media bias
civic involvement
legal action
small claims court
pre-hearing settlement
negotiation
collaborate
compromise
radical
reactionary
lobbyists
"grassroots"
penal code
run-off election
incarceration
recall election
fine
electors
civil court
political action committee
private resource
civic responsibilities
volunteers

Active Citizenship

political endorsements   propaganda   "real world experience"

"stacking cards"   patriotism   image molding

positive/negative campaigning

B. Choose the correct answer.

1. The results of an election shows that the Blue party won 30% of the vote, the Yellow party won 20% of the vote, the Red and Green parties each won 10% of the vote, and six smaller parties each won 5% of the vote. As a result, the nation's 100 seat legislative body will consist of 30 members from the Blue party, 20 members from the Yellow party, 10 members from both the Red and Green parties, and 5 members from each of the smaller parties. This country operates on what kind of political system?

   A. one-party   B. two-party   C. multi-party   D. ten-party

2. The results of an election are very close. Candidate A wins 49% of the vote, candidate B wins 48% of the vote, and candidate C wins the remaining 3% of the vote. There is a good chance that candidates A and B will have to meet again in what kind of election?

   A. a primary election   C. a general election

   B. a recall election   D. a run-off election

3. David is a liberal politician. He believes that the government should provide health care, welfare, and job training for unemployed citizens. He also believes that those who make more than $100,000/year should have their taxes raised in order to help pay for government programs. Although David could be a member of any political party, he is MOST LIKELY a member of which major US party?

   A. Democrat   B. Republican   C. Libertarian   D. Independent

4. Janice is very conservative. Although she cares about the welfare of others, she does not think it is the proper role of government to provide an income or guarantee health care. She wants to keep the government's role restricted to things like upholding law and order, protecting the rights of citizens, and providing a strong national defense. Of the two major parties, which one is Janice MOST LIKELY a member of?

   A. Democratic   B. Republican   C. Reform   D. Independent

5. Someone whose beliefs fall in between liberal and conservative is referred to as what?

   A. an independent   C. a third party candidate

   B. a moderate   D. a reactionary

6. The Democrats meet for their national convention and decide to support a woman's right to abortion on demand, oppose a constitutional amendment against flag burning, and support certain civil rights legislation. This list of policies and programs which the party supports is known as what?

   A. the party platform   C. the party agenda

   B. the party plank   D. the party delegate

7. Abigail is passionate about seeing her candidate win the upcoming primary election. She volunteers her time and energy to pass out flyers, put up campaign signs, and make phone calls. Abigail is part of what?

    A.   a television campaign

    B.   a political protest

    C.   a PAC

    D.   a grassroots campaign effort

8. Before a candidate can be his/her party's candidate for president, he/she must first defeat other members of the party who want to be the party's nominee in a series of what?

    A.   general elections

    B.   national caucuses

    C.   primaries and caucuses

    D.   run-off elections

9. The ballot for Peppersville School Board only lists the candidates' names, with no mention of their party affiliation. The school board election is an example of what?

    A.   a partisan election

    B.   a two-party system election

    C.   a multi-party system election

    D.   a non-partisan election

10. All of the following tend to be part of political campaigns EXCEPT:

    A.   propaganda.

    B.   glittering generalities.

    C.   funding from political action committees.

    D.   mandatory sentencing.

11. Phil has spent nearly three weeks serving on the jury of a criminal trial. Because he works from home as an independent contractor, the 8 hours/day he has had to be at the courthouse has meant that he has been unable to pursue new clients. It has also prevented him from spending as much time with his wife and kids. Phil is experiencing which of the following?

    A.   the benefits of jury duty

    B.   the cost of political activism

    C.   the cost of fulfilling his civic responsibility

    D.   the inconvenience of civil lawsuits

12. Voters who are aware of what is happening in their government, their judicial system, and the world around them are said to be part of what?

    A.   the United States

    B.   a two-party system

    C.   interest groups

    D.   an informed electorate

13. Which of the following is not a cost of running/serving in public office?

    A.   the ability to play a major role in setting policies.

    B.   loss of personal and family privacy.

    C.   being subject to political attacks.

    D.   sacrifices of time and energy.

14. Volunteering to mentor "at risk" youth, working at a polling place on election day, running for city council, and teaching English to immigrants, are all examples of which of the following?

    A.   political activism

    B.   participation in the judicial process

    C.   civic involvement

    D.   conflict resolution

Active Citizenship

15. Which of the following is an example of *arbitration*?

    A.   A professional athlete's agent and the team he wants to play for finally agree on a contract.

    B.   A waitress slips and falls at work. She threatens to take her employer to court to sue for $50,000 in damages. The case never goes to court, however, because the restaurant where she works agrees to pay her $30,000 to end the dispute.

    C.   Ben accuses his company of not honoring his contract. The two sides agree to present their cases before a neutral third party. They also agree that the decision of the neutral third party will be legally binding.

    D.   After three weeks of testimony, a large hospital agrees to pay the patient who is suing it one-third of the damages he is seeking, in exchange for the patient dropping the case.

Chapter 5
Conflict in the United States' Political and Judicial Systems

This chapter addresses the following competency goal and objective(s):

Competency goal 5	The learner will explain how the political and legal systems provide a means to balance competing interests and resolve conflicts.
Objective 5.01, 5.02, 5.03, 5.04, 5.05, 5.06	

5.1 ADDRESSING CONFLICTS

Conflicts inevitably arise within the US political and judicial systems. Therefore, it is important that these systems allow for different methods of **conflict resolution** (ending conflict—ideally in a manner acceptable to both sides). **Debate** is one important part of conflict resolution. It is a process in which opposing sides present their position on an issue. Both sides attempt to use facts to support their position in the hope of persuading the opposing side and/or an undecided third party to agree with them. Debate is a very important part of US politics. Candidates who are running for office often meet in public debates in order to try and persuade voters that their ideas are the best, and that they are the most qualified candidate for office. Once in office, legislators commonly engage in debate on the

Kennedy-Nixon Debate

floors of Congress, state legislatures, and local councils in an attempt to win support for their positions.

Negotiation is also important when it comes to resolving conflict. This is the process by which opponents come together to discuss how they might come to a conclusion acceptable to both sides. Successful negotiations require compromise. **Compromise** is when each side is willing to give up a little of what it originally wanted in order to reach a solution both sides can live with. Very few bills in Congress ever become law without some degree of compromise. Likewise, because of the diversity within political parties, adopting political platforms requires compromise as well. Without compromise, national, state, and local governments would accomplish very little.

Conflict in the United States' Political and Judicial Systems

Leaders usually hope that debate and negotiation will lead to a *consensus*. A "consensus" is when all parties involved are in general agreement. While not all parties may feel exactly the same way about an issue, they agree enough to take action and move forward. The process by which such general agreement is reached is called **consensus building**. Political leaders use debate, negotiation, and compromises in order to reach consensus on issues regarding public policy. Similarly, jurors in a criminal or civil trial must reach a consensus before a verdict can be rendered. Often, jurors initially disagree regarding the guilt or innocence of a defendant. Therefore, they must engage in much discussion—getting everyone's perspective—in order to reach a decision that all 12 members can live with. Consensus building is an important process, because it allows parties that were originally in opposition to come to at least some level of agreement on important matters.

Practice 1: Addressing Conflicts

1. The process in which both sides present their position on an issue and use facts to attempt to persuade both their opponent and any undecided third party to agree with them is called what?

    A. consensus building   C. discussion

    B. debate   D. negotiation

2. The process by which opposing sides come together to discuss how they might come to a conclusion acceptable to both sides is called what?

    A. debate   B. compromise   C. negotiation   D. consensus

3. The process by which people use debate, negotiation, and compromises to come to a general agreement on an issue is called what?

    A. consensus   C. consensus building

    B. conflict   D. jury process

5.2 JURISDICTION OF STATE AND FEDERAL COURTS

The United States judicial system features both the federal court system and state courts. State courts have **original jurisdiction** (authority to hear a case first) over cases involving violations of state law. Federal courts sometimes exercise **appellate jurisdiction** (authority to review the decisions of a court having original jurisdiction) over such cases, however, if it is alleged that the state court's procedures violated a defendant's constitutional rights. Sometimes state and federal courts share **concurrent jurisdiction** (both having authority to hear a case). In some cases, the federal courts enjoy **exclusive jurisdiction**, meaning that only the federal courts may hear the case. Examples of cases that fall into this category are bankruptcy cases and cases involving suits against the US government. (Review *Section 2.2, Chapter 2* regarding the judicial branch of government and jurisdiction.)

Chapter 5

STATE COURTS

State courts generally consist of lower courts, general trial courts, intermediate appellate courts, and a state Supreme Court. In North Carolina, the **lower courts** are known as *district courts*. They have jurisdiction over misdemeanor criminal cases and civil cases involving smaller claims. North Carolina's **general trial courts** are referred to as *superior courts*. These courts have general jurisdiction over more serious crimes and civil cases. They also have appellate jurisdiction over decisions made by district courts. The NC Court of Appeals acts as the state's **intermediate appellate court**. It exercises appellate jurisdiction over decisions made in district and superior courts. Finally, the NC Supreme Court is the highest court in the state. It exercises appellate jurisdiction over all lower state court decisions. It also has the power to strike down laws it views as violating the NC Constitution. State courts consist of both criminal and civil courts. **Criminal courts** hear cases involving alleged violations of the state's penal code. **Civil courts** hear disputes between private citizens, businesses, organizations, etc. (Review Section 4, Chapter 4 regarding compliance with the laws of society.)

STATE APPEALS PROCESS

NC Supreme Court
(highest state court)

NC Court of Appeals
(intermediate appellate court)

Superior Courts
(general trial courts)

District Courts
(lower courts)

FEDERAL COURTS

Like state courts, the federal court system consists of several levels. The United States is divided into geographic judicial districts with **US District Courts** acting as the federal court system's trial courts for both criminal and civil cases. Cases that fall within the District Courts' original jurisdiction include:

- Crimes that violate federal laws
- Civil cases in which the US is either the plaintiff or the defendant
- Cases that arise out of disputes occurring at sea or in other "navigable waters" within the United States
- Cases involving disputes between parties located in different states
- Disputes between a US citizen and a foreign national who does not reside in any state
- Any case in which the complaint is based on federal rather than state law

The number of federal judges serving in a particular district is determined by Congress. Meanwhile, it is the president who appoints district court judges. Like all other federal judges, they must be approved by the Senate and serve for life, until they retire, or unless they are impeached and removed for ethical misconduct.

In addition to the District Courts, there are also **Special Courts** that have original jurisdiction over only certain kinds of cases. For instance, the *Court of International Trade* hears cases involving international trade and customs. The *US Court of Federal Claims* deals with most claims for monetary damages filed against the United States. The *US Tax Court* has jurisdiction over cases dealing with contested tax assessments.

Next is the **US Court of Appeals**. Sometimes referred to as "circuit courts", they serve as the federal judicial systems mid-level appellate courts. These courts exercise appellate jurisdiction over cases heard by lower US District and Special Courts. There are currently 13 US appellate courts. Twelve of them serve a specific geographic region within the United States. The thirteenth has nationwide jurisdiction and hears appeals from the Special Courts.

Conflict in the United States' Political and Judicial Systems

Finally, there is the **US Supreme Court**. It is the highest court in the country. It has appellate jurisdiction over all lower courts—federal and state. It also has original jurisdiction over cases involving ambassadors, public ministers and consuls, and those in which a state shall be a party. It consists of nine justices—one chief justice and eight associate justices. It also has the power to declare acts of Congress and/or laws passed by states unconstitutional.

FEDERAL APPEALS PROCESS

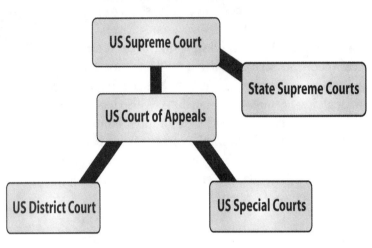

Practice 2: State and Federal Courts

1. A young man is accused of violating a state law by stealing a car in Raleigh, NC. His trial will be held in a state court that has what kind of jurisdiction over the case?

   A. original   B. appellate   C. federal   D. civil

2. A defendant is convicted of a crime in NC Superior Court. However, he claims that during the trial, the judge allowed evidence that should not have been admitted. His appeal will MOST likely first be heard in which court?

   A. US Supreme Court   C. NC Court of Appeals

   B. US Court of Appeals   D. NC Supreme Court

3. Of the following courts, which one has ONLY appellate jurisdiction?

   A. US District Court   C. US Supreme Court

   B. US Special Court   D. US Court of Appeals

5.3 THE JUDICIAL PROCESS

The United States judicial system (both federal and state) operates as an *adversarial system*. An **adversarial system** is one in which court cases are typically argued by attorneys for opposing sides (although a defendant or plaintiff can, at times, represent his/herself). Judges in such a system play the role of making sure trial procedures are conducted according to the law, rather than directly questioning witnesses or determining the facts of a case. Trial strategies are generally determined by the attorneys, with juries usually deciding the outcome of cases.

Chapter 5

CRIMINAL PROCEEDINGS: PRIOR TO TRIAL

The criminal judicial process begins with the commission of a crime. **Misdemeanors** are less serious crimes that are usually punishable by a fine, probation, or less than a year in jail. **Felonies** are more serious crimes (i.e., murder, rape, or drug trafficking) and are punishable by longer periods of incarceration and/or capital punishment (execution). Following a crime, a certain law enforcement agency will exercise jurisdiction (authority to investigate the case). This could be a local police department, state or county law enforcement agency, or a federal agency (i.e., FBI). Once law enforcement feels it has a likely suspect (someone suspected of committing the crime) it will then make an arrest and take the person into custody. In most misdemeanor cases, law enforcement must first obtain a legal document from the court called an **arrest warrant**. In the case of more serious crimes, or if the crime was committed in the presence of law enforcement, an arrest warrant is usually not needed so long as law enforcement officials have *probable cause* (sufficient evidence that the person has committed a crime) to make an arrest. Probable cause is also necessary to obtain **search warrants**. These warrants grant law enforcement officials authority to search a person's house, personal belongings, property, etc. Under the *Fourth Amendment*, search warrants are usually required before law enforcement can conduct legal searches.

If the state or federal government chooses to charge someone with a crime, that person becomes known as the **defendant**. The attorney representing the government (i.e., district attorney or US attorney) is known as the **prosecutor**. A defendant can be charged with a crime either by means of an *indictment* or a *complaint*. An **indictment** is a formal charge that someone has committed a felony. It is issued by a **grand jury**. Grand juries are special juries which hear evidence presented by a prosecutor to decide if a trial is warranted. They are composed of ordinary citizens, are usually larger than trial juries, and their proceedings are usually held in secret without the defendant or his/her attorney being present. A **complaint** is when a prosecutor files charges directly with the court rather than seeking an indictment from a grand jury. When a complaint is used to file more serious charges, the court will hold a **preliminary hearing** to determine if there is enough evidence to warrant a trial. While the Constitution requires that grand juries be used in more serious federal cases, many states have ceased to use grand juries in favor of using the complaint/preliminary hearing approach. Both grand juries and preliminary hearings are meant to protect the rights of the accused.

Once a defendant is formally charged, a judge presides over an **arraignment** in which the defendant is officially informed of the charges against him/her. The defendant is then asked to enter a **plea** of "guilty," "not guilty," or "no contest." If the defendant pleads guilty, then the judge will either impose a **sentence** (punishment for a crime) or set a future date for sentencing. If the defendant pleads "not guilty," then the court will schedule a date on the **court docket** (schedule of court proceedings) for either a trial or a preliminary hearing if one has not yet been held. A plea of "no contest" simply means that a defendant is not admitting guilt, but neither will he/she attempt to prove his/her innocence. Defendant's who use this plea normally are sentenced as if they had entered a plea of guilty, but have the privilege of not having an admission of guilt on their record.

One question the court will address prior to trial is that of *bail*. **Bail** is money paid by a defendant in exchange for not having to remain in jail until his/her trial. The money is meant to ensure that the defendant shows up for all court hearings and trial, and is usually returned after the trial is over. In most cases, defendants are granted bail. However, if the court believes a defendant will not return for trial, will commit more crimes, or will try to interfere with witnesses scheduled to testify at his/her trial, then it can choose not to offer bail. The court may also refuse bail if the crime is extremely serious (i.e., murder). If this happens, the defendant must remain in jail until trial.

CRIMINAL JUDICIAL PROCEEDINGS

In reality, many cases never go to trial. This is because defendants often plead guilty. They do this as a result of **plea bargaining**. This is a process in which defendants who know they will likely be found guilty at trial agree to plead guilty in exchange for being charged with a less serious offense, or a guarantee of less severe punishment for the crime with which they are currently charged. For instance, suppose someone knows that they will likely be found guilty of "second degree murder" if they go to trial. In exchange for being charged with the less serious crime of "manslaughter", they agree to plead "guilty" rather than make the state spend time and money conducting a trial. Such an arrangement is known as a **plea bargain**. Due to the large number of criminal cases that come before the US judicial system every year, plea bargaining is essential because it allows cases to be resolved relatively quickly.

Sometimes attorneys will file **pre-trial motions**. These are special requests made to the judge, in which one side may ask that certain evidence be omitted or certain steps be taken to ensure a fair trial. These motions are normally filed in the form of legal **briefs** that state the attorney's request in writing, as well as documenting legal reasons why the attorney feels the request is reasonable and should be granted.

CRIMINAL TRIALS

At criminal trials, prosecutors present the government's case against the accused, **defense attorneys** represent the defendant, a trial jury (sometimes called a **"petit jury"**) hears the evidence and decides if the defendant is guilty, and a judge presides over the proceedings. If a defendant wishes, he/she may waive his/her right to a jury. Also, juries are generally not used in less serious cases—i.e., cases that carry a maximum sentence of less than 6 months in jail. If a defendant cannot afford to hire a defense attorney, then the court will appoint one for him/her. In larger areas (i.e., Charlotte) this is usually a **public defender**. The Public Defender's office is responsible for representing criminal defendants who cannot afford to hire their own lawyer. If an area does not have a Public Defender, then a private attorney is assigned by the court. Bailiffs are also present in the courtroom during trials. **Bailiffs** act as the court's "law enforcement". They maintain order, assist the judge, look after the jury, and ensure courtroom security. The Sheriff is normally responsible for training and assigning bailiffs.

During a trial, both the prosecutor and defense will make opening arguments to the jury in which it summarizes its case. Each side will call witnesses and will have an opportunity to cross-examine (ask questions of) the other side's witnesses. Witnesses are called to testify by means of a **subpoena**. These are legal documents ordering a particular person to appear in court to testify. If a witness refuses to show up after receiving a subpoena, he/she can be arrested and charged with "contempt of court". Once on the witness stand, witnesses for both sides are sworn to tell the truth. A witness who lies is guilty of **perjury** and can end up in jail. Under the *Fifth Amendment*, no criminal defendant can be forced to testify.

Defendants sometimes choose to testify, however, if they feel it will help prove their innocence. Finally, each side's attorney will present closing arguments in which they attempt to persuade the jury one last time. The jury will then deliberate (meet in closed session) until it is ready to deliver a **verdict**. If the verdict is "guilty", the judge will either pronounce sentence or set a future date for **sentencing**. If the verdict is "not guilty", then the judicial proceedings are over and the defendant is free to go. He/she can never be charged with the same crime again; under the *Fifth Amendment*, they are protected from "double jeopardy". If it is a **capital offense** (crime for which the defendant can be sentenced to death) and the defendant is found guilty, then the jury must deliberate again to decide whether or not the convicted person will be executed or sentenced to life in prison. Sometimes a jury cannot come to a consensus regarding the guilt or innocence of a defendant. Such juries are referred to as **"hung juries"**. The result is a **mistrial**. If a mistrial occurs, the prosecutor may either retry the case or drop the charges against the defendant.

CIVIL PROCEEDINGS

Certain civil cases are sometimes referred to as **"torts"**. These cases normally involve alleged injuries to one's person, reputation, property, or business. Unlike criminal cases that are viewed as disputes between a defendant and the state, torts involve disputes between private citizens, businesses, organizations, etc. They come about when one side, called the **plaintiff**, feels they have been wronged and files a lawsuit seeking damages (usually money) from a defendant. Defendants usually become aware that civil action has been taken against them by means of a legal document called a **summons**. The summons informs them of the civil charges and tells them what day they must appear in court. Many times, torts are resolved by out of court **settlements.** (Review Chapter 4, Section 7 regarding pre-hearing settlements.)

APPELLATE COURTS

Defendants who are found guilty of a crime or who lose civil cases may file an **appeal**. In other words, they may ask a higher court to review, and possibly overturn, the lower court's decision. Appeals may be based on either an *issue of fact* or an *issue of law*. An **issue of fact** asserts that certain facts about a case were not given proper consideration (i.e., new evidence). An **issue of law** asserts that the decision should be overturned because trial procedures were not properly followed or the defendant's rights were in some way violated. Many citizens express outrage because they view appeals as the judicial system's way of bending over backwards to protect the rights of defendants without worrying enough about the **rights of victims**. Proponents of the appellate process answer that appeals are necessary in order to assure that innocent people are not unjustly convicted. They also point out the importance of protecting civil liberties. Victims' rights advocates counter that protecting civil liberties does not justify reversing the convictions of those who have obviously committed serious crimes.

Appellate courts are different from trial courts in that decisions are rendered by a panel of judges, rather than a jury. Attorneys present briefs ahead of time, summarizing why they believe the lower court's decision should, or should not, be reversed. They then present **oral arguments** before the judges in which they attempt to effectively present their case and answer any questions or objections the judges may have. The judges on the appellate court will then vote and come to a decision. The **majority opinion** is a written statement that presents the court's decision and how it was reached. Judges who voted differently might write a **dissenting opinion**, in which they give their reasons for coming to a different conclusion. At times, some judges issue a **concurring opinion**. This is an opinion that agrees with the conclusions of the majority opinion, but for different reasons.

The highest appellate courts are the US Court of Appeals and the United States Supreme Court. In each case, justices who are appointed to these courts by the president must endure a **confirmation process** in the United States Senate. During this process, senators will question nominees and then vote either in favor of, or against, their nomination. Once confirmed, justices to these courts exercise a great deal of authority. **Judicial review** means that the federal courts can declare laws passed by Congress or the states to be unconstitutional. Meanwhile, *writ of certiorari* is the power of higher courts to request that certain lower court decisions be referred to them for review. For example, state court cases have no expressed right under the Constitution to be heard by the Supreme Court. However, states may file a petition for *writ of certiorari* requesting that the Supreme Court invoke its power to have the case referred to it for review.

Supreme Court Building

Chapter 5

Practice 3: The Judicial Process

1. Which of the following statements BEST describes what is meant by saying that the US judicial system is an *adversarial system*?

   A. Court cases are typically argued by attorneys for opposing sides with judges playing the role of making sure trial procedures are followed according to law.

   B. Judges typically argue with attorneys who file briefs and attempt to keep evidence from being presented at trial.

   C. Appellate courts are seen as adversarial to lower courts because they seek to overturn lower court decisions.

   D. The US judicial system consists of both criminal and civil proceedings.

2. Law Enforcement officials must have which of the following to make an arrest?

   A. search warrant or an indictment
   B. probable cause or an arrest warrant
   C. *writ of certiorari* or an issue of fact
   D. complaint or a issue of law

3. A process in which a defendant agrees to plead guilty to a lesser crime or accept a guarantee of less severe punishment for the crime with which they are currently charged in exchange for pleading "guilty" is called what?

   A. an arraignment
   B. plea bargaining
   C. issue of law
   D. settlement

4. What is the role of appellate courts and how are they structured differently from trial courts?

5.4 THE LEGISLATIVE PROCESS

CONGRESSIONAL COMMITTEES

In order for a **proposal** (idea for a new law) to become a national law, it must first be introduced as a **bill** in either the House of Representatives or the US Senate. State laws follow a similar process, except that they must originate in the state legislature. The president of the United States may submit bills to Congress for consideration, but they must be formally introduced by members of either the House or Senate who support the president's proposal. Once a bill is introduced, it is sent to a **standing committee** in the house of Congress where it is being considered. These are permanent committees consisting of members of both parties, with the house's majority party having the most influence. The committee's job is to study and debate the bill. Sometimes committees will conduct **public hearings** to allow citizens who have a special interest or strong feelings about a bill to be heard prior to the committee taking action. Once a bill has been considered, the committee will take one of several actions. It may 1) recommend the bill to the entire house in its original form; 2) recommend the bill with changes; 3) send the bill on for a vote without its recomendation; or 4) ignore the bill and let it "die in committee." Standing committees will assign **subcommittees** consisting of commttee members to study bills which come before it. These subcommittees will then report to the committee as a whole, making recommendations as to what action it feels the committee should take. Standing committees are headed by **committee chairmen**. Up until the mid 70s,

Conflict in the United States' Political and Judicial Systems

committee chairmen were selected according to a *seniority system*. The member of the majority party who had been on a standing committee the longest typically became the committee chairman. Although committee chairmen are not always the most senior member of the majority party any longer, the seniority system still plays a key role in deciding which senators and representatives serve on certain committees. Since certain committees tend to wield more power and influence than others, members of Congress who have faithfully served their party the longest tend to be awarded the most coveted positions. (Review Chapter 2, Section 2 regarding the legislative branch.) One of the most powerful committees in Congress is the **House Rules Committee**. This committee actually decides the manner in which

**Louise Slaughter
2007 Chairman of
House Rules Committee**

bills come to the floor of the House of Representatives for a vote. For this reason, it exercises great influence over what bills are given a chance to pass and which ones are not. Although most committees consist of members of just one house, there are times when members of each house are involved. **Joint committees** are committees on which members of both the House and the Senate regularly serve. By comparison, **conference committees** are temporary committees consisting of both senators and representative that are established when both houses have passed different versions of the same bill (both versions may address the same issue but consist of different guidelines). The conference committee attempts to draft a version that will pass in both houses.

CONGRESSIONAL DEBATE AND VOTING ON BILLS

Once a bill makes it out of committee, it goes before the entire house for debate and a vote. The House of Representatives generally puts limits on how much time can be spent debating a bill. In the Senate, however, no such limits exist. Therefore, senators will sometimes attempt to stop a vote on bills they oppose by means of a **filibuster**. This is a strategy in which a senator will continue to talk until either the bill is withdrawn, or other senators can convince colleagues to vote "no". If, however, three-fifths of the senators present vote in favor of closing the debate, then the filibuster is ended and a vote can occur. This process is called **cloture.** If the majority in one house of Congress votes in favor of the bill, then it goes on to the other house. If the

**President Lyndon B. Johnson
Signs a Bill into a Law**

majority in that house also votes for the bill, then the bill is said to have "passed" both houses of Congress. Many times, however, bills only pass after having a number of *riders* attached. A **rider** is an additional provision that would likely not pass as its own bill, so it is added to a bill that likely will pass. Riders often have little to do with the bill to which they are attached. If either house of Congress fails to pass a bill, then that bill will either have to be reintroduced (usually with changes) or "dies" without ever becoming a law. Bills that do pass both houses are sent to the president for his/her signature. If the president signs it, the bill becomes a **law.**

PRESIDENTIAL VETOS

The president may also *veto* a bill. A **veto** is when both houses of Congress pass a bill but the president refuses to sign it. If this happens, the bill does not become law *unless* two-thirds of both the Senate and the House vote to override the president's veto. Most of the time, however, Congress does not possess enough votes to override a veto. Occasionally, the president may exercise a *pocket veto*. Under the Constitution, the president has ten days (not counting Sundays) to either sign or veto legislation. If he/she does nothing, then the bill becomes law. The one exception is if Congress adjourns (ends its session) prior to the ten days expiring. If this happens and the president takes no action, then the legislation effectively dies. A **pocket veto** is when the president intentionally takes no action on a bill because he knows Congress is not in session and his/her actions cannot be overridden. He/she is said to "put the bill in his/her pocket".

Sometimes presidents will veto legislation that they initially favored. This usually happens because Congress attached riders that the president opposes. As a result, the president changes his/her mind and rejects the bill. The president does not enjoy the power of a **line item veto**. This is a veto that allows the chief executive to reject part of a bill while accepting other parts. While some states afford this power to its governor, the president must either veto or sign an entire bill.

Any bill that is signed by the president, has had no action taken by the president after the required ten days while Congress is in session, or is still being considered, is called an **act of Congress**.

HOW BILLS BECOME LAWS

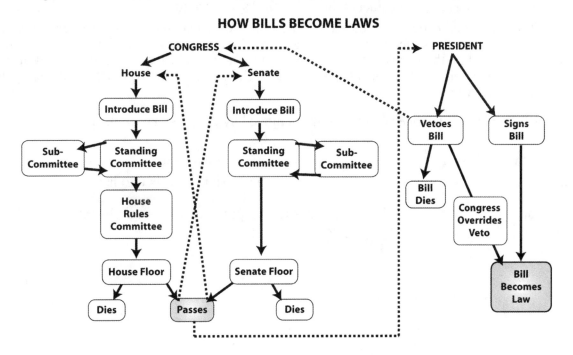

Practice 4: The Legislative Process

1. A proposal that has been introduced by a member of Congress to be considered as a potential law is called what?

   A. a resolution
   B. an act of Congress
   C. a bill
   D. a veto

2. Which of the following MOST accurately depicts the process by which a law is created?

    A. A bill is first signed by the president who then presents it to Congress. Congress then sends it to a committee in each house. If the committee approves the bill, it then goes to a subcommittee. If the subcommittee votes in favor of the bill, it then is presented to both houses of Congress for a vote. If both houses vote in favor of the bill, it becomes law.

    B. If one house of Congress votes in favor of a bill, it then goes to a committee within that same house. If the committee recommends the bill, it then goes to the other house of Congress for a vote. If that house also votes in favor of the bill, it then presents the bill to one of its own committees. If that committee recommends the bill, the bill then goes to the president who will either sign or veto the bill.

    C. Once a bill is introduced by either a senator or a representative, it then goes to a committee. The committee then assigns it to a subcommittee that will study and make recommendations to the committee as a whole. Once a committee is done debating a bill and decides to send it to the house of Congress of which the committee is a part, the bill is then debated and voted on. If it passes by a majority vote, it then goes to the other house. Once a bill passes both houses, it goes to the president who will either sign or veto it.

    D. Bills must originate in the House of Representatives. Once this occurs, they go to the House Rules Committee which then assigns them to sub-committees. Once a subcommittee recommends a bill, it then goes to the whole House for a vote. Once the House passes it, it then goes to the Senate. If the Senate passes it as well, the bill then goes to the president, who will either veto or sign it.

3. Of the following, which one is NOT a power enjoyed by the president in the process of making laws?

    A. veto   C. pocket veto
    B. line item veto   D. signing bills into law

4. What are *riders* and how can they sometimes lead to presidents vetoing bills they originally favored?

5.5 HOW LOCAL GOVERNMENTS BALANCE INTERESTS AND RESOLVE CONFLICTS

Just like state and national governments, local governments have to deal with conflicts created by controversial issues. There are **budget issues** concerning how local governments should spend money and to what extent citizens should be taxed. **Zoning issues** sometimes create conflict between business interests who want to develop land for industrial purposes and those who wish to protect residential and/or historical areas. This is because local governments usually have **zoning laws** that determine what kinds of structures may be built (i.e., residential versus commercial), where they may be built, and what standards they must meet. The question of **extra territorial jurisdiction** (existing cities expanding to exercise authority over previously outlying areas) can be a

"hot button" issue for communities where cities are growing and wanting to expand. Sometimes this involves **annexation.** (Review Chapter 3, Section 5 regarding annexation.) Extra territorial jurisdiction creates controversy because citizens often differ over whether or not they view such changes as positive. Some citizens welcome being included in a city's jurisdiction because it allows them to take advantage of its **infrastructure** (utilities, sewage, water, and other resources), as well as benefiting from such services and police and fire protection, waste management, etc. Others, however, resent such encroachments because it generally means increased taxes. Resolving controversies involving extra territorial jurisdiction and annexation normally require cooperation between county, city, and state governments.

Local governments attempt to address these and other issues in a number of ways. Smaller communities may use informal **town meetings** where the whole community is invited to come together and participate in the process of finding a solution. Most communities rely on the leadership of some kind of elected body, such as a city council or county commission. Representatives to these bodies are often elected as **"at large" candidates,** meaning that they are not elected to represent just one district or constituency, but rather the whole community. These elected bodies normally hold **public hearings** that private citizens are welcome to attend and where they can request to be heard. Sometimes local governments will

Mr. Fox

use public **forums** as well. These are special meetings conducted specifically for the purpose of allowing citizens to come and voice their opinions on topics of concern within the community. For instance, if a school board is thinking about redistricting schools, it may hold a forum to allow parents to express any concerns they might have before taking final action.

Practice 5: Interests and Conflicts

1. What are two or three issues that can cause conflicts for local governments?

2. Which of the following is NOT a method used by local governments to try and resolve conflicts?
   A. annexation
   B. public hearings
   C. town meetings
   D. public forums

5.6 IMPACT OF CITIZENS, POLITICS, AND THE MEDIA

THE ROLE OF CITIZENS

Voting is one of the most common ways individuals voice their opinion on issues. They vote for candidates who support their positions, vote to **recall** candidates they believe guilty of failing to perform the duties of their office, and/or cast their vote in a local *initiative* or *referendum*. A **local initiative** is when enough citizens in a certain community (city, town, etc.) sign a **petition** (written request initiated by citizens asking that the government take certain action) to force a vote on an issue of local importance. Meanwhile, a **local referendum** is when an entire community's electorate is asked to vote on a proposal (i.e., a new law or a change to an existing law).

In addition to voting and starting petitions, citizens also join *special interest groups*. **Special interest groups** are advocacy groups for one side of a particular issue. For example, **MADD (Mothers Against Drunk Driving)** has helped win the passage of tougher DWI (driving while impaired) laws through its efforts against drunk driving. **The Sierra Club** has fought for environmental legislation. The **NRA (National Rifle Association)** devotes its energies to defending its interpretation of the *Second Amendment*. The aim of such groups and the citizens who join them is to influence **public policy**. They want to win the passage of laws and the election of candidates who will support the group's stance on key issues.

Candy Lightner
Founder of MADD

THE ROLE OF POLITICS

Politicians and political parties often use conflict and controversial issues to try and make political gains. As a result, such issues tend to remain hot topics. Take, for instance, abortion. Traditionally, the Democratic Party tends to favor a woman's "right to choose" while many Republicans promote an unborn child's "right to life". This makes for heated debates and makes abortion an important issue both during elections and during confirmation hearings for nominees to the federal courts. Another issue that has been politicized is education. In general, Democrats have favored increased funding for existing public schools. By contrast, many Republicans have voiced support for **tuition vouchers**. Under the "voucher system" students could attend private schools with the help of public funding. Once a student enrolled in a given school, that school could then present the voucher to the government for money to assist in the child's education. Supporters believe that vouchers will improve US education. Critics say that it will lead to de facto segregation and violations of the *First Amendment*, because many private schools have a religious affiliation. One "middle-ground" solution has been the establishment of **charter schools**. However, even charter schools cause some controversy. (Review Chapter 3, Section 7 regarding charter schools.)

THE ROLE OF THE MEDIA

The media also plays a role. The **electronic media** (television, radio, the internet) has arguably had the most impact due to its ability to portray moving images of events as well as communicate and update information quickly. In addition to television, both radio talk shows that deal with current events and on-line sources of information have become increasingly popular over the last decade. The media focuses the public's attention on controversies, and potential resolutions to those controversies, by educating—and some would argue, indoctrinating (reporting with bias for the purpose of promoting a particular agenda)—the US public.

Political Radio Talk Show Host Rush Limbaugh

Practice 6: Citizens, Politics, and the Media

1. A Special election in which an entire community's electorate is asked to vote on a proposal, such as a new law or a change to the existing law, is called what?

    A.   an initiative

    B.   a tuition voucher

    C.   a recall

    D.   a referendum

2. Politically active citizens who work average jobs, live in average neighborhoods, and wish to impact public policy are MOST likely to join which one of the following?

    A.   local initiatives

    B.   charter schools

    C.   special interest groups

    D.   electronic media

3. What are tuition vouchers, and what are the arguments for and against using them?

CHAPTER 5 REVIEW

A. Define the following key terms.

conflict resolution	perjury	annexation
debate	verdict	infrastructure
negotiation	capital offense	town meetings
compromise	hung jury	at large candidates
consensus building	mistrial	forums
original jurisdiction	torts	voting
appellate jurisdiction	plaintiff	recall
concurrent jurisdiction	summons	local initiative
exclusive jurisdiction	settlements	local referendum
lower courts	appeal	petition
general trial courts	issue of fact	special interest groups
intermediate appellate courts	public policy	criminal/civil courts
issue of law	tuition vouchers	US District Court
rights of victims	charter schools	special courts
oral arguments	electronic media	US Court of Appeals

Conflict in the United States' Political and Judicial Systems

majority opinion	US Supreme Court	dissenting opinion
adversarial system	concurring opinion	misdemeanors
confirmation process	felonies	judicial review
arrest warrant	*writ of certiorari*	search warrant
proposal	probable cause	bill
defendant	standing committee	prosecutor
public hearings	indictment	subcommittees
grand jury	committee chairman	complaint
seniority system	preliminary hearing	House Rules Committee
arraignment	joint committees	sentence
filibuster	court docket	cloture
bail	rider	plea bargaining/bargain
law	pre-trial motion	veto
briefs	pocket veto	defense attorney
act of Congress	public defender	budget issues
bailiffs	zoning issues/laws	subpoena
extra territorial jurisdiction		

B. Choose the correct answer.

1. A jury has just deliberated concerning a criminal case in which the defendant is accused of robbing the victim at gunpoint. Initially, six jurors think he is guilty, four think he is innocent, and two are not sure. In order for the jury to reach a verdict that they can agree on, the group will have to engage in what?

   A. the indictment process
   B. extra territorial jurisdiction
   C. developing probable cause
   D. consensus building

2. Which of the following is not involved in a conflict resolution?
   A. debate.　　B. perjury.　　C. negotiation.　　D. compromises.

3. Miriam is convicted in US District Court of violating federal drug laws. She claims, however, that her constitutional rights were violated because the evidence used against here was improperly seized and never should have been presented at trial. Miriam appeals to the US Court of Appeals. Which of the following statements is true?

   A. The US District Court and the US Court of Appeals have concurrent jurisdiction over the case.
   B. The US District Court has exclusive jurisdiction and Miriam cannot make an appeal.
   C. The US District Court has original jurisdiction over the case.
   D. Special courts have appellate jurisdiction over the case.

4. In North Carolina, district courts serve as what?

    A.   lower courts

    B.   general trial courts

    C.   intermediate appellate courts

    D.   the courts that always have original jurisdiction over all cases

5. Which of the following is NOT a true statement regarding the United States Supreme Court?

    A.   it has appellate jurisdiction over all other courts in the country.

    B.   it consists of 9 justices.

    C.   it only has appellate jurisdiction; it has no original jurisdiction.

    D.   it can use *writ of certiorari* to request that state cases be referred to it for review.

6. Bill is a defendant in court. If Bill is found guilty at trial, the maximum he could be sentenced to is 30 years in prison and be ordered to pay a fine of at least $75,000. Bill has been charged with what?

    A.   a felony   B.   a misdemeanor   C.   a civil offense   D.   a capital offense

7. The local police department has three eyewitnesses who all say they saw Samantha break the windshield of her ex-boyfriend's car with a baseball bat and then hit him in the head with her cell phone. Since the police themselves did not witness Samantha committing this misdemeanor, they will most likely have to obtain what before they can arrest her?

    A.   probable cause   C.   search warrant

    B.   arrest warrant   D.   a new cell phone

8. Which of the following is MOST similar to the role a judge plays in a trial as part of the US adversarial system?

    A.   a boxer in a title fight

    B.   a father pulling for his son at a little league baseball game

    C.   a principle questioning a student who cut class

    D.   a referee in a football game

9. Which of the following describes a court exercising appellate jurisdiction?

    A.   A judge conducts a preliminary hearing to determine if there is enough evidence against the defendant to warrant a trial.

    B.   A grand jury considers all the evidence and decides to issue and indictment against the defendant.

    C.   A panel of judges listens to the arguments of both sides and then decides that the defendant is entitled to a new trial.

    D.   A mistrial is declared because of a hung jury.

10. Walter's defense attorney informs him that the prosecutor has a video showing Walter holding up the liquor store he is accused of robbing. As a result, Walter's attorney convinces him to plead guilty in exchange for having the prosecutor charge him with a less serious crime. Walter has just accepted what?

    A. a pre-trial settlement
    B. a tort deal
    C. a jury deliberation
    D. a plea bargain

11. Janice has just received a written notice that one of her customers is suing her for failing to honor her contract. The document informing Janice of these charges and letting her know what day to report to court is called what?

    A. a subpoena
    B. a summons
    C. a *writ of certiorari*
    D. a brief

12. Senator Maxwell has just introduced a bill for consideration. What process will his bill have to go through before it can become a law?

    A. It must first go to a committee that will consider whether or not to recommend it to the entire Senate. If the committee recommends it, then it will go to the entire Senate for debate. If there is no filibuster that prevents it, the bill will be voted on. If it passes, it then will go to the House of Representatives. It must pass in the House and be signed by the president in order to become law. If the president vetoes the bill, both the Senate and the House will need a two-thirds vote to override the veto. Otherwise, Senator Maxwell's bill is dead.

    B. It must first go to a committee that will consider whether or not to recommend it to the entire Senate. If the committee recommends it, then it will go to the House Rules Committee which will determine the rules by which it goes to the floor for a vote. If it passes, it then will go to the House of Representatives. It must pass in the House and be signed by the president in order to become law. If the president vetoes the bill, then Senator Maxwell's bill is dead.

    C. It must first go to a subcommittee. If the subcommittee recommends it, the bill will then go to a committee. If the committee approves it, the bill will then go to both houses of Congress for a vote. Once it passes in each house, the president then considers it for ten days and either signs it or sends it back to Congress to attach a rider. If the president sends it back and no rider is attached, then Senator Maxwell's bill is dead.

    D. Senator Maxwell cannot introduce a bill because all bills must originate in the House of Representatives.

13. The president is opposed to a bill that has passed both houses of Congress. Congress is pressing the president to sign the bill as soon as possible. In just eight days, Congress will recess and will not be in session again until after the election. Which of the following is NOT one of the president's options?

    A. He/she can veto the bill.
    B. He/she can sign the bill.
    C. He/she can exercise a line item veto.
    D. He/she can exercise a pocket veto.

14. The city of Banksville wants to annex all county land within a one mile radius of the city limits. Which of the following citizens is MOST LIKELY to oppose the city's plan?

    A. a county resident opposed to higher taxes
    B. a city leader who believes the city needs to expand
    C. a county resident who wants access to city water
    D. a sheriff who feels his department is stretched too thin

Chapter 6
Purpose, Development, and Implementation of Laws

This chapter addresses the following competency goal and objective(s):

Competency goal 6	The learner will explain why laws are needed and how they are enacted, implemented, and enforced at the national, state, and local levels.
Objective 6.01, 6.02, 6.03, 6.04, 6.05, 6.06, 6.07,	

6.1 INFLUENCES ON US LAW

Jurisprudence is the study of law. It is concerned with examining the theory and philosophy of law, as well as analyzing its purpose, structure, and implementation in society. US law can be traced to civilizations that existed centuries before the first American colonies.

ANCIENT LAWS

One of the earliest **legal codes** (set of written laws, rules for implementing those laws, punishments for violating laws, and so forth) was the *Code of Hammurabi*. Hammurabi was one of ancient Babylon's greatest kings, who ruled sometime between 1850 and 1750 BC. His code of law was based on previous laws and social norms that he revised and expanded. Hammurabi's laws protected the rights of individuals and are considered by many to be the first example of a king acknowledging that all human beings have certain "natural rights". They greatly influenced surrounding and future civilizations. One of these was that of the ancient Hebrews. They lived by a legal and **moral code** (set of guidelines stating what is morally

Hammurabi

"right/wrong" and directing people how they should live) called *Mosaic Law*. This code of laws included the *Ten Commandments* that are recorded in the Bible. The *Ten Commandments* have influenced not only Israel, but all societies in which Judaism and/or Christianity have had an impact. Although most Jews and Christians believe that the *Mosaic Law* was given to Moses directly by God, many scholars point out that some of its principles

Purpose, Development and Implementation of Laws

are similar to those put forth in the *Code of Hammurabi*. Many moral standards and laws (i.e., laws against stealing, murder, etc.) adopted by the United States can be traced to the nation's religious roots, and in particular, the *Ten Commandments*.

In 621 BC, a man named Draco drafted the ancient Greeks' first written code of law. Known as the **Draconian Laws**, this legal code gave a voice to the common people because it allowed them to appeal to written laws rather than upper-class judges. These laws also helped solidify the Athenian city-state because they took the responsibility for retribution out of the hands of private citizens and put it in the hands of government. Centuries later, between 529 and 534 AD, the Byzantine Emperor Justinian I, compiled centuries of Roman law into what became known as the **Justinian Codes**. These codes revived the principles of Roman law in the Middle Ages. They also firmly established the emperor as an absolute monarch with unlimited power. The *Justinian Codes* eventually influenced church government and increased the influence of Christianity over Europe. Its ideas about the absolute authority of the monarch and the union of church and state, however, were later rejected by many in the Enlightenment who advocated the principle of a **"social contract"** between governments and the people. (Review Chapter 1, Section 2 regarding social contract theory.)

BRITISH LAW

Because the 13 colonies were originally British, English models of government and law greatly influenced the US. The **Magna Carta** granted certain rights to nobles and placed the king himself under the direct rule of law. The **English Bill of Rights** further limited the authority of the king by requiring him to obtain Parliament's approval before enacting certain laws and by guaranteeing certain rights to citizens. Finally, **British common law** (law based on tradition or past court decisions rather than written statutes) also impacted US law by establishing the idea of accepting past court decisions as authoritative in cases where no formal law exists or is considered vague.

COLONIAL/NATIVE AMERICAN INFLUENCES

As people came to North America, they brought many of these ideas about government with them. The **Mayflower Compact** was a document which guaranteed the people a voice in government in Massachusetts. Meanwhile, Virginia's **House of Burgesses** was modeled after British Parliament and became the first representative body of government in the colonies. The principles on which both were based would later be expressed as reasons for both the **Declaration of Independence** and the **United States Constitution**.

However, it was not only British influences that had impact on American ideas about law and government. In the late 1500s, the Iroquois tribes of the northeast who often found themselves at war with one another agreed to stop fighting. They banded together to form the **Iroquois League**. This union served to greatly strengthen the Iroquois and make them the dominate tribe among eastern Native American peoples. The Iroquois League was so impressive that it inspired Benjamin Franklin to propose the *Albany Plan of Union* in 1754. The plan sought to strengthen British colonial ties with the Iroquois as well as attempt to imitate what they had accomplished by better unifying the colonies. Although the plan was rejected, some of its principles served as a model for the US government that formed later. By influencing the *Albany Plan of Union*, the Iroquois League also had an indirect influence on the United States.

Practice 1: Influences on US Law

1. Someone who studies the theory, philosophy, purpose, and implementation of law is said to be a student of what?

   A. social contract theory

   B. Justinian codes

   C. jurisprudence

   D. Draconian laws

2. Which of the following statements is TRUE?

   A. Due to the influence of British law, all other codes of law had no real influence on colonial codes of law and government.

   B. One of the earliest legal codes was established by a Babylonian king named Hammurabi.

   C. The Draconian Laws were a legal code that compiled centuries of Roman law into a code that greatly influenced the church and Europe.

   D. *Social contract theory* reinforces the *Justinian codes*.

3. In what way did the Iroquois impact US ideas about law and government?

6.2 TYPES OF LAW

There are various types of laws that govern society. **Criminal laws** define what actions are regarded as "criminal acts" against the state. Laws against murder, burglary, rape, identity theft, etc. are all examples of criminal laws. **Civil laws** are laws concerned with relationships between individuals, businesses, organizations, etc. A patient filing suit against a doctor for malpractice, a smoker dying of lung cancer suing a tobacco company, a homeowner suing a contractor for failing to adequately complete electrical  work, and a corporation claiming that a competitor has violated trademark laws, are all examples of civil law. One category of civil law is **family law**. Cases involving divorce, child support payments, adoptions, child custody, etc. are examples of family law. Whereas many civil cases involve monetary damages, family law often involves matters not directly related to money.

Public law is any area of law dealing directly with relationships between individuals, businesses, or organizations and the government. In addition to criminal laws, there are also other forms of public law. **Constitutional law** deals with interpretations and practical application of the *US Constitution*. For example, when the Supreme Court ruled in *Gregg v. Georgia (1976)* that capital punishment is not a violation of the *Eighth Amendment* so long as certain guidelines are followed, it was ruling on an issue of constitutional law. **Administrative law** is law that governs the operation of government agencies. These agencies oversee such things as trade, manufacturing, pollution, taxation and a variety of other areas. **International law** is also a branch of public law. It deals with laws that apply to all nations. Issues involving international trade, boundary disputes between countries, methods of warfare, how prisoners of war are to be treated, and many other international issues are all governed by international law. While the principle of international law is noble, in reality, it is very difficult to enforce. Nations that violate international law normally face few consequences unless their actions are severe enough to warrant economic sanctions or military action from other countries.

Most laws are **statutory laws**. In other words, they are laws enacted by legislative bodies (i.e., Congress or state legislatures). As we have learned, however, courts also shape the US legal code through their power to establish legal precedence.

Practice 2: Types of Law

1. Jerry agrees to paint several houses for a local developer. After completing the project, however, the developer will only pay half of the price they agreed on because he claims Jerry took too long to complete the project. Jerry, in turn, sues the developer for the difference plus the cost of legal fees. What kind of case is this?

   A. a case involving criminal law   C. a case involving administrative law

   B. a case involving constitutional law   D. a case involving civil law

2. Sadly, Janet and Tim are getting a divorce. To make matters worse, they have two beautiful children and both parents want custody. The courts will have to decide who gets the children and what kind of visitation rights the other parent will have. What kind of case is this?

   A. a case involving administrative law   C. a case involving criminal law

   B. a case involving family law   D. a case involving monetary damages

3. Which of the following does NOT involve an area of public law?

   A. Phil is charged with assaulting a police officer and may have to spend time in jail.

   B. Maya and her husband, Trent, must go to court to sign legal papers because Maya's ex-husband is surrendering his parental rights so that Trent can adopt Maya's kids.

   C. The world community demands that a leader be tried as a criminal because he is accused of violating international laws by executing large numbers of his own people.

   D. The Environmental Protection Agency fines a large corporation for improperly disposing of its waste.

4. What is constitutional law?

6.3 IMPLEMENTING AND ENFORCING LAWS

Once laws are established, they must then be **implemented** (effectively applied in society). In order to accomplish this, federal, state, and local governments rely on a number of agencies to assist in the implementation and enforcement of laws.

Chapter 6

REGULATORY COMMISSIONS AND INDEPENDENT AGENCIES

Regulatory commissions (commissions established by the government to oversee certain areas) and **independent agencies** (agencies established by legislative statute and outside the departments of the executive branch of federal or state governments) are charged with seeing that laws are efficiently implemented and held to. Below are a few examples:

- **Environmental Protection Agency (EPA)** – makes sure that laws regulating pollution, the use of certain chemicals/pesticides, and waste disposal are properly adhered to.

- **Federal Trade Commission (FTC)** – ensures **consumer protection** by making sure companies do not engage in false advertising and that they disclose crucial information (i.e., health concerns or issues regarding safety). The FTC also makes sure that businesses do not violate antitrust laws.

- **National Transportation Safety Board (NTSB)** – responsible for investigating accidents involving airplanes and other forms of mass transit. It also investigates hazardous waste spills involving modes of transportation.

- **Federal Communications Commission (FCC)** – enforces federal regulations regarding modes of communication, such as television and radio broadcasts. It also regulates all interstate and international (provided at least one of the communicating parties is in the US) telecommunications.

- **Food & Drug Administration (FDA)** – responsible for regulating food, drugs, medical equipment, dietary supplements, and other products that could impact the health of citizens.

- **Consumer Product Safety Commission (CPSC)** – regulates the sale and manufacture of consumer products to make sure that they do not pose an unreasonable risk of injury to the public.

- **Federal Aviation Administration (FAA)** – regulates and oversees US civil air travel and transportation.

- **National Aeronautics & Space Administration (NASA)** – responsible for the United States space program.

- **Central Intelligence Agency (CIA)** – primary government agency responsible for espionage. The CIA gathers information on the activities of other nations, insurgent groups throughout the world, and terrorist organizations (these are the guys they make movies about).

- **Interstate Commerce Commission (ICC)** – Created in 1887, the ICC was the nation's first independent agency. It consisted of seven members appointed by the president and approved by the Senate. Its responsibility was to regulate commerce that traveled and/or transpired between states. In 1995, the ICC was eliminated and its remaining powers transferred to the Surface Transportation Board.

LAW ENFORCEMENT AGENCIES

In addition to administrative agencies and regulatory commissions, a number of agencies also exist for the purpose of enforcing the laws through investigations and, if necessary, arrests. The **Federal Bureau of Investigation** is the nation's top law enforcement agency. It is under the **US Department of Justice** (the federal department responsible for a number of federal law enforcement agencies and the enforcement of many of the nation's federal laws) and has jurisdiction over a broad range of federal crimes including bank robberies, drug crimes within the US, and terrorism. (Review Chapter 2, Section 7 regarding federal law enforcement/FBI.) Meanwhile, another well-known federal law enforcement agency is the United States **Secret Service**. Although this agency is best known

**Alberto Gonzales
Head of US Justice Dept.**

for its role of protecting the president and various other public officials, one of its primary tasks is to enforce laws against the counterfeiting of US money and/or treasury bonds. Prior to 2001, the Secret Service operated as part of the US Department of the Treasury. However, after 9/11, it became part of the Department of Homeland Security.

Like the federal government, states also have agencies that play a role in law enforcement. The North Carolina **State Bureau of Investigation (SBI)** is the state's top investigative agency and serves as the state's equivalent of the FBI. It investigates both criminal and civil cases which fall under its jurisdiction. **State troopers** are officers of the state highway patrol and are responsible for enforcing and investigating violations of state traffic laws. State troopers also act as body guards for certain state officials and assist in searches for escaped prisoners. The state also has the **National Guard** as its military force. It consists of private citizens who work civilian jobs, but also serve part-time in the military. In times of war or in emergency situations, the president of the United States has the authority to "nationalize" the Guard and call them up for military service. For example, President George W. Bush

National Guardsman

has called up guardsmen to serve in both the War on Terror and to play a role in securing the nation's borders. Most of the time, however, it is the governor who exercises authority over the National Guard. The Guard often serves to help in times of natural disaster and/or to enforce laws and maintain order under circumstances where traditional law enforcement may not have adequate staff or resources.

Finally, there are local law enforcement agencies as well. The **sheriff's department** provides county-wide enforcement for both civil and criminal cases. Cities usually have their own **police departments** that provide city-wide law enforcement and investigate both criminal and traffic offenses. While federal agencies are in place to investigate and enforce federal laws, state, county, and city law enforcement agencies all play a role in enforcing state and local laws, the nature and location of the offense determines the law enforcement jurisdiction.

Practice 3: Implementing and Enforcing Laws

1. A television broadcast violates federal standards by using a word that is not allowed on network television. As a result, the station that aired the broadcast is ordered to pay a hefty fine and is warned that future violations could result in the loss of its license. The agency that issued this fine and warning is MOST LIKELY which of the following?

    A. FCC   B. FTC   C. NTSB   D. SBI

2. Of the following, who would MOST LIKELY be expected to investigate a six car collision that occurs on a stretch of highway in a rural part of the county?

    A. sheriff's deputy   C. state trooper

    B. SBI agent   D. police officer

3. An independent regulatory agency is one that is outside of what?

    A. the influence of the federal government

    B. the restrictions of any statutory law

    C. the influence of public opinion

    D. the departments of the executive branch of government

6.4 MAINTAINING AN INFORMED CITIZENRY

In order for laws to be effective, the US public must be an **informed citizenry**. In other words, people must be aware of the laws that govern their society. Both citizens and the government must work to make sure the public knows what is, and is not, legal. In the US judicial system, **"ignorance of the law is no excuse"**; citizens are held responsible for obeying a law, even if they did not know it existed. Therefore, citizens better make sure they remain informed.

WHAT CITIZENS CAN DO TO STAY INFORMED

There are a number of things people can do to stay informed about the law. In communities that have **town meetings**, citizens can actually participate in drafting local laws and policies. Such gatherings are normally held in smaller communities where anyone who wishes is invited to come and play a role in local decisions. Many meetings (i.e., a meeting of the city council or county commission) are held as **public hearings**, where the general public may attend and, at times, speak regarding laws and local matters. **Public forums** are another way citizens can become informed. These are meetings specifically set up to allow citizens to express their opinion about a certain law or political issue. Without question, the most common way citizens stay informed is through the **media**. People stay informed by watching television newscasts, listening to news related radio programs, reading newspapers and magazines, checking online updates, and visiting government websites.

WHAT THE GOVERNMENT CAN DO TO KEEP CITIZENS INFORMED

The government must also play a part in maintaining an informed citizenry. One method is through government **press releases**. These are statements released to the media for the purpose of relaying information to the public. In addition, advances in technology and communication over the last 10 to 15 years means that government offices are also able to reach people through **Internet websites**. Citizens can visit these websites daily to get updates and accurate information. **Accessible public officials** and **government publications** also keep people informed. By making themselves accessible (available) to the press and to the people whom they serve, public officials make it easier for citizens to be aware of laws that govern their community. Publicized **political debate** concerning laws and proposed laws help to educate citizens also. Government

Tony Snow
White House Press Secretary

officials can also use what is known as *franking privilege*. **Franking privilege** is the privilege of sending mail for free. Elected officials can use this privilege to respond to letters from constituents or send out newsletters to keep people informed about what is happening in government (i.e., what laws are being debated and passed). Sometimes, in order to make sure that it is providing the public with accurate information, the government will form **special task forces**. These are temporary groups formed for the purpose of studying/investigating a specific area. Over the years, there have been a number of special task forces assembled for the purpose of studying various crimes and issues of law.

Practice 4: An Informed Citizenry

1. What does the term "ignorance of the law is no excuse" mean?

    A. Only intelligent people can be expected to understand the law.

    B. People who commit a crime unknowingly are not subject to the same punishment as those who intentionally break the law.

    C. It doesn't matter if you didn't know your actions were illegal, you still have to answer for them.

    D. Not knowing the laws of your community is a crime.

2. Which of the following is not a way that citizens can take it upon themselves to be informed about laws and important issues?

    A. attending town meetings.

    B. participating in public forums.

    C. visiting government websites.

    D. issuing press releases.

3. What is an "informed citizenry"?

6.6 LOBBYISTS, INTEREST GROUPS, AND THINK TANKS

Although neither plays any *official* role in US government, in reality, both **lobbyists** and **interest groups** have become powerful influences in US politics. (Review Chapter 2, Section 5 regarding interest groups and Chapter 4, Section 3–4 regarding lobbyists.) Interest groups promote a particular cause or position, while lobbyists are hired by interest groups to influence legislation on any number of issues.

Chapter 6

ECONOMIC INTERESTS

Sometimes there are **economic interests** (interests involving money) at
stake. For instance, corporations with a specific **business interest** will hire
lobbyists to either ensure the passage of legislation that helps them or
prevent legislation that would cost them. An example of this occurred in
the early 90s when Congress voted down President Bill Clinton's health
care plan. While those in Congress had different reasons for opposing the
plan, most agree that an aggressive lobbying effort by US insurance
companies and other businesses played a significant role in its defeat.

Businesses also often rely on the **Chamber of Commerce**. Most chambers are local and are voluntarily
joined by businesses to promote economic growth. In addition, they also lobby governments. Many times,
chambers of commerce will join to form larger bodies, such as the US Chamber of Commerce. The US
Chamber of Commerce is one of the world's largest not-for-profit business federations, representing millions
of businesses and thousands of local chambers. It consistently ranks as one of the highest spending lobbying
groups in Washington, DC.

Big business is not the only economic interest represented by interest groups. **Labor unions** strive to unify
and represent workers who work in the same, or similar, industries. These unions increase the bargaining
power of employees by allowing them to negotiate contracts, wages, etc. as a collective group rather than as
individuals. They also lobby and endorse political candidates that they feel come closest to supporting their
political agenda. The AFL-CIO and the United Auto Workers are just two examples of unions that carry
notable amounts of political influence. **Agricultural groups** provide aid to farmers in times of economic
hardship. The American Farm Bureau Federation and the National Farmers Union are the two largest
examples of these kinds of groups. Finally, **professional groups** lobby Congress for professions that require
specialized training, such as law, medicine, and teaching. Groups like the American Medical Association
have lobbied for laws limiting malpractice litigation (medical lawsuits). The National Education Association
fights for the interests of teachers. Meanwhile, the American Bar Association fights to establish and maintain
standards for those in the legal profession.

NON-ECONOMIC INTERESTS

Some interest groups are concerned with **non-economic interests** (interests
in which money is not considered the driving factor). These groups usually
promote an **ideological belief**. In other words, they exist to promote a
principle or moral cause, rather than economic concerns. **Public interest
groups** lobby for issues that are considered to be in the "public interest".
Groups that fight for environmental legislation or the protection of civil
liberties are considered public interest groups because the issues they address
affect everyone. By comparison, **single interest groups** represent only a
specific group. The Veterans of Foreign Wars (lobbies on behalf of military
veterans) and the American Association of Retired Persons (lobbies on behalf of senior citizens) are each
examples of single interest groups.

**Former Vice President Al Gore
Environmental Activist**

THINK TANKS

Think tanks are organizations established for the purpose of researching, studying, and providing advice about important issues. Often, they are connected to universities and other institutions of research and academia. Such groups are valuable because they provide government leaders with expert opinions on matters of economics, sociology, foreign policy, etc. Some criticize think tanks and accuse them of presenting findings that are meant to ensure future funding rather than provide accurate information. Think tanks can be conservative, liberal, moderate, and/or non-partisan in nature.

Practice 5: Lobbyists, Interest Groups, and Think Tanks

1. In order to influence legislation on key issues, interest groups will often hire which of the following?

   A.   think tanks

   B.   professional groups

   C.   lobbyists

   D.   chambers of commerce

2. The US Chamber of Commerce is an example of which of the following?

   A.   an interest group representing laborers

   B.   an interest group representing economic interest

   C.   a think tank

   D.   a public interest group

3. What is a think tank, and why do critics sometimes accuse them of presenting findings that are inaccurate?

6.8: ADDRESSING CRIMINAL / ANTI-SOCIAL BEHAVIOR

Because laws are inevitably broken, society must have procedures for dealing with criminal behavior. There are three commonly recognized goals when addressing crime: 1) retribution 2) deterrence 3) rehabilitation. **Retribution** is concerned with punishing a person convicted of a crime. Those who emphasize retribution tend to favor long prison sentences, capital punishment for those who commit heinous crimes, and uncomfortable conditions for prisoners who are incarcerated. By contrast, **rehabilitation** is concerned with transforming criminals into law abiding citizens. Those who favor rehabilitation tend to emphasize  the importance of understanding *why* a person commits a crime, rather than simply punishing them. They often advocate educational programs, counseling, and job training for those in prison. Supporters of this position also stress the importance of addressing social and economic "injustices" that they believe contribute to crime. Finally, **deterrence** is meant to prevent future crimes. Those who favor retribution believe that deterrence is best accomplished by harsh punishments that will discourage people from committing similar offenses in the future. Meanwhile, advocates of rehabilitation believe that the best hope for deterrence is to change criminal behavior and improve socio-economic conditions. Both advocates of retribution and those of rehabilitation point to the rate of criminal *recidivism* as justification for their views. **Recidivism** is the rate at which criminal behavior is repeated by the same people. Statistics show that those who have been convicted of criminal offenses often commit future crimes as well. Once again, those who support retribution and those who favor rehabilitation tend to disagree on the reasons for this trend. Those promoting harsher punishments say that it is because sentences are too lenient that people continue to commit crimes. Proponents of rehabilitation argue that people return to crime predominantly because enough is still not being done to rehabilitate criminals and improve conditions in society. While there are extremists on both sides, most citizens support a balance between retribution and rehabilitation. They believe people should pay for committing crimes, but they also want to provide convicted persons with the opportunity to change and become productive citizens.

RETRIBUTION FOR LESS SERIOUS CRIMES

Judge

There are various ways that those convicted of criminal behavior can be punished. In less serious cases, a convicted person might simply have to pay **monetary compensation**. In other words, they have to pay money in the form of a fine, restitution, or compensation. **Restitution** is money or property a person gained as a result of their crime which they must give up. For instance, someone convicted of charging $50 in purchases to a stolen credit card may be ordered to pay back the person to whom the card belongs. In the same way, someone convicted of shoplifting hundreds of dollars in clothes may be forced to pay the store from which they stole them. **Compensation** is when a defendant is ordered to pay for another's loss as a result of their crime. Suppose a young man is speeding to get away from the police. He loses control of his car and smashes into the front of a convenience store, shattering all of the glass. The court then orders him to pay for all of the damages, as well as $10,000 to make up for the money the store owner lost because he had to close his store for three days. The defendant must "compensate" the store owner for his losses.

In addition, a person who commits a less serious offense may have to perform **community service**. This means that the court orders the convicted individual to perform a set number of hours working for a charity, cleaning public areas, serving at a city shelter, volunteering for a non-profit organization, etc. In some cases, the court will punish people by placing them on **probation**. Instead of going to prison or jail, the court gives convicted persons a set of conditions that they must meet within a certain amount of time. If they do, then they will not have to be incarcerated. If they do not, however, the judge may choose to revoke the probation and send the person to jail or prison. (Review Chapter 4, Section 4 regarding probation.) It is important to remember that while monetary compensation, community service, and probation can all be sentences imposed for less serious cases, they can also be imposed for more serious crimes if there are mitigating circumstances (circumstances that make the defendant's actions more understandable and/or less offensive) or if it is a defendant's first offense. Sometimes they may also be imposed together, or as part of a tougher sentence that also includes incarceration.

RETRIBUTION FOR SERIOUS CRIMES

Felonies and more serious misdemeanors often involve some form of **detention** (restriction of a person's liberty to leave a given location—i.e., police often detain suspects for questioning). Sometimes these detentions take the form of **house arrests**, in which convicted persons are confined to their home and/or designated areas. Often, house arrests are 24 hours/day. In some cases, however, a person on house arrest may be allowed to leave long enough to go to work or school. The most common form of detention is *incarceration*. **Incarceration** means a convicted criminal is sentenced to spend time in a particular facility without being free to leave. **Long-term incarcerations** (a year or more) are usually served in state run **prisons**. Meanwhile, persons who receive shorter sentences (less than a year) often serve them in county administered **jails**. Generally, the more serious the crime, the longer the period of incarceration one is sentenced to. In reality, however, most convicted criminals do not spend their entire sentence behind bars. This is because most are granted *parole*. **Parole** means a prisoner is released early from prison but is still considered to be serving his/her sentence. For example, say that the court convicts Jim of burglarizing homes and sentences him to 20 years in prison. After 5 years, Jim's case goes before a parole board. The board reviews Jim's case and finds that he has been a "model prisoner" while incarcerated. They decide to let Jim out of prison *on the condition* that he obeys the law and reports regularly to a parole officer who will supervise him and make sure he follows all the conditions of his parole. If Jim abides by the rules of his release, then he will spend the remaining 15 years of his sentence living in society while on parole. If he violates his parole, however, he can be sent back to prison. Many US citizens are upset that so many convicted prisoners are paroled after serving only a small portion of their sentence. Proponents of the parole system point out, however, that prisons are overcrowded and that without parole, there would be no place to house new prisoners. Debate over the parole issue becomes especially heated when paroled convicts are arrested and convicted of additional crimes; especially when those crimes are violent or similar to the crimes for which they were originally sent to prison. In response to such protests, some states have enacted **"three-strikes laws"**, requiring long prison sentences—many times without the chance of parole—for those convicted of three or more serious offenses.

Sometimes conviction (being found guilty) of a crime can result in **confiscation of property**. Confiscation means the state takes a person's home, money, possessions, etc. as punishment for criminal behavior. For instance, those convicted of tax evasion may have property confiscated and sold to pay their debt to the government. Cars used during illegal drug deals and weapons used or possessed illegally are other examples of property that might be confiscated.

Gas Chamber

The most serious form of retribution is *capital punishment*. Better known as the **"death penalty"**, capital punishment is when an individual is sentenced to die for their crime/crimes. The death penalty is not used in every state (it is used in North Carolina) and is usually reserved for those convicted of premeditated murder (although some states, the federal government, and the US military have crimes other than murder for which a person may be executed). If a defendant is found guilty of a capital offense, then the same jury that found

him/her guilty must also decide whether he/she will be executed (put to death) or sentenced to life in prison (often without the chance of parole). Lethal injection, a process by which poisonous chemicals are injected into a condemned person's veins, is used in nearly every state as the method of execution; although many states also have alternate methods as well (North Carolina has the gas chamber). The death penalty has long been an issue of intense debate. Those who advocate abolishing (doing away with) the death penalty claim that it constitutes "cruel and unusual punishment", is uncivilized, and that it inevitably results in the execution of innocent people who have been wrongly convicted. They also highlight statistics suggesting that the death penalty is not fairly applied because men and minorities are more likely to be sentenced to death than women and whites. Some even claim that by the time you add up the cost of appeals, life sentences actually cost the state less money than executions. Proponents of the death penalty claim that it is justice for those who have committed horrible crimes, prevents recidivism, and that it would be unquestionably cheaper than housing and feeding prisoners sentenced to life if the appeals process was properly modified. Many of them also respond to statistics regarding the disproportionate number of minorities on death row (area of a prison where those sentenced to die live and await execution) by suggesting that the solution is to increase the number of whites executed for committing heinous crimes, rather than abolishing capital punishment.

ADDRESSING JUVENILE OFFENSES

Juvenile offenses are those crimes committed by individuals under a certain age. While the age at which one is no longer considered a juvenile differs from state to state, it usually falls somewhere between the ages of 15 and 19. In some cases, juveniles who commit extremely serious crimes can be tried as an adult. Like adults, courts can sentence juveniles to fines, paying monetary compensation, community service, probation, etc. If a juvenile is sentenced to incarceration, he/she usually goes to a **juvenile detention center** rather than a prison or an adult jail. Judges sometimes send juveniles to **boot camps** as an alternative to juvenile detention centers. These are military-style camps designed to rehabilitate juvenile offenders through instilling discipline and respect for authority. Juveniles who go to boot camps usually do so as part of a probation imposed by the court.

Metal Detector at School

Schools have also had to take a more active stance in dealing with anti-social juvenile behavior. Whereas years ago, the worst offenses included fighting and smoking in the rest rooms, today, schools must deal with issues involving guns on campus, illegal drugs, hate crimes (crimes directed at someone because of their race, sexual orientation, etc.), and even terrorist threats. As a result, schools have had to use stiffer penalties, such as **long-term suspensions** (not allowing students to return to school for extended periods), legal searches of student lockers and backpacks, use of metal detectors, and taking out arrest warrants.

MENTAL ILLNESS IN THE CRIMINAL COURTS

While crime is a major problem in society, some anti-social behavior is not the product of evil intent, but rather, mental illness. Even for the worst of crimes, most states allow criminal defendants to plead "not guilty by reason of insanity." Defendants who use this defense must prove that mental illness was the reason for their criminal act. If they are found to be mentally ill, or to have been mentally ill at the time of their crime, then the court may confine them to a **mental institution** where they will hopefully receive the help that they need. Perhaps the most famous defendant to successfully plead insanity was John Hinckley after he attempted to assassinate President Ronald Reagan in 1981.

Purpose, Development and Implementation of Laws

Practice 6: Criminal/Anti-social Behavior

1. Paul believes that crime would decrease if the government would just impose tougher laws. He believes that anyone convicted of murder should automatically get the death penalty. He also thinks that other crimes should carry longer sentences with fewer chances for parole. Paul is a proponent of what?

   A. restitution   B. compensation   C. retribution   D. rehabilitation

2. Brenda is released from jail after serving three months for writing bad checks. Over the next five years, Brenda is arrested eight more times for the same crime. What are Brenda's actions an example of?

   A. restitution   C. juvenile offenses

   B. probation violations   D. criminal recidivism

3. Parker and Joe are both convicted of breaking into a house and stealing possessions inside. However, because Parker has never been in trouble before and did not personally remove any property himself, he receives a list of conditions that he must follow and an officer to whom he will report for three years of supervision. If he completes the conditions and reports as he should, he will not go to prison. Joe, on the other hand, has a long criminal record and is sentenced to two years in prison. Joe, however, only serves nine months before he is out early for "good behavior". Which of the following statements is true?

   A. The court seeks rehabilitation for Parker but retribution from Joe.

   B. Parker is on probation while Joe is on parole.

   C. Parker is only incarcerated for a short time while Joe is incarcerated for a long time.

   D. Joe is obviously an adult and Parker obviously a juvenile.

4. What are some of the arguments for and against the death penalty?

CHAPTER 6 REVIEW

A. Define the following key terms.

jurisprudence

Federal Bureau of Investigation (FBI)

rehabilitation

deterrence

recidivism

State Bureau of Investigation (SBI)

Draconian Laws

state troopers

National Guard

sheriff's department

police department

informed citizenry

incarceration

United States Constitution

Iroquois League

criminal laws

civil laws

family law

public law

constitutional law

administrative law

international law

special task forces

regulatory commissions

business interest

agricultural groups

non-economic interests

Food & Drug Administration (FDA)

National Aeronautics & Space Administration (NASA)

Ideological belief

retribution

"ignorance of the law is no excuse"

Code of Hammurabi

moral code

Ten Commandments

National Transportation Safety Board (NTSB)

restitution

compensation

community service

probation

detention

house arrest

Declaration of Independence

town meetings

public hearings/forums

media

press releases

Internet websites

accessible public officials

government publications

political debate

franking privilege

implementing law

economic interest

chamber of commerce

professional groups

public/single interest groups

Consumer Products Safety Commission (CPSC)

Central Intelligence Agency (CIA)

legal codes

Environmental Protection Agency (EPA))

Department of Justice

Secret Service

monetary compensation

Federal Communications Commission (FCC)

Justinian Codes

Magna Carta

English Bill of Rights

British common law

Mayflower Compact

House of Burgesses

prisons/jails

long-term incarceration

parole

"three-strikes" laws

confiscation of property

death penalty

juvenile detention center

boot camps

long-term suspensions

statutory laws

lobbyists & interest groups

independent agencies

labor unions

Federal Trade Commission (FTC)

think tanks

Federal Aviation Administration (FAA)

Interstate Commerce Commission (ICC)

Purpose, Development and Implementation of Laws

B. Choose the correct answer.

1. The study of the theory, purpose, and implementation of law in society is called what?
   - A. legal code
   - B. common law
   - C. jurisprudence
   - D. public law

2. Written laws, rules for implementation of laws, punishments for breaking the written laws, etc. are called what?
   - A. *Hammurabi codes*
   - B. legal codes
   - C. juris codes
   - D. social contracts

> *"As the colonies' first representative body of government, it helped to provide a model by which later state governments, and even our national government, would be organized."*

3. The above quote is referring to which of the following?
   - A. the *Mayflower Compact*
   - B. the Iroquois League
   - C. the House of Burgesses
   - D. the First Continental Congress

4. Which statement would Benjamin Franklin have MOST agreed with?
   - A. "Thank goodness for our British heritage; surely there in nothing we have found amongst the natives of this land that would suggest that they have anything to offer us in the way of civilized government."
   - B. "I believe that this plan proposed today in Albany will not only unite the colonies in their war against France, but will also serve to unite the previously divided Iroquois people as well."
   - C. "It appears that the Iroquois nation has done well by uniting in a common league. Such union for the colonies, however, should be approached cautiously. We dare not give too much power to a unifying body."
   - D. "The Iroquois people have forged a unity that the British colonies would do well to imitate, and a nation with which we should form an alliance in this war against the French."

5. Susan and her neighbor get into an argument. The argument escalates and the neighbor begins yelling curse words. In response, Susan gets a screwdriver out of her garage and attacks the neighbor, stabbing him several times but causing no serious injuries. The police arrest Susan and charge her with misdemeanor assault. Which of the following is a true statement about this case?
   - A. It is an issue of public law that will be addressed in criminal court.
   - B. It is an issue of civil law because it involves a private dispute between neighbors.
   - C. It is an issue of criminal law that, if Susan is convicted, will likely result in a long-term incarceration.
   - D. Because Susan has violated a statute, it will be addressed as a matter of constitutional law.

Chapter 6

6. A year long undercover operation has revealed the leaders of a US drug ring. Finally, on a specific day, law enforcement raids a meeting where several of these drug lords are meeting to exchange narcotics, military-style firearms, and large amounts of money. The drug lords are arrested and charged with multiple counts of violating federal drug laws, murder, money laundering, etc. Which law enforcement agency MOST LIKELY conducted the year-long investigation and made these arrests?

   A. FBI

   B. Secret Service

   C. SBI

   D. the police department in the city where the meeting occurred

7. Jeanette is driving along an open stretch of interstate 85. Because she is not within any city limits, traffic is light and she forgets to monitor her speed. Eventually, she notices blue lights flashing in her rear view mirror and looks down at her speedometer to see that she is driving 83 mph in a 70 mph zone. She pulls over and the officer who stops her issues her a citation. This officer is most likely part of what law enforcement agency?

   A. sheriff's department   C. state highway patrol

   B. police department   D. State Bureau of Investigation

8. A judge would MOST LIKELY use the term "ignorance of the law is no excuse" in which of the following situations?

   A. when addressing a police officer who obtained evidence illegally

   B. when addressing a defendant who claims that he was mentally ill and unable to understand what he was doing at the time of his crime

   C. when addressing a lawyer who fails to adequately prepare a defense for his client

   D. when addressing a defendant who claims she did not know her actions were illegal

9. Ricardo works as the president's press secretary. It is his responsibility to make sure that the press stays informed regarding what the White House is doing and why. To adequately fulfill this role, which of the following methods is Ricardo NOT likely to use?

   A. make himself accessible to the press with press conferences several times/week.

   B. make himself accessible to the public by appearing on television.

   C. attend public forums regularly to express his opinion on important matters.

   D. issue press releases.

10. The National Society of Dog Lovers wants to see the government pass legislation which will increase fines and jail times for those convicted of mistreating animals. Because so many citizens own dogs, they are a large and well-funded group. In order to get the laws they want passed in Congress and state legislatures, they will likely do which of the following?

   A. attend town meetings to express their views

   B. hire lobbyists

   C. form special task forces

   D. fight for economic interests

Purpose, Development and Implementation of Laws

11. Organizations devoted to researching and studying areas such as economics, sociology, and foreign policy for the purpose of advising public officials who make policy decisions affecting these areas are called what?

    A. universities
    B. special task forces
    C. think tanks
    D. interest groups

12. Someone who favors retribution over rehabilitation would likely favor all of the following positions EXCEPT:

    A. the use of capital punishment.
    B. a more restricted appeals process.
    C. longer prison sentences.
    D. more paroles.

13. Someone who favors rehabilitation over retribution would likely favor all of the following positions EXCEPT:

    A. fewer government programs like welfare and Head Start.
    B. classes allowing those who are incarcerated to get their high school diploma.
    C. counseling for paroled convicts to help them adjust to society.
    D. abolition of the death penalty.

14. Billy and Juanita are convicted of robbing a liquor store together. Billy is 21 and is sentenced to eight years of incarceration. Juanita, however, is considered a juvenile and is sentenced to two years. Which of the following statements is MOST LIKELY true?

    A. Billy will have to serve his sentence in a county-run adult jail while Juanita will be sent to a juvenile detention center.
    B. Billy will be in prison for eight years while Juanita will likely be paroled and placed on probation.
    C. Juanita will have to go to a boot camp before she goes to prison.
    D. Billy will go to prison but likely be out in less than eight years.

15. What is true regarding people who commit a criminal offense because they are mentally ill?

    A. They are punished the same way as any other criminal.
    B. They are punished if the crime caused physical injury but are not if only property was damaged.
    C. They must prove in court that they were mentally ill at the time of the crime or face the same punishment as anyone else.
    D. They cannot use their mental illness as a defense in cases involving murder or attempted murder.

Chapter 7
Making Economic Decisions

This chapter addresses the following competency goal and objective(s)

Competency goal 7	The learner will investigate how and why individuals and groups make economic choices.
Objective 7.01, 7.02, 7.03, 7.04, 7.05, 7.06	

7.1 RESOURCES & FACTORS OF PRODUCTION

Economics is the study of how individuals, firms, and nations can best allocate their limited resources. In other words, how people can get the most of what they want or need from the limited amount available, and at the lowest cost. **Needs** are the things people must have to live (food, shelter, clothing, etc.). **Wants** are all of the goods and services one desires and would obtain if he/she could. While wants might be unlimited, resources for obtaining them (i.e., money) are. Therefore, people have to make choices about how to spend the resources that they have to obtain their needs and wants. This is why we study economics.

RESOURCES

Resources are defined as those things which humans can put to productive use. Resources include money, people (particularly their labor), time, information, machines, and natural resources. **Natural resources** are all of the raw materials in nature used to produce what humans need or want (timber, water, iron ore, crude oil, natural gas, coal, fish, uranium, and arable [farmable] land). There are two kinds of natural resources: *renewable* and *nonrenewable*. A renewable natural resource is a resource that can be replenished (replaced) over time. A good example of a renewable

natural resource is timber. We cut trees down to make furniture, decks, baseball bats, paper, and so on. However, we can plant more trees and replenish the supply for future use. A nonrenewable natural resource, on the other hand, is a natural resource that cannot be replenished over time. An important example of a nonrenewable natural resource is petroleum (crude oil). It takes millions of years for petroleum to form, so there is a fixed supply of petroleum under the ground. When it is gone, there will be no more. It is important to remember that even renewable natural resources can be expended if they aren't given a chance to renew.

FOUR FACTORS OF PRODUCTION

Most resources need to be properly processed in order to produce things that are needed and/or wanted. There are **four basic factors of production**: *land, labor, capital*, and *entrepreneurship*. These four factors are elements of virtually any business, whether it is a small gift shop or a massive multinational corporation.

When economists use the term *land*, they use it in a much broader sense than most people. **Land** includes not only the property on which a production plant is built, but also all other natural resources involved. So remember, in terms of economics, "land" is more than the ground you stand on.

Labor is the contribution of human workers to the production process. While one tends to think of hard, physical work when one hears the term "labor," economists use this term more broadly as well. For an economist, labor includes mental efforts as well as physical ones. It includes both highly skilled and unskilled labor. Open-heart surgery, assembly-line work, janitorial services, and the writing of this book all fall under the category of labor.

Capital refers to all the structures and equipment involved in the manufacturing process. Imagine a factory like the one seen in the photo to the right. The building, the machinery, the tools, the lighting, and the assembly line are all capital. Capital includes the nail guns used by roofers, rags used by employees at a car wash, and the computer used to enter data.

Entrepreneurship is the last factor of production. It consists of the creative, managerial, and risk-taking capabilities that are involved in starting up and running a business. It is easy to confuse *labor* and *entrepreneurship* because they are both human activities, and because entrepreneurship is, in fact, a kind of of labor. However, while all entrepreneurship may be labor, not all labor is entrepreneurship. Entrepreneurship involves organizing the business, developing a business model (i.e. a plan for the conduct of business operations), and raising the funds needed to open for business. Famous entrepreneurs include Bill Gates of Microsoft™, Sam Walton of Wal-Mart/Sam's Club™, and Ray Kroc of McDonald's™.

One resource you may have noticed is not included in the four factors of production is *time*. Time becomes an issue when we measure how quickly resources can be turned into usable goods and services. **Productivity** is the rate at which goods/services can be produced. It may be considered in terms of labor or in terms of capital. Productivity is a key factor in determining economic growth. Increased productivity means that there are more goods available to buyers and — assuming a competitive labor market — financial rewards for laborers (i.e., larger incomes and bonuses).

Practice 1: Resources and Factors of Production

1. Those things that people must have to live are called what?

    A. natural resources

    B. wants

    C. needs

    D. renewable natural resources

2. The study of how individuals, firms, and nations can best allocate their limited resources is called what?

    A. entrepreneurship

    B. economics

    C. study of production

    D. capital

3. Which of the following is NOT one of the four basic factors of production?

    A. land   B. labor   C. time   D. entrepreneur-ship

7.2 SCARCITY AND DECISION-MAKING

Every child who grabs a toy in the store only to hear Mom say, "Put that back, we can't afford it," has experienced the frustration of *scarcity*. **Scarcity** is the lack of adequate resources to obtain all of one's **wants** and/or **needs**. Sometimes people confuse the terms "*scarce*" and "*rare*". Hurricanes are *rare* (only a few of them each year), but they are not *scarce* because people do not want even those few. No one produces hurricanes, and even if they could, it's not likely they would sell very well — at least not on the coast.

Gold, by comparison, is *scarce*. Although there is a lot, there is still not nearly as much gold as people want. Because of this scarcity, people are willing to pay a lot for gold. This is how pricing works. The more scarce an item is, the more it costs. An item's scarcity increases, thereby making the item more costly, either by becoming rare (there is less of it to go around) or because people want more of it than is available. Conversely, an item's scarcity decreases and it becomes less costly as it becomes more common and/or demand for it diminishes.

Pricing sets monetary value on producers' output by establishing the amount of money for which they will be willing to exchange their goods and services with consumers. The **consumer** is the economic actor purchasing or receiving goods and/or services, while the **producer** is the economic actor who makes or provides the goods and/or services. Producers have to consider a number of factors when setting price, including **salaries** and **wages** (money paid to people in exchange for their labor to produces output).**Goods** are material products made to satisfy wants and needs. Examples of goods include hot dogs, frisbees, automobiles, medicines, textbooks, etc. **Services,** on the other hand, are activities performed to satisfy wants and needs. Medical care, education, trash pick up, and massages are all examples of services. Producers want to sell their goods and services for as high a price as possible. Meanwhile, consumers seek to pay as low a price as possible to obtain them. In theory, prices in a free-market economy will be set when producers realize the highest price they can charge and yet still sell their product, and consumers find the lowest price possible at which producers are willing to exchange their goods.

Making Economic Decisions

The result of scarcity is that economic actors (households, business firms, and governments) must often make choices between two or more options that offer less than they would like. Consider this dilemma. Tom takes a date to the varsity football game. He decides to go to the concessions stand at half-time. He asks his date, Melissa, what she would like, and then hurries to beat the rush. Melissa wants a soda and nachos. Tom, being really hungry, would like a hot dog, nachos, and a soda. He sees the price list. Hot Dogs....$1.50; Nachos...$2.00; Chips...$0.75; Soda...$1.00 Looking in his wallet, Tom realizes he has only

$5.00. Tom is facing the classic economic problem. Because of **limited resources** (in this case, money), he is forced to make a decision that requires him to choose between options that are all less than ideal. The reality of limited resources requires consumers to follow, either consciously or unconsciously, an economic **decision-making model** that consists of several steps. Using the example of Tom, we can see this model at work.

DECISION MAKING MODEL

First, Tom must _define the problem._ Doing a quick calculation, he can see that what he wants costs $7.50, and he only has $5.00. Either he or his date will not get what he or she wants.

Second, he must _list the alternatives._ He could choose Option #1: get what he would like for himself — the hot dog, nachos, and soda, which cost only $4.50. However, this leaves him with only $0.50 left over. He wouldn't even be able to get Melissa a bag of chips. He also would probably not get another date with Melissa (or any girl Melissa knows for that matter). He could choose Option #2: get Melissa's nachos and soda for $3.00, and have $2.00 left over. If so, he can get a hot dog and a drink from the water fountain. He can also choose Option #3: get both of them a hot dog and a soda, and cope with Melissa's disappointment about the nachos. Of course there are other possibilities as well, such as borrowing money from a friend, but time is limited and Tom must choose from these three options.

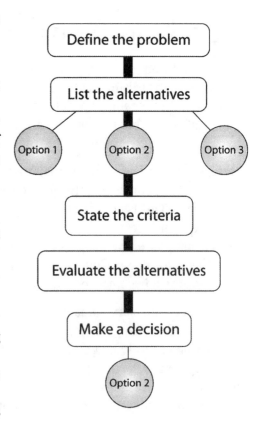

Third, he must _state the criteria._ What are his priorities? Is filling his stomach most important to him? Is pleasing Melissa? Is not feeling like a selfish person? Tom realizes he doesn't want to be selfish more than he wants to eat. He also realizes that he really likes Melissa and wants another date with her. He decides that his criteria will be to please Melissa, not feel selfish, and feed his stomach, in that order.

Fourth, he must _evaluate the alternatives_. In each option (1, 2, and 3), there is a _trade-off_. A **trade-off** is the act of giving up one thing of value to gain another thing of value. In Tom's case, he values making a good impression on his date, having a full stomach, and feeling good about himself, but each scenario involves a trade-off. An **opportunity cost** is the value of the alternative option that is lost when one makes the decision. In Tom's case, if he chooses to fill himself, his opportunity cost is a future date with Melissa and his guilt. On the other hand, if he chooses to buy Melissa her nachos and soda, then his opportunity cost is his hunger pangs. If he chooses the middle road, his opportunity cost is feeling partially hungry and partially disappointing Melissa.

Finally, Tom must *make a decision*. He decides that the benefit of Melissa's gratitude outweighs the cost of giving up a soda. He chooses Option #2 and gets a drink from the water fountain. Now, you might initially think that Tom chose a want (pleasing Melissa) over a need (food). *Ah, what we do for love.* In reality, however, even the food Tom desired would be classified as a want. This is because he did not really *need* the soda nor the nachos. After all, he wasn't starving and he can always grab something to eat at home. While everyone needs food and clothing, an appetizing snack or the latest fashions are often wants, not needs.

Practice 2: Scarcity and Decision Making

1. If a desired item is in such short supply that there is not enough to meet demand, then that item is said to be what?

    A. scarce   B. rare   C. renewable   D. affordable

2. The item mentioned in question #1 will likely be which of the following?

    A. cheap   C. a renewable natural resource

    B. expensive   D. an opportunity cost

3. List the five steps in the economic decision-making model.

7.3 Costs and Decisions Facing Producers

Reggie is a producer of delicious, homemade lemonade. During the summer, he opens a lemonade stand on his street corner. Because his street borders a popular park that has no other vendors, Reggie can make a fair amount of money throughout the hot summer. This is because Reggie has found a way to meet a specific want/need. For some, Reggie's lemonade is simply a **want**. They could drink the water in their backpack or wait till they get home, but they desire the taste of that sweet lemonade. For others, it could be a **need**. They play so hard in the park that they get overheated and feel faint. They have nothing else to drink and spot Reggie's lemonade stand as the one place they can get important fluids. In either case, because of the hot summer days, Reggie's

product sells because it provides many people with **immediate gratification**. In other words, it is in demand because it offers immediate relief from the heat and the thirst that people feel.

It is not all easy for Reggie, however. Like any producer, he faces costs for the factors of productions: land, labor, capital, and entrepreneurship. He can set up the stand for free on the sidewalk of the street corner, but recall that land for economists means more than physical land. His land costs also include the natural resources he needs to make lemonade: water, ice, sugar, and lemons, as well as lemonade mix. These costs are what economists call variable costs. **Variable costs** are costs that vary (go up or down) when the amount of products that are produced changes. Lemons, sugar, and lemonade mix all cost money, so the more lemonade Reggie sells, the more lemons, sugar, and lemonade mix he will need to buy. There are also **fixed**

Making Economic Decisions

costs, that do not change regardless of how many goods are produced. For instance, consider Reggie's capital costs. Recall that capital is the equipment needed to carry out production. In this case, Reggie needs a lemon squeezer, several large pitchers, a stirring spoon, a cooler to keep the lemonade cool, and the lemonade stand itself. All of these Reggie buys at the beginning of the summer, and they last the whole season. Regardless of how much lemonade Reggie produces, these costs remain the same — they are *fixed*. **Variable costs** and **fixed costs** together equal **total cost** of producing a certain amount of lemonade. Reggie's fixed costs equals $80 and his variable costs of producing 120 glasses of lemonade in a day are $60. Therefore, his total cost after one day of production is $80 + $60 = $140. For two days of production, his variable cost is $60 + $60 = $120 and his fixed cost is still $80 (because it is fixed). So, his total cost for two days is $120 + $80 = $200. If Reggie continues producing 120 glasses per day, then after three days his total cost will be $260, after four days $320, and so on.

Cost is only half of the equation for producers. Reggie sells lemonade, after all, to make money. He does so by selling his lemonade at a price above what it costs him to make it. Otherwise, he would have no incentive to produce. **Incentives** are what motivate economic actors to act. A producer's incentive is generally to make a profit (more money than they started with). A producer will always have an incentive to sell one more unit if the cost of one more unit is less than the price of one more unit. The cost of producing "one more unit" is known as **marginal cost.** For Reggie, the cost of one more glass of lemonade is his marginal cost ($0.50). For many products, the marginal cost changes depending on how many products are made. In Reggie's case, however, his marginal cost is constant. Although any price above $0.50 per glass of lemonade would result in a profit for Reggie, he wants to make as much money as possible (wouldn't you?). Since Reggie lives in North Carolina and it is the summer, he finds that people are willing to pay $1.50 per glass for his cold lemonade. He makes a healthy profit of $1.00 per glass. Still, Reggie believes that more people would stop by his lemonade stand if only they knew it was there. For $40, he prints out 500 fliers to pass out in the surrounding neighborhoods and throughout the park. This $40 is now a fixed cost. As a result of his advertising, Reggie is now selling 150 glasses per day — with the potential to sell more! Unfortunately, however, he is unable to serve so many customers; he cannot make the lemonade fast enough. People come to his stand, but because they have to wait for Reggie to finish making more lemonade, some leave to go find a soda machine. As a result, Reggie loses their business.

Using the same decision-making process that Tom did at the football game, Reggie begins by defining the problem: he needs more labor than he himself can provide. He then lists the alternatives. Option #1 would be to do nothing and be content with the business and profit that he has. Option #2 would be to pay his little brother, DeMetrius, a wage to work for him. **Wages** are payments made by producers in exchange for one's labor and time for the production of goods and services. Wages are generally tied to the amount of hours worked or the amount of product produced. Option #3 would be to pay DeMetrius a **salary**, which is a set amount that the producer agrees to pay a laborer that is not tied to hours or specific production.

Reggie's criteria is very simple: He wants to do whatever will make him the most money. He evaluates the alternatives by determining how much money DeMetrius will be willing to work for. Can he still make the profit he wants if he pays DeMetrius the wages/salary required to get his labor? Reggie decides the most effective means of paying his brother will be a wage based on the amount of product sold because he believes it will create an incentive to work hard and sell more. By contrast, he fears that paying DeMetrius a salary or an hourly wage would create an incentive to relax and work slowly since there is no additional pay (incentive) for working harder. Therefore, his two real alternatives are to pay DeMetrius per glass sold, or to keep the present arrangement. Each option has a **trade-off**. If Reggie hires DeMetrius, he will be able to make more glasses of lemonade, but he will make less money per glass because he now has to pay DeMetrius. Conversely, if he keeps the present arrangement, he can keep all the money for himself, but he will sell fewer glasses and continue to lose customers. If Reggie chooses to hire DeMetrius, then the money that he must part with to pay his brother will be his **opportunity cost**. On the other hand, if he does not hire DeMetrius, his opportunity cost will be the additional glasses of lemonade and the lost customers.

DeMetrius decides that he wants $0.25 per glass sold to work for his brother. DeMetrius' wage would add $0.25 to the marginal cost of each glass, putting the marginal cost at $0.75, and the profit (not counting fixed costs) at $1.50 - $0.75 = $0.75. Reggie estimates that adding DeMetrius would enable him to sell at least 60 more glasses of lemonade per day. Without DeMetrius, Reggie can sell 150 glasses per day at a profit of $1.00 per glass. 150 X $1 = $150 of profit per day. With DeMetrius, Reggie can sell 210 glasses per day at a profit of $0.75 per glass. 210 X $0.75 = $157.50 of profit per day. Since hiring his brother will enable Reggie to make more profit, he decides to give DeMetrius the job.

Practice 3: Costs and Decisions Facing Producers

1. Costs faced by a producer that can change depending on the circumstances are called what?

   A. variable costs

   B. fixed costs

   C. marginal costs

   D. total costs

2. The costs of producing each additional unit ("just one more") of a particular product is called what?

   A. fixed costs

   B. marginal costs

   C. total costs

   D. variable costs

3. John has been told by his friends that he makes some awesome t-shirts. John decides that he might want to sell some of them. If John uses the decision-making model and decides that after spending money to buy the shirts and the dye necessary, he can sell the shirts for $1 more than what it cost him to make them, then which of the following statements is true?

   A. John won't sell the shirts because his marginal cost is too high.

   B. John can make a profit on each shirt, but will likely not sell them because his total cost is higher than the combined total of his variable and fixed costs.

   C. John has an incentive to sell the shirts because he stands to make a profit.

   D. John has an incentive, but it is unclear whether or not he will make a profit.

7.4 INCREASING PRODUCTIVITY

Producers always have an incentive to reduce their total costs and increase their profits. How does this occur? Reducing total costs comes from increasing **productivity** (the ability to turn input into output in a certain amount of time). How is productivity increased? One way is through *specialization of labor*. **Specialization** is the devotion of certain resources to a specific task. Take, for example, the earliest humans. They were nomadic hunters/gathers who roamed about in search of food sources. While all that roaming sounds adventurous, as soon as people learned to cultivate plants and domesticate animals, they were able to begin a *division of labor*. **Division of labor** is the act of splitting up work into smaller and more specialized tasks. Instead of each family trying to produce everything it needs, people perform a specific task for which they receive a wage or salary and buy what they don't produce themselves. As a result, more gets produced and with better quality. When labor becomes more specialized, laborers become more efficient. Because he/she gets more practice at a specific task, the laborer learns to perform that task more smoothly and effectively than others. As industrialization began to take place, products like textiles that were once made in individual homes began to be made in factories where workers tend to do repetitive, specialized tasks. A **factory** is a facility designed and used for producing particular goods and services. Factories allow for **mass production** (the production of large quantities of a particular good) because materials can be amassed and assembled in one place, thereby making production cheaper and much faster. As a result, products can be produced and distributed to consumers quicker and in much greater numbers.

Another innovation has been the **business organization**. Whereas in the past, individual merchants or groups of merchants would produce and sell their own products, legal business organizations enable owners to gain profits from production and pay their laborers a monetary wage or salary. In modern business firms, there are usually workers whose specialization is to manage and direct those whose labor produces the goods or services. These people are commonly referred to as "management". The owners or chief executives of businesses are often the entrepreneurs. One example of how specialization combined with good business organization can lead to profitable mass production is entrepreneur Henry Ford's assembly line. Prior to Ford's assembly line, workers would assemble an entire automobile piece by piece. In an **assembly line**, the product moves down the line and is assembled by a series of laborers, each of whom carries out one specific task. This allows more to be produced, thereby allowing producers to lower prices and make products more affordable. Ford's innovation made cars affordable to the "average man" and revolutionized the role of the automobile worldwide.

Chapter 7

Innovations like the assembly line and other improved methods of production are due to another major factor: advances in *technology*. **Technology** is the application of scientific breakthroughs to commerce and industry. Examples of how technology increases production include Eli Whitney's cotton gin in the late 1700s, the introduction of the electric sewing machine in the early 20th century, and the impact of computers and the internet today. Technology is constantly redefining what our economy is capable of producing through both *invention* and *innovation*. An **invention** is any new form of technology created to meet a need. For instance, when Eli Whitney created a machine that removed seeds from cotton much quicker than by hand (the cotton gin) the machine was said to be his "invention". By comparison, an **innovation** is something that profoundly changes and improves the way things

iPod

are done. Innovations can be an invention or simply a change in process. Once again, an example would be Henry Ford's assembly line. Before Ford, assembly lines consisted of workers moving from station to station to work on a product, while the product itself sat still. Ford's innovative assembly line, however, allowed workers to stay in one spot while the products came to them. It was innovative because it forever changed the way factories operated and improved production.

White Collar Worker

Economic growth can also result from investments in human capital. **Human capital** refers to that which makes laborers more productive, in and of themselves. For instance, improved health care is an investment in human capital because it reduces the number of days that workers are out sick and extends the age to which they can continue working. Improved education and training is also an investment in human capital because it equips workers to use

Blue Collar Worker

the latest technology or provide specialized services. Education and training is important because there is a huge disparity in the wages of **unskilled workers** (workers whose jobs require minimal amounts of training and few specific skills) and **skilled workers** (workers whose jobs require greater training and/or education and more skills). Examples of unskilled workers include waiters/waitresses, construction workers, garbage collectors, and the guy who asks, "would you like fries with that?" Examples of skilled workers include doctors, engineers, and executives. Workers can also be divided into *blue collar* and *white collar* workers. **Blue collar jobs** are occupations that require manual labor, whereas **white collar jobs** typically do not (although even a lawyer has to occasionally carry boxes up a flight of stairs). It is important to remember that some blue collar workers, such as electricians and plumbers, are considered *skilled*. By comparison, most white collar workers are considered *skilled* as well; although some may not be. While almost any job well done is honorable and worthy of respect, those who receive advanced training and education generally stand to make much more money in their lifetime.

Making Economic Decisions

As technology develops, producers often replace unskilled workers with less costly machines. Many factories have turned from human workers to the use of **robotics** (machines that can be programmed to produce goods without the need for constant human interaction). The process of replacing human labor with machines is known as **automation.** Automation occurs whenever businesses conclude that machines can complete the same task as a person but with greater production and/or at less cost (i.e., machines at "self-checkout" stands in grocery stores). One industry that has been greatly impacted by automation is agriculture. **Agribusiness** is the replacement of small, labor-

Agribusiness

intensive family-owned farms with larger, capital-intensive company-owned farms. Although there was a time when most Americans supported themselves through farming, very few work in agriculture today. This is because machines and other forms of technology have reduced the need for human labor.

Just as individuals and companies face trade-offs, so growing economies also produce "winners" and "losers." While new inventions, technological advancements, innovative modes of production, and automation often increase productivity and stimulate economic growth, they also cause some to lose their jobs. It is important that workers acquire skills and educate themselves if they hope to remain a valued source of labor in our ever changing economy.

Practice 4: Increasing Productivity

1. Selling laptop computers at discount prices and producing so many of them so as to still make a huge profit is an example of what?

    A.   assembly line technology   C.   the practice of mass production

    B.   adequate business organization   D.   the application of automation

2. Of the following, who would MOST LIKELY earn the highest wage/salary?

    A.   an uneducated blue collar worker

    B.   a skilled white collar worker

    C.   someone who graduated high school and has very little additional training

    D.   someone who works as a hired hand on a farm

3. What is automation and why do businesses turn to it?

7.5 THE IMPACT OF INVESTMENT

How can a firm or worker increase productivity? Through *investments*. **Investment** is using resources that could bring immediate benefits for the purpose of gaining greater benefits at a later time. One example is financial investment, such as when people buy stocks or put money in 401k plans at work. Productivity growth, however, comes through **capital investment**. This is investment in capital goods and human capital. **Capital goods** are those products used to make other goods or provide services. For example, bolts and metal used to produce car engines, plastic and wiring used to manufacture computers, and a van used by a courier service to deliver packages are all examples of capital goods. Investing in capital goods can increase productivity by allowing a worker to do more work in a given timeframe. Capital goods should be distinguished from **consumer goods**, which are those items purchased for final use by individuals, households, and/or firms. A pair of skis, a toaster, or a bottle of your favorite soft drink, are all examples of consumer goods. In today's world, many consumers and businesses practice *recycling*. **Recycling** is when a good (either capital or consumer) is reprocessed and reused. Aluminum, paper, and plastic products are all goods that are often recycled.

Laborers also invest to increase productivity. They do this by spending time, energy, and money on **education** and **training**. Through education and training, people increase their knowledge, skills, and value as workers (employers are willing to pay more for labor that is highly educated and well-trained). For example, by choosing to spend time and energy (and money if you bought it yourself) reading this book, you are making an *investment* that will hopefully make you better educated and more productive. This will, in turn, make you more valuable to potential employers when you go to look for a job. It is important to remember, however, that not all education and training requires a classroom or a book — it can take place on the job or through real-world experiences. In addition to education/training, taking care of one's physical condition is also an investment in human capital. Through exercise, eating right, getting enough rest, etc., workers tend to be more alert and productive.

For both producers and laborers, there are always trade-offs and opportunity costs to investments. Choosing to buy new machinery means less immediate returns on production. Spending time studying for a test means giving up doing something more enjoyable or relaxing. Investments are made when the likely return is considered more valuable than the otherwise immediate gratification.

Costs of Investment, PPI, and the Law of Diminishing Returns

To decide how much money to spend on investment versus how much on production and consumption, a business will compare the *cost of investment* versus the *estimated future benefits*. To estimate the costs of goods that producers might purchase or sell, the US government maintains the **Producer Price Index (PPI)**. The PPI measures the average changes in prices for different goods. However, the cost of investment is not only the amount that a producer

spends on capital goods, but also the opportunity cost of not using that money to produce more goods to be sold (i.e., immediate profit). The opportunity cost of lost production can be found by comparing the ratio of **output versus input.** *Input* is all of the factors of production that go into making a good or service. *Output* is simply the amount of the good or service being made. While increased input often results in increased output over the long-run, in the short-run, producers have to be aware of what is called the *law of diminishing returns*. The *law of diminishing returns* states that as more and more of a *variable input* (input whose amount, frequency, etc. can change) is combined with a *fixed input* (input that is unchanging), the amount of output per input decreases. Take, for instance, chefs in a kitchen. Initially, if you add a second chef, you produce more meals. Continue to add chefs, however, and they start to bump into each other, drop food, argue over stove space, and feel crowded and frustrated because they can't get anything done. Now, in the long-run, you can build a bigger kitchen — that would be an investment in capital goods. In the short-run, however, adding a tenth chef is not likely to help — and might even hurt — production. In this example, the chefs = variable input because the number of chefs can change. Meanwhile, the kitchen space = fixed input because, unless you remodel, your kitchen is not getting any bigger. The *law of diminishing returns* is also true for consumers. Say you love chocolate ice cream. Your first bowl of triple chocolate fudge brownie ice cream will likely taste incredible! Your second bowl may taste good. The third bowl will probably not add much more to your enjoyment. After the fifth bowl, you may even be sick. The ice cream is variable (you can eat different amounts), but your stomach is fixed (a certain size). Of course, if you keep eating bowls of triple fudge brownie ice cream, you might wake up when you're 40 to discover that your stomach size is not nearly as "fixed" as it use to be.

Practice 5: The Impact of Investment

1. Using resources that could be used for immediate benefit for some greater benefit at a later time is called what?

    A. productivity
    B. investment
    C. capital good
    D. diminishing returns

2. Mark's company produces lawn mowers. In order to increase production and profits, Mark invests thousands of dollars in a new machine that assembles lawn mower engines much more efficiently than any previous system his company has used. The machine which Mark has purchased is what?

    A. an example of improved training
    B. an example of diminishing returns
    C. an example of input over output
    D. an example of a capital good

3. Define the *law of diminishing returns*.

7.6 DIFFERENT ECONOMIC SYSTEMS AND ECONOMIC FACTORS

MARKET ECONOMY AND ADAM SMITH

The US economy is theoretically a **market economy**. In a market economy, producers are free to produce what they choose to produce and consumers are free to consume what they choose to consume. The two parties, producer and consumer, make these **choices** in a *market*. The **market** is the organized exchange of goods, services, and resources within a given region at a given time. An economic **exchange** is simply a trade of one thing for another. In a market economy, this exchange is most often a good, service, or resource in return for money. Every time you buy something, you are choosing to make an economic exchange in a market. If there are multiple producers, consumers can choose between them to decide the products they will buy: cornflakes or donuts, newspapers or teen magazines. Producers have an incentive to produce what consumers want, because to do so will make them money (this is known as **profit motive**). Ultimately, over the long-run, consumers will control what products are produced via **consumer sovereignty**. In other words, producers will decide what to produce based on how much consumers demand the product. If there is no demand, then no one will buy it. This equals no profit, which results in no incentive to produce. Producers often try to manipulate

this process through advertising. Advertising aims at convincing consumers that they *need* or *want* a producer's product. The power of advertising can be seen in fads where everyone suddenly "needs" the newest jeans or the latest cell phone.

Adam Smith

Since exchanges in a market economy generally involve money, the pricing of goods, services, and resources is crucial. The question, then, is, "how are these prices set in a free market?" In 1776, a Scottish economist named **Adam Smith** published *An Inquiry into the Nature and Causes of the Wealth of Nations*. Known better as ***Wealth of Nations***, it remains one of the world's most comprehensive defenses of free market economics. In it, Smith argues that the market is led by incentives. Producers' incentive is to make the most profit possible, and consumers' incentive is to buy the goods they need and/or desire at the lowest possible price. Smith believed that allowing these incentives to take their natural course would produce the most efficient output of goods and services. This unseen force directing the market came to be called the "**Invisible Hand**". This "hand" relies on the existence three conditions. First, the market economy must have **competition** — many buyers and sellers all competing to get what they want or to make the most profits. Second, the market economy depends upon private property. In other words, the consumers and producers must own the goods, services, and resources they exchange and use for production. This ownership of capital by producing firms is referred to as **capitalism**. Third, the market economy must allow **free enterprise** (freedom to buy and/or sell what one wishes).

Under Smith's definition, even the US is not a perfect market economy. This is because the government limits free enterprise. How? Take illegal drugs, for instance. You're not allowed to buy or sell them, are you? Cuban cigars are another example. Although there is definitely a demand for them in the United States, they cannot be legally sold because of US sanctions against Cuba. The government sometimes interferes in other ways, as well. For instance, during the Great Depression, President Roosevelt initiated a number of programs designed to manipulate the economy and help people out of economic hardship. Today, the government dictates the minimum wage employers may pay workers, prevents companies from establishing monopolies, sometimes uses subsidies to protect farmers, and occasionally uses tariffs to limit foreign competition. This kind of action goes against what Adam Smith advocated. He promoted what is called *laissez-faire* economics. **Laissez-faire** is a French term meaning "leave alone"; it implies that the government should not attempt to manipulate nor regulate the market. Smith believed that to do so would disrupt the market's efficiency and lead to a less desirable outcome. The role of government in the market is always an issue of intense debate among economists and political leaders.

COMMUNIST-COMMAND ECONOMY

German philosopher, **Karl Marx**, had economic and political views that were radically different than Smith's. In 1848, together with Friedrich Engels, he published *The Communist Manifesto*, a work that attacked capitalism as an unjust system that privileged the rich and exploited the poor working class. He advocated a revolution in which the working class would rise up and establish *socialism*. Under **socialism**, government controls all capital and owns all property. Marx believed that socialism would, in time, evolve into *communism*. **Communism** is socialism at its ideal stage. It refers to a society in which everyone does their best to contribute to the common good. Under a "perfect" communist economic system, resources are owned by everyone, governments ultimately disappear, and income is distributed according to need rather than production. Marx believed that profit motive and other incentives would be

Karl Marx

unnecessary, because people would produce just as much through **cooperation** (working together towards a common goal). In reality, no country has ever achieved such a state of communism. Countries that are called "communist" (i.e., China, Cuba, North Korea) are labeled as such because it is the Communist Party that rules. In these countries, the government continues to exist and control the economy through socialist policies. Economies where prices and production are controlled by the government are called **command economies.** More and more, true command economies have proved to be failures. In the former Soviet Union, economic woes led to the nation's collapse and fragmentation (breaking up). North Korea's population is incredibly poor and the country far less developed than neighboring South Korea, which practices capitalism. Meanwhile, even China's Communist Party has found it necessary to allow elements of a market economy to exist within the country.

MIXED ECONOMIES

Market in China

The truth is that most economies (including the United States) are actually **mixed economies**. In other words, they feature elements of both free-market and command economies. They differ, however, in which type of economy they resemble most. As mentioned earlier, the US is closest to a free-market society; but in reality, the government does impose certain regulations and restrictions on the market. Conversely, China is a communist nation that allows elements of capitalism. Thus, some mixed economies are more capitalist in nature, and some are more socialist/communist.

Chapter 7

KEYNESIAN THEORY

An important figure in increasing the involvement of government in market economies was British economist, John Maynard Keynes. The **Keynesian theory** advocates an aggressive governmental fiscal policy. **Fiscal policy** is a government's strategy for using changes in public spending (purchases by the government) and taxation to influence aggregate demand. Keynes believed that if the economy is struggling, the government should increase public spending and decrease taxes. This, he believed, would stimulate the economy. However, this also means that government is spending more money while taking in less tax revenue. Such a practice of governments spending more than they have in revenue is called **deficit spending.**

John Keynes

Practice 6: Economic Systems and Economic Factors

1. The organized exchange of goods, services, and resources within a given region at any time is known as what?

   A. production   B. capitalism   C. a market   D. competition

2. Which of the following BEST describes the "Invisible Hand"?

   A. government controls cause people to fear revolutions
   B. the ideal society that eventually evolves according to Marx
   C. the desire of producers to make a profit and consumers to buy products at the lowest cost which ultimately determines market pricing
   D. the freedom to buy and sell whatever one wants

3. Which of the following men would agree the MOST with the following statement?

   "While I certainly do not advocate government control of the economy, I do believe there are times when government can stimulate the economy through spending more and lowering taxes."

   A. Karl Marx   C.   John Keynes
   B. Adam Smith   D.   Friedrich Engels

CHAPTER 7 REVIEW

A. Define the following key terms.

economics	productivity	economic exchange
needs	specialization	profit motive
wants	division of labor	consumer sovereignty
natural resources	factory	*Wealth of Nations*
renewable natural resource	mass production	"invisible hand"
nonrenewable natural resource	business organization	competition
four basic factors of production	assembly line	capitalism
land	technology	free enterprise
labor	invention/innovation	laissez-faire
capital	human capital	*The Communist Manifesto*
entrepreneurship	unskilled workers	socialism
scarcity	skilled workers	communism
pricing	blue collar/white collar jobs	consumer
robotics	cooperation	producer
automation	command economies	wage/salary
agribusiness	mixed economies	goods/services
investment	*Keynesian theory*	limited resources
capital investment	fiscal policy	decision-making model
capital goods	deficit spending	trade-off
consumer goods	opportunity cost	recycling
immediate gratification	education & training	variable cost/fixed cost
Producer Price Index (PPI)	total cost	output versus input
incentives	*law of diminishing returns*	marginal cost
market economy	productivity	economic choices
Karl Marx		

B. Choose the correct answer.

1. Robert moved from an apartment building to a house. He now has to decide between maintaining his own yard or hiring a professional landscaping service. Which of the following can Robert use to make a wise decision?

    A.   free-market system   C.   the "invisible hand"

    B.   economic decision-making model   D.   factors of production

2. George has just saved enough money to buy the car he's dreamed of. He puts down $5000 in cash and finances the rest through his local credit union. George's car is what?

    A.   a consumer good   C.   a production cost

    B.   a capital good   D.   a renewable resource

3. In order for Jamie to paint one additional portrait, it will cost her $50.00. The good news is that, if she paints it, she can probably sell it for $250.00. Which of the following equals Jamie's marginal cost?

   A. $50   B. $200   C. $250   D. $300

4. David decides to start his own business. He opens a shop that manufactures sports equipment. He pays Frank an hourly wage to make baseball bats and Gene a salary to manage his finances. Three days after his grand opening, he is ecstatic because Mike, who runs the town's parks and recreation department, calls him and orders equipment for 6 little league baseball teams. Which of the following statements is true?

   A. David is a producer, Frank is labor, Gene is the entrepreneur of the business, and Mike has just ordered capital goods.
   B. David is a producer, Frank and Gene are consumers, and Mike has just made an investment.
   C. David is the entrepreneur, Frank and Gene are both labor, and Mike is a consumer.
   D. Frank and Gene are both entrepreneurs, David is the owner, and Mike has just made a capital investment.

5. Thorndike Corporation has just finished a year of record profits. Rather than use the resources to immediately raise production, they decide to purchase land and materials to build a new plant and purchase updated technology. Thorndike's actions represent what?

   A. failure to recognize opportunity costs
   B. capital investment
   C. consumer investment
   D. investment in human capital

6. Trent is a diabetic. One day, while on vacation, he goes to buy insulin which he needs to keep his medical condition in check. Next to the pharmacy, he notices a surf shop with the exact pair of designer sunglasses he's been wanting to buy. Trent has enough money for his insulin and a cheap pair of sunglasses, but he cannot afford both the insulin and the designer glasses. Which of the following statements is true?

   A. Trent must choose between his two needs.
   B. Trent is experiencing a scarcity of insulin.
   C. Trent is experiencing a scarcity of money.
   D. Trent must buy either the cheap or the designer sunglasses.

Making Economic Decisions

7. Michelle opens up a new beauty salon. She purchases all of the chairs, hair dryers, scissors, etc. that she needs. She also purchases enough shampoo and other beauty products to get her through the first month, and will purchase more as she needs them. As time goes on, Michelle finds that she has to purchase more of these products and that her supplier raises the price every third or fourth purchase. Fortunately, Michelle is still doing well enough that she can pay the increase in price and still make a profit. Enough profit, in fact, that she concludes it is in her best interest to hire a second hairdresser named Lisa. Which of the following statements is NOT true?

   A. By offering to pay for Lisa to take additional courses in hair styling, Michelle is making an investment in human capital.

   B. Michelle's chairs, scissors, and hair dryers are fixed costs while her shampoo and beauty products are variable costs.

   C. Michelle is an entrepreneur who has considered the trade-offs to hiring an employee and determined that the benefits of hiring Lisa outweigh the costs.

   D. Michelle's marginal cost of cutting an additional customer's hair is greater than the potential profit. Therefore, it makes sense to hire Lisa.

8. Which of the following statements would Adam Smith most DISAGREE with?

   A. "When the economy suffers, the only role government should play is to spend and cut taxes. Anything more interferes with the most desirable economic outcome."

   B. "Leave the economy alone! Let the desire of producers to profit and the desire of consumers to buy goods for as little as possible take the market on its natural course."

   C. "The invisible hand can be trusted to steer the market without the interference of government."

   D. "Laissez-faire economics is a good thing."

9. The island of Mogo is ruled by a king and a council of five elders. The king and this council determine what the islanders need and what can be produced. They also determine at what price things will be sold. Although they allow some people to own private property, they are strict about how such property can be used. It sounds like Mogo has what kind of market?

   A. free-market

   B. mixed market that is predominately command

   C. command market only

   D. true communist market

10. Adrian is an economist at Burnfield University. When asked a question about the US market, she replies that what products are produced will ultimately be decided by what the public buys. In other words, she believes that it is the US public's demand and willingness to pay for certain goods that will control production, rather than the producers themselves. Adrian obviously believes in what?

   A. the influence of consumer sovereignty

   B. the power of capital investment

   C. the benefit of command economies

   D. the philosophies of Marx

Chapter 8
The US Economy

This chapter addresses the following competency goal and objective(s):

Competency goal 8	The learner will analyze features of the economic system of the United States.
Objective 8.01, 8.02, 8.03, 8.04, 8.05, 8.06, 8.07, 8.08, 8.09	

8.1 COMPARING ECONOMIC SYSTEMS

There are four basic types of economic system: *traditional*, *command*, *market*, and *mixed*. As we learned previously, the US is usually referred to as a market system; although in reality, it is a mixed system because the government does regulate the market to some extent. Because a country cannot produce everything that its residents want and need, the US and other nations face three fundamental questions.

- What will be produced?
- How will it be produced?
- For whom will it be produced?

In addition, who owns the means of production, what motivates producers, and government's role in the market also influence and define economies.

TRADITIONAL ECONOMIES

Traditional economies have existed throughout history. Generally, what is produced is whatever has been produced in the past. Laborers in traditional economies usually produce at a subsistence level, making just what they need to survive. A small wealthy class (aristocracy) that hands down property and wealth from one generation to the next often owns or controls the factors of production. Because both their occupation and their social status are inherited from their parents, laborers have little opportunity for economic advancement. The upper classes benefit from this system because it protects their wealth and position. Productivity is motivated by both the need to survive and a sense of purpose. Since one's lot in life is predetermined, it is not one's duty to advance to a higher social status, but rather to become an expert in one's assigned role. For example, if you are a ditch digger by birth, then you should strive to be the best ditch digger around.

The US Economy

Traditional economies are not as common today because they usually grow unstable once citizens become aware of other kinds of economic systems. Lower economic classes tend to be either attracted to the opportunities of market systems, or drawn by the equality instituted by command systems. Meanwhile, the middle and upper classes tend to desire the opportunities for even greater wealth and success present in a market system.

COMMAND ECONOMIES

A second type of economy is the **command economy**. In command economies, the government owns the means of production. Private ownership of property is minimal because land and capital are generally owned by the state. Government plays the dominant role in that it alone determines what is produced, how much it costs, and how it will be distributed. Distribution is based on **equity**. In other words, output is meant to be distributed equally among the citizenry (at least in theory). Although laborers tend to remain employed, they may or may not have a say in what kind of job they hold and/or under what conditions they work. The incentives to produce are expected to be a sense of duty to the country and/or a sense of personal pride. Historically, command economies have proven to be less efficient than market economies. Although they initially attract poorer individuals because of their emphasis on economic equality, in reality, command economies have been susceptible to corruption and greed just as much as market economies. In addition, while national loyalty and personal pride are noble principles, they consistently fail to provide as much motivation for productivity as the promise of financial profit and personal advancement. Finally, command economies, because they are centralized, tend to be slow to react to changes in demand. As a result, they often produce too much of something that is not desired and too little of something for which there is a market. For example, in the former Soviet Union, it was not uncommon to see people lined up around the block waiting to buy scarce products like a loaf of bread or a roll of toilet paper.

Former Soviet Union Flag

MARKET AND MIXED ECONOMIES

Next is a **market economy**. In a market economy, producers and consumers determine what gets made and for whom. Property and factors of production (land, labor, capital, and entrepreneurship) are privately owned, with the government owning only enough to carry out its limited and defined role. Producers decide what to produce based on what consumers demand and what prices consumers are willing to pay. The motivating factor for producers is profit and for laborers, higher wages/salaries and/or personal advancement.

As mentioned before, just about every economic system is, in reality, a **mixed economy**. In other words, they have elements of more than one system that make up their economic framework. The US is a mixed economy in that it offers great freedom to economic actors (producers and consumers) while at the same time implementing enough government control to hopefully avoid economic catastrophes (i.e., depression, massive inflation, crucial shortages of needed goods, etc.).

Chapter 8

Practice 1: Comparing Economic Systems

1. What are the four types of economic systems?

    A. production, market, command, free

    B. market, traditional, mixed, command

    C. command, labor, capital, traditional

    D. free, command, communist, mixed

2. Which of the following MOST resembles a *traditional* economic system?

    A. Susan became a nurse because her mother and grandmother were nurses. Although she could have chosen any profession, she wanted to follow in their footsteps. One day, she plans on returning to medical school and becoming a surgeon.

    B. Arthur is a talented man. He is intelligent enough to do almost anything, but the government has assigned him to work in an automobile factory. He hates his job but has no choice since the government makes all economic decisions and stresses the importance of everyone working for the good of the country.

    C. Nathan is an excellent cobbler. Because his family has practiced this profession for generations, it is all he ever hoped or was expected to be. The shop he works out of is on land owned by a wealthy landlord and, although he takes great pride in his work, Nathan will likely never advance beyond where he currently is in life.

    D. Paula has pulled herself up by the bootstraps. Although she was born poor, she worked hard in school and earned a scholarship. She graduated with honors and now works for a large corporation. Taking advantage of the opportunities afforded her, she was able to buy her parents a new house and send her baby brother to college as well.

3. What are some reasons why command economies have traditionally been less effective than market economies?

8.2 THE FREE ENTERPRISE SYSTEM

The United States economy is a mixed market economy. It is a market system in which the government plays a limited role. As such, the US features a **free enterprise system** that is driven by **voluntary exchange**. In other words, individuals and businesses freely choose to exchange goods, services, resources, etc. for something else of value (usually money). The government does not tell consumers what to buy nor producers what to produce. Both consumers and producers decide for themselves — they make *voluntary decisions*. Because consumers have the economic freedom to buy what they want (so long as it is legal) and producers the freedom to pursue a profit, entrepreneurs and laborers are motivated to produce goods and/or services that consumers/employers demand. The **goal of consumers** is to buy the goods they want/need at as low a cost as possible. Meanwhile, the **goal of producers** is to sell the goods they produce so as to make as

much profit as possible. A voluntary exchange occurs when a consumer finds a product they want/need at a price they are willing to pay and for which the producer is willing to give them the product.

The US Economy

EFFECTS OF THE FREE ENTERPRISE SYSTEM

The nature of the US free enterprise system produces several things. For one, it encourages the ownership of **private property** (land, labor, capital, etc. owned by private citizens/businesses rather than the state). To produce the goods and services that are in demand, producers must be able to acquire and own the means necessary to manufacture them. Secondly, it also encourages increased **productivity and efficiency**. Since producers stand to make more profit if they produce more output, they are motivated to increase their productivity (produce more goods in a given amount of time). To do this, they are forever seeking more efficient means of production. This, in turn, encourages technological **inventions and innovations**. *Inventions* are new products (i.e., machines) that perform a task or fulfill a need that no previous product could perform/fulfill, or at least could not perform nearly as well (remember the example of Eli

Levittown

Whitney's cotton gin). An *innovation* is any invention or change in process that greatly improves something that already exists (i.e., a faster way to package potato chips). One example of innovation came about in the late 1940s when a developer named William Levitt revolutionized home building. Taking advantage of a demand in the market, Levitt introduced a way to build homes much faster and more affordable. As a result, he made a fortune selling homes to middle class citizens who formerly could not afford a house. Levitt's approach forever changed the way developers and consumers approached the housing market. His methods were *innovative* and made him lots of profit by allowing him to increase productivity (i.e., make more homes in less time).

The market also encourages **specialization and division of labor**. As discussed in Chapter 7, specialization is focusing on the performance of a particular task, rather than trying to master and perform several tasks. Division of labor is the process of splitting up work into smaller and more specialized tasks. Since specialization and division of labor increase productivity, they are important elements of a free enterprise system.

GOVERNMENT'S ROLE IN THE US FREE ENTERPRISE SYSTEM

Compared to many other countries, the government's role in the US economy is relatively limited. In general, it allows the market to determine what will be produced and at what price it sells. Meanwhile, it enacts and enforces laws to prevent fraud and/or coercion (forcing people/economic actors to make decisions against their will), protect property rights, and enforce legal contracts, patents, and copyrights. A **patent** is guaranteed ownership and control of an invention, innovation, or production technique for a specified amount of time. In other words, if you invent a car engine that can run on sand and you obtain a patent, then no one else can duplicate your product without paying you big bucks. A **copyright** is the legal right granted to a writer, musician, artist, etc. to exclusive publication, production, sale, or distribution of a literary, musical, dramatic, or artistic work. If you write a poem and obtain a copyright, then no one else may publish it without your consent and/or compensating you financially. Copyrights and patents protect those who want to use original ideas in the marketplace.

The government does regulate the economy to some degree, however. For example, federal laws prohibit monopolies, set a minimum wage, prevent discrimination in hiring, and outlaw certain products. In addition, the government also impacts the economy through taxation, trade policies, subsidies, and interest rates.

Disadvantages of the US Free Enterprise System

Most people agree that the United States economic system is arguably the strongest and most impressive in the world. However, like anything, the US free enterprise system has disadvantages as well. For one, since the market rather than the government determineseconomic conditions, market economies offer less **security** (protection from negative change) than command markets. Although command markets strictly limit people's choice of careers, they do tend to guarantee **full employment** (everyone who can work having a job) because jobs are government assigned. In a

free market system, no such guarantee exists. A thriving market with lots of production might produce a lot of jobs. However, the following year when the market dips, people who found themselves previously doing well might find themselves laid off and without work. Also, a free enterprise system fails to produce **equity**. In theory, a command economy promotes economic equality. In a market economy, however, no such equality is guaranteed. People's economic status is not set by the government, but rather is determined by how hard they work, what job they can get, how efficient and innovative they are, how driven they are, what ideas they have, etc. To those who succeed in a market system, this is not seen as a disadvantage but as a benefit. To those who struggle, however, it is often seen as a downside of the free enterprise system.

Practice 2: The Free Enterprise System

1. Which of the following is NOT an element of the US free enterprise system?

    A. voluntary exchange

    B. freedom

    C. full employment

    D. motivation to make profits

2. Which of the following is naturally encouraged by the free enterprise system?

    A. government control of the economy

    B. increased efficiency and productivity

    C. economic equity

    D. economic security

8.3 Circular Flow of Economic Activity

There are three fundamental economic actors: *households*, *businesses*, and *government*. A **household** is an individual or family unit (blood-related or not) that occupies a single housing unit (apartment, condo, or house) and shares common living expenses. A **business** is an individual or group that works to produce a certain good or service. The **government**, meanwhile, provides law and order, structure, and even necessary goods and services that might otherwise not be provided by what the market demands (i.e., national defense, maintaining public parks and monuments, etc.). Typically, individuals in households receive **wages** or a **salary** in exchange for their labor. Thus, households supply labor to businesses in exchange for money. These businesses then use this labor to produce goods which households and other businesses buy and consume. Both households and businesses pay taxes to the government that then uses these tax dollars to provide things that are meant to benefit society. In addition, the government also uses revenue to purchase goods from private businesses and pay wages/salaries to households in exchange for the labor of government workers. As you can see, households, businesses, and government depend on each other in order for the economy to function smoothly. This mutual need is referred to as **economic interdependence**. Households provide labor and act as consumers. Businesses act as producers *and* consumers (i.e., they need to purchase

The US Economy

things necessary to run their business), and government acts as both a producer and a consumer as it provides structure and some regulation. The economic flow of money between households, businesses, and government is called the **circular flow of economic activity.** This "flow" is depicted in the diagram below.

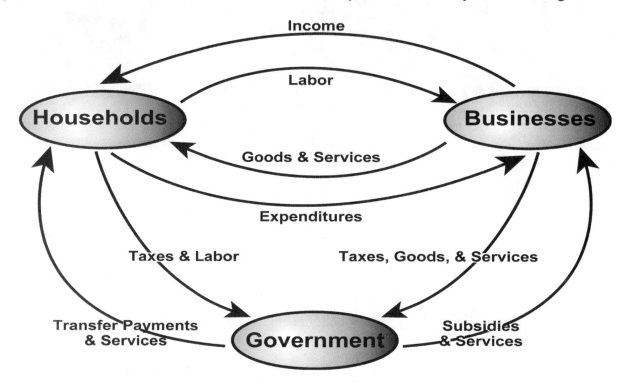

PRODUCT AND FACTORS MARKETS

Goods which are sold for final consumption to consumers are said to be sold in the **product market**. Running shoes sold to a jogger, pencils sold to a student, frozen dinners sold to a busy mom, etc. are all examples of goods sold in a product market. The product market is where producers earn profit. However, some goods are sold to producers so that they can improve or increase production. Such goods are said to be sold in the **factors market** because they involve factors of production (land, capital, labor, entrepreneurship). The factors market is where producers invest.

Practice 3: Economic Activity

1. What are the three major economic actors in the US economy?

    A. government, the market, entrepreneurs
    B. land, capital, labor

    C. households, businesses, government
    D. consumers, producers, businesses

2. The fact that these three actors need each other in order for the economy to function smoothly is referred to as what?

    A. circular reliance
    B. economic need

    C. economic interdependence
    D. product and factor markets

3. Describe how businesses act as both producers and consumers?

4. What role does the government play in the circular flow of economic activity?

8.4 SUPPLY AND DEMAND

LAW OF SUPPLY AND DEMAND

In a market economy, buyers and sellers determine what will be produced and for whom. This occurs through what Adam Smith called the "invisible hand." (Review Chapter 7, Section 6 regarding the market economy and Adam Smith). This phenomenon is more commonly referred to, however, as the *law of supply and demand*. **Supply** refers to how much a certain good is available to consumers. **Demand** refers to how much consumers want the particular good. The *law of supply* states that producers will only produce a good that will yield them profit. This means that, in order for there to be any supply of a certain good, producers must be convinced that producing the good will make them money. They have no incentive to produce a product that will cost them more to produce than the amount for which they can sell it. Likewise, they also have no incentive to produce more of a certain product than people are willing to buy at the price producers are willing to sell. In other words, producers will stop producing a good once their marginal cost begins to equal or exceed their expected profit. By comparison, the *law of demand* states that consumers will only demand/buy a product for which they have a need or want and that is set at a price they can afford. The more they desire a product and the more scarce that good is, the more they will be willing to pay. However, the more available a product is (i.e., can get it from several competing producers) or the less they desire the good, the less they are willing to pay. Thus, the *law of supply and demand* states that supply (what is produced) will be determined by what is demanded (what consumers will buy). If there is sufficient demand for a good, then producers will supply it so long as they can make a profit. On the other hand, if there is no demand, or if demand is not great enough to earn a profit, producers will not supply it. If the profit that a company can receive is considered high, many producers will enter the market to produce that good or service. However, if the profit they receive is relatively low, only a small number of producers (i.e. those who can make the product for the lowest cost and highest profit) will enter the market.

Producers will also cut back on production once supply begins to exceed demand. For instance, say a company invents an electrical heater that allows you to heat your whole house without ever turning on the gas, thereby saving you hundreds of dollars in heating bills. The product might sell like hot cakes in December and January, but come April, demand will fall off drastically. The *law of supply and demand* suggests that the producer of this product will produce much larger amounts of the product during the winter months when there is high demand than during the summer months when demand is small. During the winter, the potential profit is far greater than the marginal cost of producing each heater. However, as the weather grows warm, the heaters don't sell fast enough to justify making them at the same pace. Therefore, production will drop to the level of demand.

INFLUENCES ON SUPPLY AND DEMAND

Several factors influence supply and demand. One important factor is *price* (the amount of money for which producers are willing to sell their products to consumers). There may be demand for a good, but if producers don't believe they can earn a sufficient profit, it will either not be produced, or will only be produced by those firms that can mass produce enough to make the profit they require. The price at which producers are willing to make the same amount of product that consumers demand, thereby resulting in every unit produced selling, is called the **equilibrium (market) price**. It may be easier to understand this concept if one considers it graphically. The graph to the right shows a supply curve and a demand curve. The **supply curve (or supply schedule)** tells us how much of the product that sellers are willing to part with at various price levels. The **demand curve (or demand schedule)** tells us how much of the

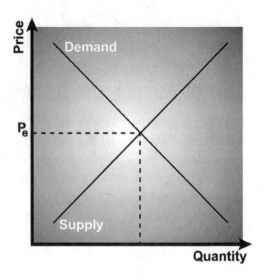

product buyers are willing to purchase at various prices levels. The point at which the two curves meet is the equilibrium price. Any price below the equilibrium price will result in less supply because producers are not making enough to continue producing the product. Conversely, any price above the equilibrium price will result in lessening demand because fewer consumers are willing to pay for it. According to Adam Smith's theory of the "invisible hand", prices are set as supply and demand naturally steer the market towards the equilibrium price.

Income is another factor. **Personal income** is all of the money received by a household (wages, salary, etc.). **Disposable income** is all of the income a household has after paying taxes. It is the income that consumers can choose to spend as they wish. Of course, households also have certain fixed expenses that are necessary to live (i.e., rent/mortgage, electrical bills, sewage and water, etc.). The income left after paying for "necessities" is referred to as *discretionary income*. Discretionary income impacts supply and demand because how much discretionary income consumers have determines how much they are willing to spend on "wants" after they have taken care of their "needs."

Another factor is **competition**. How many producers are supplying a particular good? The more suppliers there are, the more options for consumers. The more options for consumers there are, the more producers must compete for business. In order to compete, producers must either lower prices as much as they can while still making sufficient profit, or quit producing the particular good. Take, for instance, Wally's small coffee shop on the corner. It is a local business with only one location. Unfortunately for Wally, he has to close his business because a huge coffee house chain has opened up down the street. Why must he close? Because the chain is so big and sells so many cups of coffee, it can offer customers lower prices, special deals, etc. Wally cannot afford to compete because he can't make up in volume what he would lose in profit if he charged the same low price. Because consumers want to pay as low a price as possible and because they have a choice, they stop going to Wally's and go to the big chain. Thus, Wally has no choice; he closes, thereby lessening the supply of coffee in the neighborhood. Now the big chain is the only producer of a good cup of coffee. In turn, it can now raise prices because, while demand for coffee is the same, there is now only one supplier. Since there are now fewer options for consumers (only one coffee shop instead of two) people are willing to pay the big chain more than they would have when they could have gone to Wally's.

Chapter 8

Supply and demand will also be affected by *complimentary* and *substitute goods*. **Substitute goods** are goods that can be used in place of other goods. For example, both hot dogs and tacos are foods that can be bought at the convenience store for lunch. If one buys a hot dog, then they are less likely to buy a taco (unless they are really hungry and/or enjoy heartburn). The more substitute goods there are for a particular product, the more competition producers face in trying to convince consumers to buy their particular good. **Complimentary goods**, on the other hand, are goods that work together to fulfill a certain need. For instance, DVDs and DVD players are both useless unless used together. Therefore, the more the demand for DVDs goes up, the more the demand for DVD players increases as well. Whereas consumers purchase substitute goods *instead* of buying another product, they purchase complimentary goods *because* they have another product.

Practice 4: Supply and Demand

1. The idea that what is produced will be determined by what consumers need/want, provided they are willing to pay enough for producers to make a profit, is called what?

    A. the market
    B. the law of demand
    C. the law of supply and demand
    D. the influence of disposable income

2. The price at which total supply equals total demand is known as what?

    A. the middle price
    B. the consumer price
    C. consumer demand
    D. the equilibrium price

3. What is the difference between personal, disposable, and discretionary income?

4. How does competition influence production?

8.5 FACTORS THAT AFFECT PRICES

SHORTAGES & SURPLUSES

When supply of a certain good falls short of demand, the market is said to have a **shortage** of that product. Conversely, when supply exceeds demand, there is said to be a **surplus**. The graph to the right shows not only the equilibrium price, but also the results of prices above or below the equilibrium price. A price above equilibrium results in a surplus. A price below equilibrium results in a shortage. If prices are too high, people will not buy the product. Therefore, producers will not be able to sell all that they have. On the other hand, if prices are too low, people will buy up all that is available faster than producers can produce more. Thus, many people who demand the product will be left without. When there is a shortage, prices increase because the product in demand is more scarce and people are willing to pay more to get the small amount that is available. When there is a

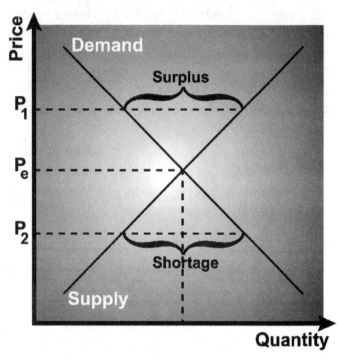

surplus, prices fall because there is more than demanded and those consumers that do want the product have a lot of options regarding where to get it. Therefore, producers must compete (i.e., lower prices) to convince these consumers to buy from them. Otherwise, producers will be stuck with goods/services that they paid to produce but from which they make no profit.

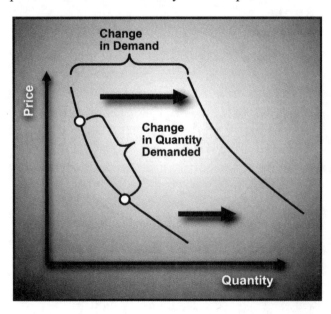

As you can see, the quantity (amount) available of a good is one factor that impacts price. It is important to note that there is a difference between change in *quantity demanded* and change in *demand*. Change in quantity demanded simply means that the amount demanded has changed, although the amount people want may not have. This can occur because of changes in supply without any change in overall demand (i.e. people may want the same amount of the good, they just buy more or less because the supply is larger or smaller). Sound confusing? Maybe this example will help illustrate what we're talking about. Imagine that a hail storm moves through Florida and severely damages the orange crop. The damaged crop does not cause people to want less orange juice, but consumers will end up buying less and at a higher price because there is less orange juice available. By contrast, a *change in demand* is a change in the amount of product that consumers actually want. For instance, residents in Wilmington, NC might not demand much plywood. However, when a hurricane is headed toward the coast, the demand for plywood in Wilmington increases drastically. People want more of this product at any price than they did previously. There is also a difference between *quantity supplied* and *supply*. A *change in the quantity supplied* is a change in the amount producers sell that may or may not be linked to a change in the overall willingness to supply products at different price levels. Take, for instance, oil companies in the US. Since just about every adult in the US drives a car, there is an overwhelming demand for their product. However, suppose a war breaks out in the Middle East (which often happens) and imports of oil fall. Although demand alone would dictate a high level of supply, other circumstances intervene to cause the quantity supplied to be less than market forces alone would have dictated. By comparison, *a change in supply* is a change in the amounts that producers are willing to sell at all prices. Say ten years from now, a company begins to mass market a car that runs on water instead of gas. Now, the number of businesses producing oil drops, but for totally different reasons. This time, it is because demand has dropped and the market dictates that there is not enough profit to continue production.

CONSUMER TASTES

Price is also affected by *consumer tastes*. **Consumer tastes** refers to individual consumers' preferences. What is desirable to one consumer may not be desirable to another. Consider this example of how consumer taste can impact price. Teresa is 17 years old and wants to get a new pair of blue jeans. She sees the pair she wants at a well-known, upscale fashion store for $125. Since she forgot to bring her credit card, Teresa decides she will come back the next day and buy them. That evening, she runs to Discount Kingdom to buy some hairspray and notices in the clothes section that they have a cheaper brand of jeans that look exactly like the pair she wants for only $35. Based on what we've learned, the decision seems simple; forget the $125 pair and buy the lower priced jeans. However, what if Teresa's top priority is not price?

Ferrari

What if she can afford either pair and her top priority is the status symbol of wearing jeans from the upscale store? If so, Teresa will choose the $125 pair of jeans rather than the $35 jeans. While some might argue Teresa is too shallow and not very practical, this is a perfect example of how consumer tastes impacts price. The upscale store can afford to set prices above what they normally would in the market because they know that enough consumers want the status of their label, prefer the way their jeans fit, have been convinced by advertising that anything less than their jeans won't do, and so on. How much a consumer values status, what a consumer considers comfortable or attractive, and what producers a consumer trusts are all ways in which a consumer's individual taste can help set price.

The US Economy

INFLATION AND INTEREST RATES

A general rise in prices for most products throughout an economy is called **inflation**. When you ask for $20 to go to the movies and get a lecture from your parents about how, when they were kids, movies cost $2 and a box of popcorn 75 cents, you are listening to (or, at least pretending to listen to) your parents rant about inflation. As the costs of production increase, firms are willing to produce less at given prices. Therefore, to cover their costs and still make a profit, they raise prices. However, inflation should also lead to increased employment and wages, which means people have more money to spend. In a perfectly even inflation, the prices will end up higher but the amount of production will end up exactly the same. The opposite is true of **deflation,** which is a general fall in prices. An even deflation should lead to lower prices but the same amount of production. In reality, there are many factors that can affect inflation/deflation, preventing them from occurring "evenly." In rare times, the economy will experience *stagflation*. This is when prices rise and employment/wages fall at the same time.

Gerald Ford
President During Stagflation

Interest rates are another economic factor. An **interest rate** is the amount paid to a lender in exchange for the use of that lender's money. Credit card companies, banks, lenders who offer school loans, and the credit union that financed your car all charge interest rates. Consumers, however, also earn interest when they open bank accounts. For instance, if you put $100 into an account that paid 2% interest annually, at the end of one year, you would have $100 X 0.02 = $102. When interest rates are higher, consumers are more likely to save rather than spend. They want to earn interest on the money they've saved rather than pay high interest rates on credit cards or large purchases (like homes or cars). On the other hand, if interest rates are low, consumers are more willing to spend. Therefore, when interest rates are high, prices tend to fall to encourage consumers to spend money they are inclined to save. Conversely, when interest rates are low and consumers inclined to spend already, prices tend to rise.

GOVERNMENT'S IMPACT ON PRICES

As mentioned before, the US government regulates and manipulates the economy to some degree. It sometimes does this through **wage and price controls**. For example, the government sets a **minimum wage**. This is the minimum amount that producers must pay employees for their labor. Those who support a minimum wage argue that anything less would not provide an adequate standard of living. While the intent of this wage control might be good, in reality, it also creates a surplus of labor that leaves many unemployed. This is because businesses only have so much money to spend on labor. For example, say Pedro owns a business. He wants to hire Mike, Frank, and Kevin. However, if he hires all three, he cannot afford to pay them all the minimum wage required by the government. Therefore, Pedro hires Mike and Frank at the minimum

wage and leaves Kevin unemployed. Had Pedro been free to pay them what he wanted, he could have also hired Kevin. The government has also been known to set *price floors* (minimum price below which the price of a good or service is not permitted to drop) and *price ceilings* (maximum price above which the price of a good is not permitted to rise). For instance, the government might set a price floor on agricultural products to protect US farmers from bankruptcy, or a price ceiling on rents to ensure lower income families can afford a home. While such solutions as price ceilings and price floors may sound appealing, it is important to remember that they do not adhere to normal laws governing the marketplace and, therefore, have economic costs as well as benefits.

Finally, the government also affects market prices through *fiscal* and *monetary policy*. How much the government spends and how much the government taxes households and businesses will affect supply, demand, and price. As mentioned before, President Roosevelt's fiscal policy was to engage in deficit spending and use government programs to stimulate the economy. By contrast, President Ronald Reagan trusted in a fiscal policy known as *supply-side economics*. **Supply-side economics** is an economic approach that seeks to increase production by cutting corporate taxes so that businesses can have more money to spend on production and labor. Reagan believed that by enabling businesses to spend more on capital and labor, it would have a **"trickle down effect"** by which everyone in society would benefit. Both Roosevelt's "New Deal" and Reagan's "Reagonomics" are examples of fiscal policy. Monetary policy has to do with how the federal government controls the money supply. We will discuss monetary policy later in this chapter and in Chapter 9.

Practice 5: Factors that Affect Prices

1. Dana's company has produced a large number of pink, rubber shoes. However, the demand for pink, rubber shoes in the marketplace is drastically less than the current supply. Which of the following situations does Dana find herself in?

    A. She needs to raise prices to make up the difference between supply and demand.

    B. She needs to cut prices because she is experiencing a surplus.

    C. She needs to cut prices because she is experiencing a shortage.

    D. She needs to raise prices because she is experiencing a surplus.

2. Every year when Bonnie goes to the mountains, she stops off at her favorite country store to buy one of their awesome apple pies. Although she could buy an apple pie at the grocery store for a third of the price, she insists that no other pie compares. She willingly pays the extra money. Many others feel the same way and thus, the country store can continually sell pies charging more than the average market price. The store's price is largely due to what?

    A. the market equilibrium price for apple pies   C. price controls

    B. change in quantity demanded   D. economic impact of consumer taste

3. This year, when Bonnie arrives at the country store mentioned in #2, she discovers that the pies cost $1 more than they did the previous year. Bonnie is noticing what?

    A. a price ceiling   B. a price floor   C. inflation   D. stagflation

4. Describe how supply-side economics works.

8.6 COMPETITION IN THE MARKET

A market system is one in which **buyers** (consumers) and **sellers** (producers) come together to exchange things of value (i.e., money for goods). In a perfectly competitive market, no individual buyer or seller buys or sells enough to change the price of a particular good or service. For a perfectly competitive market to occur, four factors must be present:

- There must be a large number of buyers and sellers.

- Products must have the same quality.

- There must be no major barriers to entering market.

- There must be a free exchange of price information. That is, consumers and producers must have access to what each producer is charging for their goods.

In many cases, these conditions more or less exist. Consider, for instance, the wheat market. There are so many wheat farmers that no single one of them can raise or lower the market price of wheat by how much they individually supply. At the same time, so many different companies around the world are bidding for wheat that none of them can lower the price by withholding their bid. The wheat market is relatively competitive.

MONOPOLIES AND OLIGOPOLIES

While no one company can corner (control) the market on an entire industry under perfect competition, there are situations where perfect competition does not exist. A **monopoly** is a market structure under which there is only one producer of a given good or service, and in which there are no adequate substitutes. For example, if only one company supplied electricity or made cars, these would be examples of monopolies. For a monopoly to exist, there must be barriers that prevent other firms from entering the market. Since a monopoly is the only supplier of a good or service that is in demand, it is able to dictate the industry price of that good or service by how much it produces. In general, monopolies charge higher prices, produce less output, and provide less quality than a competitive market. This is because they have no competition. If consumers aren't

John D. Rockefeller Established a Monopoly in the Oil Industry

totally satisfied, the monopoly doesn't have to worry or improve. After all, the consumer has nowhere else to go for the good.

Another market structure that prevents perfect competition is the *oligopoly*. An **oligopoly** is a market in which there are only a few producers. Typically, oligopolies form in industries which must necessarily be large (i.e., companies that provide utilities like electrical power or natural gas). Oligopolies operate in a manner between competitive markets and monopolies. Unlike perfect competition, the oligopolist firms can affect the price of a product. However, unlike a monopoly, the oligopoly must observe and take into account the actions of its competitors. Oligopolists must be responsive to price changes because they will lose market share quickly if they are not. It is also relatively easy for the members of an oligopoly to conspire to control prices just as a monopoly would. For this reason, there are laws to prevent such actions.

CONGLOMERATES AND MERGERS

Sometimes, previously separate — and perhaps even competing — companies combine to form larger companies. **Conglomerates** are large companies that consist of several businesses, many of which may be unrelated in what they produce (i.e., General Electric, which owns NBC, companies offering financial services, and health care services). The process through which one firm buys and/or joins with another is called a **merger**. A **vertical merger** is when a company buys out another company that was previously its supplier, or that it previously supplied. For example, if Ford Motor Company™ bought out Firestone™ Tires, it would be a vertical merger. A **horizontal merger** is the merging of two firms that make similar products. For example, when the oil company British Petroleum™ (BP) bought out the American Oil Company™ (Amoco) in 1998, it was a horizontal merger. BP is an example of a **multinational conglomerate** because it is a conglomerate with companies operating in more than one country.

Practice 6: Competition

1. A market structure in which only one producer supplies a good that is in demand, thereby permitting them to set the price by how much they supply, is called what?

   A. competition   B. monopoly   C. oligopoly   D. conglomerate

2. Bertolett Ice is a large manufacturer of winter sports equipment. They produce hockey sticks, skis, snowboards, sleds, etc. They have just bought out McKinney Blade, a company that use to be their main supplier of blades to make ice skates. The process of Bertolett buying McKinney is known as what?

   A. oligopolistic activity   C. vertical merger

   B. conglomeration   D. horizontal merger

3. Why do monopolies tend to produce less output, charge higher prices, and provide less quality than competitive market structures?

8.7 ECONOMIC INSTITUTIONS AND BUSINESS ORGANIZATIONS

TYPES OF BUSINESSES

Thousands of US businesses operate every year. These businesses are organized in a number of different ways. The simplest form of business is the *sole proprietorship*. A **sole proprietorship** is a business owned by an individual or the members of a household. Remember Wally's coffee shop? That was a sole proprietorship because it was owned only by Wally. The advantages of a sole proprietorship are flexibility, personal charm, direct interaction between owners and consumers, and the fact that business decisions can be made quickly by one owner. However, proprietorships have disadvantages as well. First, the proprietor has **unlimited liability**. In other words, he/she is responsible for all debts incurred by the business. Proprietorships also have a **limited life**, which means that they cease to

function at the same time that their owners do. For the company to continue after the original owner's death or retirement, it must be reorganized under new ownership. Third, proprietors usually have limited funds available to them and have to obtain startup money by taking out loans from banks or other financial institutions. The government provides help for sole proprietorships and smaller partnerships through the **Small Business Administration (SBA).**

Some businesses are organized as *partnerships* or *cooperatives*. A **partnership** is a type of business in which two or more people pool their resources and share the risks and profits of the business. Law firms, doctors offices, and accounting firms are often partnerships. There are also many businesses that exist as **cooperatives**. In a cooperative, a much larger number of producers pool their resources than in a typical partnership. These owners then make decisions and elect a board of directors from within their membership to oversee the company. The advantages of cooperatives and partnerships are that they can raise more money than sole

proprietorships and combine expertise. However, there are disadvantages as well. First, unlike a sole proprietorship, it may be difficult to reach decisions that satisfy the whole firm. A second disadvantage is the legal complication of dissolving the partnership if it should break up. Proprietorships simply perish if the owner quits or dies, but a partnership must decide whether to remain in business and, if not, who gets what. This is not as much a problem for cooperatives, as their membership is generally large enough for them to continue without interruption. The third major disadvantage of the partnership is that the partners are completely responsible for the debts incurred by the business. Although several individuals share the debt, because partnerships and cooperatives tend to be larger, their debts are usually greater as well.

Chapter 8

The third type of business is a *corporation*. A **corporation** is a firm that exists as a legal entity in the same way a person does, and which is usually owned by a number of shareholders (although much smaller businesses and even individuals can incorporate, as well). **Shareholders** buy **stock** in the corporation, thereby granting them a share of ownership proportional to how much stock they own. Many corporations sell their stock on a **stock market** (a market where anyone can buy or sell stocks in available companies). Stock markets are important institutions in a market economy because they are primary vehicles for investment. The rise or fall of major stock markets (ie, the New York Stock Exchange) is a major indicator of how the economy is doing overall. A major advantage of the corporation is that it offers

NY Stock Exchange

limited liability. Individual shareholders can only lose what they invest in the corporation and are not liable for all the debts that the corporation incurs. In other words, if you buy $1000 worth of stock in a corporation that has $1,000,000 in debt and the corporation goes under, you only lose $1000; you aren't stuck with the whole million. Bonds are another way that some companies raise money. Whereas buying stocks makes the purchaser part owner in a company, **bonds** are a means of *loaning* money. A person loans a certain amount of money to either the government or a private entity in exchange for the bond. They then collect interest on the loan in addition to cashing in the bond (getting their money back) at a later time. There are other advantages to corporations, as well. Selling shares means they can raise large amounts of money in a short period of time. Without the corporation, people would not be willing to invest in gigantic firms because of the huge personal risk such investments would entail. Corporations also have **unlimited life**. They live on past the death of individuals. There are also disadvantages of corporations, however. One is double taxation. The corporation, as a legal entity, is taxed based on the profits it earns. Shareholders are often then taxed again on any **dividends** (payments made to shareholders from the profits of the firm) and/or capital gains (money earned by selling an asset at a higher price than one purchased it). Corporations may also suffer from internal conflict. The shareholders (owners) and the hired management may not agree on how to proceed with the business. Shareholders may prefer that profits be paid as dividends, while managers may want to reinvest profits in capital goods. Over time, shareholders can also lose control of the corporation as other stockholders acquire larger shares and gain more influence.

Finally, there are **franchises**. These are businesses in which sole proprietors or partnerships purchase the local rights to a trademark corporation. For instance, McDonalds™ is a massive multi-national corporation; but the local McDonalds where you grab a Big Mac and fries is probably franchised to an individual owner or partnership. The franchise owner must pay a licensing fee and maintain contractual agreements with the trademark corporation. The benefits of a franchise are the name recognition and backup support that national chains can provide. The disadvantage is the lack of flexibility and limited creativity that owners have, given that they must uphold a national chain's identity and sell only certain products.

The US Economy

ANTI-TRUST LAWS

As discussed in the previous section, monopolies prohibit a competitive market. In order to ensure competition, the US government began passing **anti-trust laws** in the late 1800s. These are laws that prohibit monopolies. Originally, they were either not enforced or proved ineffective. Beginning with President Theodore Roosevelt, however, the federal government finally started challenging monopolies during the early part of the 20th century. Since then, courts have used anti-trust laws to break up illegal monopolies in tobacco, oil, railroads, etc.

"Buck" Duke
Headed a Tobacco Monopoly
in North Carolina

LABOR UNIONS

Union Members Then

"Molly Maguires" Coal Workers

A **labor union** is an organization of workers who come together to engage in collective bargaining with employers. **Collective bargaining** is negotiating wages and working conditions as a group rather than as individuals. If one worker refused to work 80 hours/week in a factory or coal mine, it would have little effect. However, if all workers refuse to work such long hours, they might force a change. The purpose of unions is to look out for the interest of workers who are members of its organization. Traditionally, they have fallen into two basic categories: *craft unions* and *industrial unions*. **Craft unions**, such as the International Brotherhood of Electrical Workers, are groups of skilled laborers of the same occupation. **Industrial unions**, such as the United Auto Workers, are workers in the same industry who may be of various skill levels. In the past, some unions were able to secure "closed shop" workplaces (employers could only hire union members), thereby increasing the union's ability to carry out collective bargaining. The influence of unions was also enhanced by the **National Labor Relations Act** of 1935. This law gave employees the right to join unions without interference from employers and to choose representatives for the purposes of collective bargaining. In 1938, Congress passed the **Fair Labor Standards Act**. It included laws restricting child labor, establishing a minimum wage, and regulating workplace safety. In addition, the 1935 **Social Security Act** provided income for retirees and widespread unemployment benefits (this was especially important given that 1935 was the middle of the Great Depression). Not all legislation has favored unions, however. For instance, the **Taft-Hartley Act** of 1947 weakened unions when it prohibited closed shop rules that forced employees to hire only union workers. Due to the efforts of unions, the US government has implemented a number of regulations and passed many laws regarding labor. As a result, US workers enjoy a better quality of life and higher standard of living than most of the world's laborers.

Unions are not without criticism, however. Collective bargaining and government regulations have disadvantages as well. As mentioned before, requiring employers to pay a minimum wage increases unemployment because employers cannot afford to hire as many people. In addition, US producers often find themselves at an economic disadvantage when competing with foreign companies that do not have to abide by the same labor regulations. Go to a discount clothing store and check the labels. See how many of the shirts, pants, etc. are made overseas. In fact, do this with just about any product. Stores sell large numbers of foreign goods even though their quality might be similar to US goods. Why? Because there is a demand for them from consumers. Why do consumers want these products if US quality is similar? In general, because they are more affordable. Why are they more affordable? Because the manufacturers

Union Member Today

did not have to pay as much to make them. Why didn't they have to pay as much? In part, because they didn't have to pay their workers a minimum wage or abide by as many regulations. This doesn't necessarily mean that minimum wages are wrong (after all, producers in some countries keep cost down by treating their workers unfairly and dishonestly), but it does demonstrate one of the negative consequences of laws that limit how producers manage, hire, and pay workers.

Critics of unions also argue that they hurt quality. It is no coincidence, they claim, that US goods and services tend to be inferior in industries that are highly unionized. For example, foreign cars on average score better in terms of customer satisfaction than American cars. Those who blame unions say it's because it is easier for foreign companies to fire, demote, replace, or cut the wages of employees who fail to perform up to company standards. In the US, however, regulations put in place largely by unions protect workers in the auto industry. Finally, unions can sometimes be susceptible to corruption. Although most unions were founded with noble intent and have helped bring about needed changes, some unions have fallen under the influence of corrupt leaders and even organized crime.

DISPUTES BETWEEN LABOR AND BUSINESS

Sometimes, collective bargaining between unions and businesses fails to produce a compromise both sides can live with. When this happens, the two sides often turn to *mediation*. **Mediation** occurs when a neutral third party gets involved to help labor and employers come up with a solution. Sometimes they rely on **arbitration**. Arbitration is similar to mediation in that it involves a third party; but it is different in that the decisions of the third party are considered legally binding by both sides. If collective bargaining, mediation, and/or arbitration still do not solve the problem, then both unions and business owners may turn to more drastic measures. For example, a union may call a *strike*. A **strike** is when workers refuse to work until owners meet their demands. At times, strikes involve "picket lines" (striking laborers stationing themselves outside their employer's business in protest). Because people's livelihood is at stake, strikes are usually heated and can even turn violent. Business owners, on the other hand, might authorize a **lock-out**, in which employees are not permitted to return to work. Both strikes and lock-outs are based on the belief that one side can wait out the other, thereby forcing them to give in.

Practice 7: Economic Institutions and Business Organizations

1. Frank has owned the same Italian bistro in the heart of the city for nearly 23 years. Although it's small, it's known for the best lasagna in town. What kind of business does Frank operate?

    A. sole proprietorship
    B. partnership
    C. cooperative
    D. corporation

2. Barry and two associates have been operating a business that is not going well. Barry is stressed out because the company is over $200,000 in debt and he knows that if it goes under, he and his two associates will have to pay it out of their own pockets. It sounds like Barry and his two associates have what?

    A. sole proprietorship
    B. partnership
    C. cooperative
    D. corporation

3. Miriam is happy because she just received notice in the mail that the stock she bought last year for $1000 is now worth $1200. The additional $200 is what?

    A. Miriam's investment
    B. Miriam's stock
    C. Miriam's dividend
    D. Miriam's capital gain

4. What is a union and what is its purpose?

5. In what ways have unions helped make positive changes? What are some criticisms of unions?

8.8 MONEY: SPENDING, BORROWING, AND INVESTING

Most of us take the existence of money for granted. We fail to realize the its invention was one of the greatest innovations in world history. Prior to its existence, most early civilizations relied on a **barter system**. People had to trade goods that they possessed for goods that they wanted. As you might imagine, it wasn't always easy to find the person with the good or service you wanted who was willing to exchange it for the good or service you had to offer. Money became a **medium of exchange** that solved this problem because it could be assessed a value and then exchanged for any number of goods in a market place. Most people use the term "money" interchangeably with *"currency"* . **Currency** refers to both **coins** (metal currency, such as pennies, dimes, etc.) and notes (paper money). Economists, however, use the term **"money"** much more broadly. Anything that acts as both a medium of exchange and a standard of value is considered money. Nearly everyone exchanges and invests money on a daily basis. Individuals, businesses, and even the government must make decisions about how to invest and spend money.

Chapter 8

INDIVIDUAL SPENDING, BORROWING, AND INVESTMENT

When individuals spend money, they use either currency, checks, credit cards, or debit cards. Checking accounts are often called **demand deposits** because one's money is available "on demand." Hence, when one writes a **check** authorizing a transfer of funds from his/her checking account, it is treated in the same manner as currency. A **debit card** is a card that looks like a credit card, but really serves the same function as writing a check. Each time the card is used to make a purchase, money is deducted from the card owner's checking account. **Credit cards**, however, work differently. Whereas debit cards are simply a convenient way for consumers to access their own money, credit cards are a loan. The cardholder is actually deferring payment until a later date. For this reason, the cardholder must  pay interest on the cost of the purchase. Say, for example, that Eric sees a flat-screen TV that he really wants for $1300. The only problem is, Eric only has $100 in his checking account, $80 in his savings account, and doesn't make enough money to both buy the television and pay all his bills. Using a credit card, Eric *charges* (defers payment on) the $1300 and gets the TV. Eric will have to pay a portion of the charged amount back to the credit card company every month. The good news is that he now has the TV he wants and only has to pay $50 per month. The bad news is that Eric is being charged 18% interest by the credit card company. As a result, Eric will not only have to pay the credit card company the $1300 that he charged, but also all of the interest. In essence, by using a credit card, Eric ended up getting the television sooner, but paying a lot more for it. Today, many consumers buy on **credit**. Instead of paying for items at the time they acquire them, they pay at some later time and/or in installments in exchange for paying interest. While buying on credit can have positive effects (ie, it promotes a thriving economy and allows consumers to buy big items — like houses and cars — that they otherwise could not), credit cards often lead to irresponsible spending that leaves some buried in debts they can't repay.

Contrary to demand deposits, **time deposits** are accounts that individuals only have access to after a set amount of time. For instance, certificates of deposits, or CDs (no, not the kind that play music), are one example of time deposit accounts. People who invest in a CD put their money in an account for a set amount of time (usually, at least a year) and cannot withdraw it for that amount of time. Why would someone do this instead of keeping their money in a deposit account where they can get it anytime they want? They usually do so because such accounts offer a higher interest rate, which is good when you are investing. Say Tommy has $5000. If he wants, he can put it in his savings or checking account and have constant access to it. However, his checking account offers almost no interest and his savings account is not much better. Since Tommy feels that he does not have to use this money for a while, he elects to deposit it in a one year CD yielding 5% interest. After one year, if Tommy puts the money in a demand deposit account, he will roughly have $5000, give or take a few bucks (provided he didn't spend it). However, by putting the money in the CD for a year, he now has $5250 ($5000 + 5% , which is $250).

BANKS, CREDIT UNIONS, AND SAVINGS & LOANS

Most US adults have financial accounts. Demand deposit accounts (checking, savings, etc.) and some time deposit accounts (ie, CDs) are usually held at either a *commercial bank, credit union,* or a *savings and loan.* **Commercial banks** are financial institutions whose main functions are to receive deposits of money, extend credit, and provide loans. Commercial banks are similar to corporations in that stockholders own and manage them in order to make a profit. Banks make money mostly through granting loans that charge interest. In addition to loans to businesses, banks commonly grant loans to individuals to buy houses (mortgages), purchase cars, etc. Usually, before banks will grant loans to individuals or businesses, they require that they possess enough *collateral.* **Collateral** is anything of value

that could be used to cover the value of the loan should one be unable to repay. For example, when you borrow money to buy a car, the car is collateral. If you don't pay, the bank can take the car and sell it. Another example is if you fail to pay your mortgage, the bank can foreclose and sell your house. Collateral is how a financial institution protects itself against financial loss.

Credit unions, on the other hand, are cooperative associations that serve only their members. Like banks, they offer checking and savings accounts, as well as grant loans. Because they are technically non-profits, credit unions do not have to pay the same taxes as commercial banks. This means that they can usually offer higher interest rates. Credit unions, however, are exclusive; only certain individuals may join. For instance, the North Carolina State Employees Credit Union is open only to those who either are, or have been, employees of the state.

Finally, **savings and loan associations** are saving institutions designed to aid home building (in the classic movie, *It's a Wonderful Life,* George Baily runs a savings and loan). Historically, savings and loans lend their money out as mortgages on homes. In the 1980s, many savings and loans made bad investments and ended up going bankrupt. Because they were not government insured at the time, taxpayers had to bear the burden of bailing them out. The bad taste left by the 80s, along with the fact that credit unions and commercial banks offer similar services, has caused a decline in the popularity of savings and loan associations.

George Bailey
in *It's a Wonderful Life*

STOCKS, BONDS, AND MUTUAL FUNDS

As mentioned before, **stocks** are shares in a company that an individual/organization purchases giving that person/entity part ownership. People buy stocks hoping to see its value increase over time. For instance, in the 1950s, the American Family Life Assurance Company started by selling stock at a very low price. As a result, many people bought a good number of shares for only a few hundred dollars. Today, those that kept their stock in AFLAC have made millions. The problem with stocks is that they can be risky, and few people know enough to be "experts in the market". While it is great that those early investors in AFLAC did so well, investors in Enron (a huge corporation that went bust after years of promise) had quite a different experience. Some even lost their life's savings! To help minimize risks, many investors put their money in *mutual funds*. **Mutual funds** pool money from a number of investors to buy a range of stocks. Thus, an investor's money is dispersed among several companies. This reduces risk because, if one company does poorly, others are likely doing better. Because they are generally managed by a financial expert, investors are free to focus on other things without having to constantly keep an eye on their investments. The downside to mutual funds is that they generally offer a lower rate of return. **Bonds**, as we learned earlier, are loans to either a company or the government.

INSURANCE

Insurance involves transferring risk to others. An individual or household has something of great value and wants to make sure that, if it is lost or damaged, it will be financially covered. For this reason, they invest in **insurance**. They pay money to an insurance company (usually monthly) for the assurance that, if what they value is lost or damaged, the insurance company will pay for their loss (either in full or in part). Insurance is especially popular when it comes to things that households or businesses would likely not have the available funds to pay for on their own. **Life insurance** is meant to provide money to one's family if one dies. Say Martin provides the

main income for his family of six. If Martin didn't work, his family could not pay their mortgage, car payment, etc. Well, what happens if Martin dies? How will Martin's family make it? To make sure they would be ok, Martin buys life insurance. Martin pays money monthly to the insurance company which, if he dies, will provide his family with the money they need to live. Martin may either buy *term* life insurance, which simply pays money to his beneficiary (the person Martin wants the money to go to); or he may buy what is often called *whole* life insurance, which is generally more expensive and builds cash value like an investment. **Health/medical insurance** is meant to cover health and medical expenses, many of which can be outrageously expensive. A broad category of insurance is *liability insurance*. For instance, paying for auto liability insurance will cover accident related damages a person causes to other people or their property. Homeowner insurance policies often include liability as well. If someone falls in your yard and then successfully sues you to pay for their injuries, then your liability insurance will pay the cost. In general, then, **liability insurance** provides protection from claims arising from injuries or damage to other people or property. **Comprehensive liability** insurance covers a much wider range of catastrophes. Businesses need comprehensive liability to cover injuries that occur on business property, accidents due to employee negligence, property damage caused by company workers, losses or injuries caused by defective products, and any professional mistakes (ie, medical malpractice on the part of a doctor).

BUSINESSES AND INVESTMENT

Like individuals, businesses invest in a variety of ways as well. In addition to stocks, bonds, etc. one of the biggest ways businesses invest is through **capital investment**. They take money earned from profits and reinvest it in capital to help make the company more efficient, Review *Chapter 7, Section 5* regarding impact of investment. Many businesses also provide *pension funds*. **Pension funds** are mutual funds set up by employers to allow their employees to save for retirement. Employees pay into the fund and gain interest just as if they had invested in a mutual fund on their own. Many times, the employers will contribute on the employee's behalf as well. When the employee retires, they get a monthly pension payment that is similar to a paycheck.

THE GOVERNMENT AND MONEY

In order to ensure that banks, credit unions, and savings and loan associations are able to cover their deposits, the government established the **Federal Deposit Insurance Commission (FDIC)**. The FDIC came about after the Great Depression, when many banks had to close after mass numbers of citizens starting withdrawing their money. The FDIC helps prevent such mass withdrawals by assuring depositors that their money is insured by the government up to a certain amount. The FDIC also requires banks to hold a certain percentage of their reserves in real currency. In other words, they have to keep a certain amount of money on hand rather than loaning it out. The amount that banks are required to keep on hand is called the **reserve requirement**.

The executive and legislative branches of government can affect the economy through **fiscal policy** (how it spends money and imposes taxes). However, the US government also features a central bank that is independent of the influence of any branch of government. This bank is known as the **Federal Reserve** and its purpose is to strictly control the money supply through **monetary policies** that protect the economy from excessive inflation. By raising the reserve requirement of banks, the Federal Reserve forces banks to hold on to more money, thereby pumping less money into the economy and decreasing inflation. This is called a **"tight money" policy**. Conversely, the Federal Reserve might lower the required reserve, thereby freeing banks, etc. to loan more money. This increases inflation and is called an **"easy money" policy**. It is important that the Federal Reserve be independent because the executive and legislative branches of government both have incentives from time to time to engage in inflationary spending and the printing of more money.

**Ben Bernanke
Chairman Federal Reserve**

Practice 8: Spending, Borrowing, and Investing

1. Money can BEST be defined as which of the following?

    A. currency
    B. a medium of exchange
    C. something that transfers risk from one party to another
    D. interest

2. Someone who puts their money in an account that they have no access to for a certain amount of time is said to have put their money in what?

    A. a stock   C. a bond
    B. a demand deposit   D. a time deposit

3. Which of the following is NOT a difference between commercial banks and credit unions?

    A. Credit unions are only open to those who qualify for membership, whereas banks are open to the public in general.

    B. Banks provide loans, whereas credit unions only provide a means for saving and investing.

    C. Credit Unions are considered "non-profits" and therefore don't have to pay the same taxes as banks.

    D. Credit Unions are normally able to offer higher interest rates than banks.

4. What is a mutual fund and how is it riskier or safer than investing in regular stocks?

5. What is the role of the Federal Reserve and what is the difference between "tight money" policy and "easy money" policy?

CHAPTER 8 REVIEW

A. Define the following key terms.

traditional economy

market economy

voluntary exchange

goal of producers

Small Business Administration (SBA)

inventions and innovations

full employment

business government

circular flow of economic activity

supply

law of demand

supply curve/schedule

disposable income

substitute goods

consumer tastes

interest rate

supply-side economics

monopoly

vertical/horizontal merger

unlimited liability

cooperative

stock/stock market

unlimited life

anti-trust laws

craft/industrial unions

Social Security Act

arbitration

barter system

currency

time deposit

credit/credit cards

credit union

pension funds

fiscal policy

"tight money"/"easy money" policies

command economy

mixed economy

economic freedom

private property

specialization and division of labor

patent

security

wages/salary

product market

demand

law of supply and demand

demand curve/schedule

competition

shortage

inflation

wage and price controls

"trickle down effect"

oligopoly

multinational conglomerate

limited life

corporation

bonds

dividends

labor union

National Labor Relations Act

Taft-Hartley Act

strike

money

coins

check

commercial banks

savings and loan association

capital investment

Federal Reserve

Federal Deposit Insurance Commission (FDIC)

equity

free enterprise system

goal of consumers

productivity and efficiency

insurance (life, health/medical, liability, comprehensive liability)

copyright

household

economic interdependence

factors market

law of supply

equilibrium (market) price

personal income

complimentary goods

surplus

deflation

minimum wage

buyers/sellers

merger

sole proprietorship

partnership

shareholders

limited liability

franchise

collective bargaining

Fair Labor Standards Act

mediation

lock-out

medium of exchange

demand deposit

debit card

collateral

mutual funds

reserve requirement

monetary policies

Chapter 8

B. Choose the correct answer.

1. Economic system based on equity and in which the government decides what gets made and sets prices is called what?

   A. market system

   B. traditional economy

   C. political economy

   D. command economy

2. A small country in the Western Hemisphere is ruled by a communist government. The government, therefore, practices strict control over the economy. However, in reality, the government does allow some capitalism to exist because it finds that it helps bring much needed money into the country. This nation's economic system can MOST ACCURATELY be labeled as which of the following?

   A. command economy

   B. capitalistic economy

   C. mixed economy

   D. market economy

3. Bill's business chooses to produce fluorescent toothbrushes that allow people to brush their teeth in the dark because he believes there is a demand for them. He decided to embark on this business adventure on his own, despite some skepticism from those who know him. Since the government does not force consumers to buy what they don't desire, Bill will have to convince people to purchase his toothbrushes of their own free will. This scenario is MOSTLY an example of what?

   A. a mixed market economy

   B. a free enterprise system based on voluntary exchange

   C. productivity and efficiency

   D. a corporation at work

4. Monica has written a inspiring poem. Friends of hers encourage her to get it published. Monica is hesitant because she does not want another person to steal her poem and then publish it under his/her own name. She fears that, if this happens, someone else will make all the money and she will have nothing. Monica needs to obtain what?

   A. a patent

   B. a copyright

   C. a bond

   D. a creative license

5. Which of the following is NOT encouraged by the free enterprise system?

   A. ownership of private property

   B. new inventions and innovations

   C. workers specializing in different tasks

   D. equity of wealth

6. Jordan works for the state of North Carolina as a probation officer. His labor provides the government with a much needed service. In return, the state pays Jordan a salary. With his salary, Jordan purchases the goods he needs/wants from private firms. He also pays taxes that allow the government to continue to provide protection and government services. Jordan's economic interdependence with the government and private businesses is referred to as what?

   A. the money flow

   B. the monetary cycle

   C. circular flow of economic activity

   D. economic independence

The US Economy

"If the public wants this football team to remain in this city, then they will buy season tickets. If they do not, then the tickets will not sell. However, this organization will not continue to lose money on this team. If this city does not appreciate what they have, then we are prepared to move to another city where the fans are waiting in expectation for us to come, and they are anxious to pay to see the product we put on the field."

7. The above quote is an indirect reference to which of the following?
    A. a factors market
    B. law of supply and demand
    C. disagreement over equilibrium price
    D. security encouraged by a free enterprise system

8. Albert is paid $1400 every two weeks. After taxes are taken out, he actually has $900 to take home. Once Albert pays for necessities (mortgage, groceries, water, etc), he is left with roughly $150 every two weeks. Which of the following statements is true?
    A. Albert's personal income is $1400, his disposable income is $900, and his discretionary income is $150.
    B. Albert's disposable income is $1400, his personal income is $900, and his debt is $150.
    C. Albert's disposable income is $1400, his discretionary income is $900, and his personal income is $150.
    D. Albert's discretionary income is $1400, his disposable income is $900, and his personal income is $150.

9. Byron has just received an annual bonus at work for $2000. Currently, interest rates are very high. The year before, Byron received a bonus check for $1200 when interest rates were very low. Which of the following statements is MOST LIKELY true?
    A. Byron spent his bonus last year and will spend it again this year.
    B. Byron saved his bonus last year and will save this year's check, too.
    C. Byron spent his bonus last year, but this year will save it.
    D. Byron saved his bonus last year, but this year will spend it.

10. A fiscal policy that claims the best way to stimulate economic growth is by lowering taxes on producers so that they can spend more on labor and capital is referred to as what?
    A. Roosevelt's New Deal
    B. deficit spending
    C. supply-side economics
    D. "easy money" policy

11. Which one of the following would anti-trust laws be designed to prevent?
    A. two competing firms engaging in false advertising against one another
    B. foreign producers enjoying unfair advantages over US producers because they are not subject to the same regulations
    C. banks not keeping enough money in reserve to cover their deposits
    D. one producer eliminating all competition and preventing other producers from entering the market

" I love owning my own business; I just wish I had more freedom to do my own thing. I'm grateful for the support the corporate office provides, but I wish I could decide for myself what kind of food we serve and what kind of atmosphere to provide."

12. The above quote is most likely from which of the following?

    A.   a partner in a cooperative

    B.   owner of a franchise

    C.   stockholder at odds with management

    D.   owner of a sole proprietorship

13. Who would be most likely to engage in a lock-out?

    A.   a worker who is convinced that mediation is a bad idea

    B.   an owner who can no longer afford to keep his sole proprietorship open

    C.   a union member who feels that even a strike is not enough

    D.   an employer who wants to "get tough" with the union

14. Gary wants to save for retirement. However, he is no expert in investing and needs someone who knows more than him helping him handle his money wisely. Gary doesn't desire to get rich quick; he just wants to know that his money is growing over the next thirty years until he is 65. Since Gary's top priority seems to be steady growth and security for his money, the BEST option for him would be what?

    A.   to put all of his savings in the stock of whatever company is currently performing the best on the New York Stock Exchange

    B.   to put all of his money in a relatively unknown stock that is likely to do well

    C.   to invest in a mutual fund

    D.   to purchase collateral

Chapter 9
Factors Influencing the US Economy

This chapter addresses the following competency goal and objective(s)

Competency goal 9	The learner will analyze factors influencing the United States economy.
Objective 9.01, 9.02, 9.03, 9.04, 9.05, 9.06, 9.07, 9.08	

9.1 ECONOMIC INDICATORS OF THE BUSINESS CYCLE

The US economy is similar to a roller coaster. Sometimes it makes its way uphill on a slow, steady rise. Then, just after it reaches the peak, it comes racing back down! Such economic ups and downs are called the **business cycle**. The business cycle has four main parts; *trough, expansion, peak*, and *contraction*. The amount of time each part lasts varies depending on the circumstances. The steady ride up is called **expansion**, because the economy is growing. Many times it leads to a **recovery** because this growth often occurs after a less prosperous period. An expansion/recovery is sparked by something that happens to jump-start the economy. Government spending programs, corporate tax breaks, increased investments, and/or even a war that increases demands for production (i.e., WWII) can lead to recovery. Whatever the reason, the economy improves as companies produce more goods, employment increases, and people are able to buy more. As the "roller coaster" inches its way to the top, the expansion reaches its **peak**. This period is defined by **prosperity**, in which production is high, unemployment low, and wages increase. The peak period only last for a time, however, before the economy starts to come down. This period is known as **contraction** and is characterized by a fall in production, rising interest rates, declining profits, and a slowdown in capital investments. Demand falls as consumers stop buying goods. As businesses sell less, they make less. As a result, they stop hiring and even lay employees off; thereby raising unemployment. If this trend lasts for 6 to 8 months, the economy experiences a **recession**. Eventually, the economy hits its low point: its **trough**. The trough period is a time of high unemployment, low economic production, and falling stock prices. If it continues to worsen and last a long time, the nation may even slip into a **depression**.

GDP, CPI, AND THE NATIONAL DEBT

Economists use several **economic indicators** (facts, data, etc. that helps show the present and/or future health of the economy) to track business cycles and measure how well the economy is doing. One means is by calculating the nation's **gross domestic product (GDP)**. The GDP is the total value of all final goods and services produced in an economy. Many economists prefer to calculate economic growth using **Per capita gross domestic product**. Per capita GDP is meant to calculate the number of goods produced per person and is determined by dividing a nation's GDP by its total population Some economists prefer to use per capita GDP because GDP alone does not adequately compare the **standard of living** (level of economic prosperity at which people live) in different nations. Another economic indicator is the **consumer price index (CPI)**. This index measures monthly changes in the costs of goods and services by monitoring the prices of goods/services that are typically purchased by consumers. Finally, economists look at the **national debt** (amount of money owed by the federal government). How much money the government owes affects fiscal policy which inevitably affects the economy and the business cycle. Economists study the GDP, CPI, and monitor the national debt for the purpose of predicting economic trends and proposing solutions to economic problems.

Practice 1: Economic Indicators of the Business Cycle

1. The ups and downs that the nation's economy goes through is officially referred to as what?

    A. a roller coaster

    B. expansion

    C. the business cycle

    D. economic madness

2. Which phase of the economic cycle is characterized by prosperity?
    A. contraction   B. peak   C. trough   D. recession

3. What is the difference between GDP and per capita GDP? Why do some economists prefer to measure economic growth using per capita GDP?

9.2 GOVERNMENT REGULATION

As mentioned before, the US government reserves the right to regulate the economy under certain circumstances. Supporters of such moves believe they are necessary to ensure competition in the market, help lower-income households, protect civil rights in the marketplace, and so on. One area of government involvement is in **environmental protection.** Through the EPA (Environmental Protection Agency), the federal government enforces federal laws and standards dealing with the environment. Producers have to take into account more than just the most economical way to produce their goods. They also have to make sure they are meeting government standards. As a result, they might have to use more expensive or less efficient means of production than they otherwise would have. This reduces profits, which in turn impacts capital investments, employment, how much money consumers have to spend, etc.

The government also impacts the economy through its efforts to ensure citizens' safety. The Occupational Safety and Health Administration (OSHA) and the Consumer Protection Safety Commission (CPSC) are just two examples of government agencies concerned with safety. OSHA enforces government standards regarding **workplace safety**. Meanwhile, the CPSC oversees **consumer protection** by making sure no products on the market are potentially harmful or defective. Again, while such regulations are arguably necessary and good, they also require producers to spend money on extra safety measures, conduct additional product safety tests, and pay personnel to make sure that their businesses meet safety guidelines. These additional expenses are inevitably passed on to consumers in the form of higher prices.

Finally, there is the government's impact on the labor force. Businesses must abide by certain laws and regulations when it comes to who they hire and how they treat their employees. For instance, federal law prohibits employers from discriminating against job applicants based on race, gender, etc. Some employers even go so far as to have **affirmative action** policies (policies designed to hire and/or recruit minority candidates for job openings) for the purpose of promoting racial and/or cultural diversity. Affirmative action and/or policies geared towards providing a more multicultural workplace means that  employers may not simply hire the most qualified person, or the person who is willing to work for the lowest wage. Instead, they might actually hire someone who is less qualified and/or more expensive in order to meet government/public expectations concerning diversity and/or equality. Meanwhile, some consumers may actually be willing to pay more for goods and services from a producer they believe promotes equality, rather than purchase similar products from producers they believe guilty of discrimination.

The federal government also regulates **labor disputes**. As noted in *Chapter 8*, the US government has passed laws setting limits on what actions both employers and unions may take. Such regulations mean that the labor market is not simply subject to the natural forces of supply and demand, but rather are under the influence of government as well.

Government also makes an impact when it chooses to **deregulate** (stop or decrease its regulation of) an industry. One example of this occurred in the 1970s when President Jimmy Carter deregulated the airline industry. Before Carter took such action, the airline industry benefited from a system in which the government practically guaranteed it a profit. It was the government that set fares, determined routes, and finalized schedules. As a result of this setup, however, consumers found themselves paying higher prices and often dissatisfied with service. By deregulating the airlines, Carter suddenly threw the airline industry into the realm of free-market competition. This had great economic impact as suddenly airlines found themselves having to produce more efficiently and compete to survive. Railroads, trucking, and energy production are all industries which have experienced various degrees of government deregulation.

Jimmy Carter

Practice 2: Government Regulation

1. Which of the following statements is true?

    A. The EPA impacts the US economic system by enforcing regulations regarding discrimination in hiring.

    B. The economy was greatly impacted in the 1970s when President Carter decided to regulate the airline industry as a public utility.

    C. Government regulations regarding affirmative action and consumer safety have no impact whatsoever on the US economy.

    D. Any action taken by the US government to regulate how producers conduct business inevitably affects the economy.

2. What is affirmative action and how might it have economic consequences?

9.3 IMPACT OF HUMAN AND CAPITAL RESOURCES

Throughout history, population shifts have impacted the United States economy. **Population shifts** are changes in the population of different regions due to large amounts of people either moving in or exiting. Population shifts are brought about by both **migration** (the movement of people from one location in a country to another) and **immigration** (people coming to the US from another country to live permanently). When large numbers of people move from one area to another, it inevitably has economic consequences. The United States Census Bureau has recorded in recent decades that more and more US citizens are leaving the traditionally more populated areas of the North for the South and western states. As the US economy relies less on factory workers and manufacturing, people are leaving the **"Rust Belt"** states of the northern Midwest and the **"Frost Belt"** states of the upper North that have traditionally thrived off of these types of jobs. With automation and increases in foreign competition, fewer jobs are now available in many of the plants and factories which helped build these regions. As a result, more and more people have migrated south to the **"Sun Belt"** states. The "Sun Belt" stretches from North Carolina, through the Deep South, all the way to California. Because of this migration and the immigration of many Hispanics from Latin America, the populations and economies of these states have grown drastically. Initially, rapid increases in population can cause serious problems as economies are faced with more demand for jobs, housing, and services than they can provide. However, population growth tends to eventually lead to economic growth as well, because people bring their money, labor, willingness to invest, skills, etc. with them when they move.

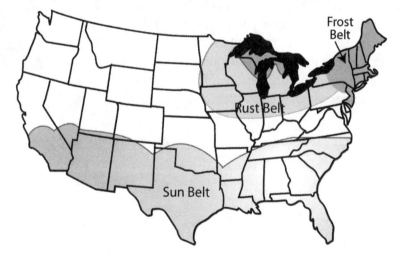

Because the United States economy increasingly depends on innovations and revolves around new technologies, areas that provide jobs in computers and technology have boomed over the last two decades. **Silicon Valley**, in northern California, is known worldwide as the hub of the US computer industry. It is home to such businesses as Apple™ Computer, eBay™, Google™, and Yahoo™. Similarly, **Research Triangle Park**, located in the Raleigh-Durham area of North Carolina, is one of the most prominent hi-tech research and development centers in the country, and the largest research park in the world. As centers of technological development, both Silicon Valley and Research Triangle Park have attracted people who work in ever growing technology-related fields. Meanwhile, their geographic areas have benefited economically from the additional money and investments that these areas attract. **Service industries** (restaurants, doctors' offices, auto mechanics, various forms of entertainment, etc.) also thrive in such areas because, as population increases, so does the demand for services and goods.

Practice 3: Human and Capital Resources

1. Changes in population due to large amounts of people either moving in or exiting are called what?

    A. migration   B. immigration   C. population shifts   D. growth

2. Which of the following has contributed to the migration of people from the "Rust Belt" and "Frost Belt" to the "Sun Belt"?

    A. increases in US manufacturing
    B. increased focus on hi-tech research and technology in the US economy
    C. increased immigration from Mexico
    D. increased reliance on US factories to provide labor

3. Why does a sudden growth in population initially create economic problems for an area? Why do population and an area's economy tend to ultimately grow simultaneously?

9.4 IMPACT OF CURRENT EVENTS ON THE ECONOMY

Consumers and producers are also influenced by current events. Wars, scandals, political unrest, etc. are all events that have the potential to disrupt trade, alter production, and influence spending. As a result, what happens in the world around us affects us economically.

THE WAR ON TERROR

On September 11, 2001, the nation and the world stood in disbelief as terrorists used hijacked jetliners to crash into the World Trade Center and the Pentagon. Sadly, we later learned that additional lives were lost when another plane crashed in Pennsylvania after brave passengers attempted to subdue their hijackers. While nothing can begin to compare with the tragic loss of life that occurred on that day, the fact is that the terrorist attacks of 9/11 had economic affects as well. Anything that causes instability affects people's confidence and willingness to invest or spend. Fewer investments and/or less spending mean less money for business. Less money for business affects production, which affects prices, which affects demand, and so on. One business that was impacted by 9/11 was the airline industry.

Factors Influencing the US Economy

Because the 9/11 terrorists used hijacked planes in the attacks, consumers initially lost great confidence in the industry to provide for passenger safety. To help, the government established the **Department of Homeland Security** in 2001 to oversee airline safety and the nation's defenses against future terrorist attacks. By establishing this department, the federal government hoped to bolster the nation's confidence. The more confident and secure citizens feel, the more it helps the economy.

9/11 eventually led to a declared "war on terror". Congress passed the **PATRIOT Act**, which increased law enforcement's ability to track and investigate possible terrorist plots. In 2001, the US attacked Afghanistan to root out terrorists living in that nation. In 2003, **Operation Iraqi Freedom** got under way when a US led international force invaded Iraq to bring down Saddam Hussein. Such events have economic as well as political consequences. Instability in the Middle East causes gas prices to rise. This affects consumers and those who produce goods and services that rely on oil. Terrorist alerts may cause people who would normally fly, not to. Meanwhile, airlines and

other businesses have to pay more for added security measures. The additional costs affect consumers in the form of higher prices and taxes. These are just a few examples of how events like the War on Terror can affect the US economy.

LEGAL DECISIONS

Bill Gates
Co-founder Microsoft™

Legal decisions can also affect the economy. For instance, when courts use anti-trust laws to break up monopolies, previously closed markets suddenly open up to competition. This inevitably affects prices, production, and the quality of goods as consumers suddenly begin to have options. Although monopolies are not as common as they were at the beginning of the 20th century, such cases are occasionally still brought. One of the most recent anti-trust cases of note was the **Microsoft™** case. In 1998, The US Justice Department and 20 US states filed suit against the computer giant, charging that it had established an illegal monopoly. Initially, the courts agreed and ordered Microsoft™ to be broken up into two units. Microsoft™ appealed, however, and the case was eventually settled out of court. A number of Microsoft's™ competitors were upset, claiming that the settlement prevented free market competition. In addition to anti-trust cases, lawsuits against a large corporation, criminal allegations against members of a certain industry, and charges that the leader of a particular corporation is involved in some kind of scandal, can all affect the actions of consumers and producers.

OUTSOURCING AND DOWNSIZING

How do businesses deal with economic challenges caused by current events and factors in the market? Like consumers, producers have to adapt to survive in the market system. One way they do this is by **downsizing**. In other words, they reduce their number of employees and/or operations. While this makes sense for producers and is sometimes necessary to stay in business, it is often tragic for workers who lose their jobs.   In addition, the closing of facilities often has economic affects beyond simply those who have been laid off. For instance, say you live in a small town where 60% of the population is employed by the rubber plant. Because of certain factors, the demand for the company's product drops. To stay alive, the corporation must close several of its plants. Unfortunately, your town's plant is one of them. Right away, 60% of the population is out of work. Some will find other jobs in town, but most will be forced to move away. However, it is not just those workers who feel the affects. What about the owner of the local diner who depends

Textile Mill

on factory workers for 90% of his business? What about the car dealership that sells the vast majority of its cars to those employed at the plant? What about the local dentist whose clientele is almost entirely employed by the rubber company? Downsizing has economic effects not only on workers, but on geographic areas as well. **North Carolina's textile and furniture industries** have been hit especially hard in recent years. Once thriving businesses and huge contributors to North Carolina' economy, these industries have shrunk considerably over the last few decades due to increased trade, lower tariffs, and the affordability of foreign products. As a result, North Carolina is a state that is becoming less and less dependent on traditional blue collar industries like textiles, and more dependent on white collar industries like those of Research Triangle Park and the financial institutions of Charlotte (Charlotte is one of the nation's top financial centers and is home to both Bank of America and Wachovia).

US Made Furniture

Another method that has become more popular in recent years is *outsourcing*. With **outsourcing**, businesses pay outside firms to perform tasks that the company would have traditionally done itself. For example, some US companies outsource customer service calls to companies in India because it is cheaper than paying people in the US. Why do companies outsource? Usually, because it is more economical, frees the company up to focus on other aspects of their business, and hopefully, improves quality.

Practice 4: Impact of Current Events on the Economy

1. How has the airline industry been affected by the terrorist attacks of 9/11 and the War on Terror?

    A. The have not been affected because consumers want to travel more than they worry about terrorism.

    B. It has thrived because of all the increases in security and awareness about terrorism.

    C. It has struggled because production costs have risen while consumer confidence has decreased.

    D. The have struggled because the government took over ownership of the airlines after 9/11, and they are now no longer privately owned and run.

Factors Influencing the US Economy

2. Which of the following would LEAST affect the overall US economy?

    A. Terrorists successfully blow up a major US oil pipeline and several major US oil refineries.

    B. The Supreme Court upholds a ruling that a huge corporation has established an illegal monopoly in a revolutionary new technology market and must be broken up.

    C. Several airline pilots resign because they are tired of working in an unstable industry.

    D. The president signs a bill lowering tariffs, thereby making it easier for products from other countries to be sold in the US.

3. When companies hire outside firms to handle jobs the company has traditionally done itself, it is called what?

    A. downsizing

    B. outsourcing

    C. technological advancement

    D. profit necessity

4. What is downsizing and what effects can it have on workers and geographic areas?

9.5 THE US AND INTERNATIONAL ECONOMIES

While the United States has arguably the strongest and most influential economy in the world, it is by no means independent. The US is affected by how the economies of other countries are doing. For this reason, the US has an interest in other countries' economies remaining healthy and stable. Many times, the same companies that operate in the US also operate or own interests in other nations as well. For example, **multinational conglomerates** own a variety of companies in more than one nation that are often unrelated in what they produce. Such business practices, along with the availability of worldwide communications and the capability to travel relatively quickly anywhere in the world, has resulted in the economic **globalization** (world-wide connection) of business. As a result, global economies are **interdependent** (rely on one another) as never before.

FOREIGN TRADE

International trade is the process by which nations exchange goods with one another. *Exports* are goods that a nation sells to other countries. *Imports* are those goods that a nation buys from other countries. The process of the United States trading goods with other nations is referred to as **foreign trade**. The rate at which a nation trades with other nations can be either favorable or unfavorable. A **favorable balance of trade** is when a country is exporting more than it imports. It is considered favorable because such an arrangement means that a nation is producing and receiving payment for more than it is spending on foreign products. A favorable balance of trade is usually an indication that a nation is producing goods (this means more jobs and investments) and is bringing more money into the economy than it is spending in foreign markets. By contrast, an **unfavorable balance of trade** is when a nation's imports exceed its exports. Why do countries engage in trade with one another? Because no country produces everything it needs on its own (although some come closer than others). In other words, some countries enjoy an *absolute advantage* in the production of certain products; they produce them better and more efficiently than anyone else. However, sometimes nations agree to trade based on a **comparative advantage**. In some situations, there might be a country that can do a better job producing just about anything than the nation with which it trades, but in order to focus on producing the goods it is *most* efficient at, it still finds it in its best interest to import certain products rather than producing them itself. For example, say that country X can produce 100 bags of wheat for every 1 bag country Y produces. At the same time, country X can also produce 2 boxes of fruit for every 1 that country Y produces. X can produce both products in greater numbers and more efficiently. However, in order to focus on its wheat production, it still decides to import fruit from country Y, because Y does almost as good a job as X at producing that particular good. Although country Y cannot produce as much fruit as X, it can produce fruit at a lower opportunity cost. Therefore, *comparatively*, it has an advantage. This is a crude example of how comparative advantage works; but hopefully it helps you understand the principle.

Comparative Advantage

Country *X*   Country *Y*

Wheat   100 bags   1 bag   = absolute advantage
                                                     for *X*

          or   or

Fruit   100 boxes   50 boxes = comparative
                                                     advantage for *Y*

One important factor in trade is the international **exchange rate** of currency. In other words, how much is a given amount of money in one nation is worth in another nation. If a producer in the US is told that his product can be sold in Japan for X amount of yen, then he/she better know how many yen equal a dollar. After all, he/she is paying his/her production costs in dollars, not yen. The buying power of one nation's currency against another nation's currency affects how much producers charge for their products and, ultimately, the balance of trade between nations.

International trade without restrictions is known as **free trade**. Many times, however, governments will intervene to regulate trade. **Tariffs** are special taxes placed on products imported from another country. Governments sometimes use tariffs to raise the price of foreign goods and make domestic products more competitive in the marketplace. Labor unions have traditionally favored tariffs because they help US manufacturers and tend to protect jobs. Some US businesses, however, oppose tariffs because other countries tend to respond with tariffs of their own, thereby making it more costly for US producers to sell their own goods abroad.

Oil Tanker

Embargoes are another means by which governments impact trade. **Embargoes** are sanctions against a country that prevents another country/countries from trading with it. For instance, in 1973, US citizens found themselves waiting in long lines just to obtain gas for their cars because countries in the Middle East imposed an oil embargo. In 1979, the United States stopped shipping grain to the USSR after the Soviets invaded Afghanistan. Despite any demand that might exist in the marketplace, embargoes prohibit certain nations from trading with one another. Finally, there are **treaties**. Treaties are formal agreements between nations. Usually, they are intended to ensure peace and prevent the outbreak of war. Often, they include economic agreements as well.

INTERNATIONAL ORGANIZATIONS AND AGREEMENTS

There are several organizations that exist to facilitate international trade and a number of agreements in place to help regulate its practice. Below are just a few examples.

World Trade Organization (WTO)	International organization that establishes rules for international trade and helps resolve disputes between member nations.
European Union (EU)	Trading union consisting of 25 European nations that facilitates trade and commerce as it seeks to create a unified regional, rather than national, economy.
International Monetary Fund (IMF)	International organization that oversees the international financial system by monitoring exchange rates and payment balances between nations. It also offers financial assistance in certain situations.
United Nations (UN)	International diplomatic body centered in New York City. Its member nations seek to engage in diplomacy to deal with international issues. In addition to potential military conflicts, it also seeks effective solutions to economic matters as well. Its ability to provide workable solutions and negotiate peaceful resolutions to armed conflicts helps determine how the worldwide economy responds to international circumstances.
North American Free Trade Agreement (NAFTA)	Trade agreement ratified during the Clinton administration, which lowered trade barriers between the US, Canada, and Mexico. It caused concerns in the US as some feared it would result in the loss of US jobs. Proponents of the agreement argued, however, that NAFTA would benefit the economy by allowing US businesses greater access to foreign markets.

Chapter 9

AID TO DEVELOPING COUNTRIES

The US is one of many nations that are considered to be **"developed countries."** These are countries which have greater material wealth and whose citizens experience a higher standard of living. They tend to have more stable governments, greater economic opportunities, increased production, and access to the latest technological advances. By contrast, many countries are considered to be **"developing countries."** These nations are poorer and often depend on **foreign aid** in the form of money, food, technology, capital, etc. for survival. One organization that is geared towards helping developing nations is the **World Bank**. It provides finance and counsel to poorer countries attempting to improve their economic condition. By safeguarding foreign investments, the World Bank helps provide greater incentive for businesses to invest in developing nations.

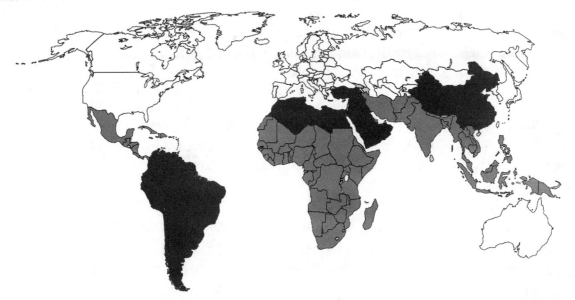

Areas Often Considered Developing Countries

Historically, it has been in the best interest of the US to help developing nations for several reasons. For one, the more advanced the economies of these nations become, the more markets it ultimately creates for US businesses. Secondly, the less developed a nation's economy, the poorer its population tends to be. This often gives rise to discontent that can lead to political instability. In the past, such instability made underdeveloped nations susceptible to communism. For this reason, the US has often attempted to bolster the economies of developing nations in the hopes of building alliances and preventing the spread of governments unfriendly to the US. Finally, there are also moral reasons. Many in the US believe that it is the nation's responsibility as the most abundant country on earth to help poorer countries succeed as well.

POLITICAL ISSUES THAT AFFECT TRADE

Trade is also impacted by political concerns. At times, the US has restricted trade with certain nations in the name of **human rights** (rights every living human possesses). For instance, the US has not traded with Cuba for more than 40 years on the grounds that Fidel Castro's regime is a communist government guilty of oppressive policies and human rights violations. In addition, some countries might practice abusive policies towards minorities or women. Others might use **child labor** (requiring children to work) or pay their workers almost nothing in order to maximize profits. While some applaud US efforts to limit trade in the name of human rights, others are critical and point out inconsistencies in US policy. Cuba, for instance, is ostracized for alleged human rights violations; while China, which commonly imprisons people for their political beliefs, continues to trade regularly with the United States. Most agree that this is because of political factors. Cuban immigrants who fled the Castro regime are a formidable political force in the state of Florida. Because of its population, Florida has a large number of seats in Congress and a large number of votes in the Electoral College. For this reason, no politician wants to alienate the Cuban community by acting to re-establish trade with Cuba while Castro is alive (the 2000 presidential election between Al Gore and George W. Bush was decided by who won in Florida). At the same time, due to its size and military strength, China is a country with whom the US seeks to maintain good relations. As you can see, economics is greatly affected by political realities.

Fidel Castro

Practice 5: The US and International Economies

1. The existence of multinational conglomerates, worldwide communications, and the ability to travel anywhere in the world in a reasonable amount of time all contribute to what?

    A. trade restrictions
    B. tariffs
    C. economic globalization
    D. an unfavorable balance of trade for the US

2. Explain the difference between a "favorable balance of trade" and an "unfavorable balance of trade."

3. A business in Winston-Salem is experiencing record profits, largely because they have discovered a high demand for their product in Canada. Since they don't have to pay any Canadian tariffs, they are able to sell their product at a reasonable price that matches demand. This business is benefiting from which of the following?
    A. WTO   B. EU   C. NAFTA   D. IMF

4. Which of the following would be considered a "developed country"?
    A. Ethiopia   B. Haiti   C. France   D. Afghanistan

5. Why is it in the United States' best interest to help developing countries improve their economies?

9.6 EFFECTS OF MONETARY AND FISCAL POLICY

As discussed earlier, the United States government influences the US economy through both its **fiscal policy** (how the government chooses to spend money and how it chooses to tax households/businesses) and its **monetary policy** (how much it restricts or releases the flow of money into the economy). In general, the federal government directs fiscal policy at accomplishing long term economic goals, while monetary policies tend to be geared toward more immediate economic relief.

FISCAL POLICY

Taxation is the first part of government fiscal policy. As the government decreases taxes, producers have more money to spend on labor, capital, etc. and households have more disposable income. This results in economic growth as it helps increase employment, production, and consumer demand for goods and services. However, if not careful, it can also lead to severe inflation. Raising taxes, on the other hand, has the opposite effect. That's why governments will sometimes raise taxes to deal with rising prices. The government collects taxes in the form of **personal income taxes, excise taxes, sales taxes,** etc. (Review Chapter 2, Section 6 regarding taxes.) These taxes are either **progressive** (the percentage of tax one pays increases as their income rises), **regressive** (the percentage of tax one pays decreases as their income rises), or **proportional** (everyone pays the same percentage proportional to their income) in nature.

Government spending is the other part of fiscal policy. The money which the government takes in (mostly in taxes) is **revenue.** By spending more of its revenue, the government pumps money into the economy and promotes growth. However, if the government both cuts taxes and increases spending at the same time to try to bolster the economy, it often results in deficit spending (spending more money than the government has in revenue). When this happens, the nation experiences a deficit and an increase in the national debt. On the other hand, a government might also reduce government spending. When this happens, less money is pumped into the economy as government spending decreases, and those who normally benefit from government spending have less money to spend in the market.

MONETARY POLICY

As discussed in Chapter 8, it is the **Federal Reserve** that sets monetary policy and controls the amount of money circulating in the economy. It does this in three primary ways. First, the "Fed" controls the money supply by either raising the **reserve requirement** (amount of cash banks are required to keep on hand rather than loan), or by lowering it. A **"tight money" policy** (high reserve requirement) limits the money supply, whereas an **"easy money" policy** (low reserve requirement) increases it because more people can borrow and spend money. Consider this simplified example. Say that 100 people want to buy a house. They all go to the bank to take out a loan for the purchase. The Federal Reserve, however, has just instituted a "tight money" policy. This means that the bank has to keep more money on hand and has less money to lend. As a result, the bank does not have the resources to grant all 100 households a loan. It can only loan money to 60 households. What consequences does this have? In addition to disappointing the 40 households that couldn't get a loan, it also means that 40 houses will not be bought that otherwise would have been. This means less money for the developer, fewer construction workers hired, less contractors employed, less demand for house inspectors, and less income for real estate agents. These people, in turn, will now have less income to spend in the market place, and so on, and so on. On the other hand, if the Federal Reserve institutes an "easy money" policy, then the bank loans more money, more homes are bought, incomes increase, etc.

Factors Influencing the US Economy

The second way the Federal Reserve impacts the nation's money supply is through the *discount rate*. The **discount rate** is the interest rate that banks and other financial institutions pay the Fed in order to borrow money. In other words, the Federal Reserve acts like a "bank for banks". Banks and other financial institutions can borrow money from the Fed, and then—just like a household or business that borrows from the bank—pay it back with interest. Remember, an **interest rate** is a percentage that determines how much money one must pay a lender in exchange for a loan. The higher the discount rate charged by the Fed, the higher the interest rate charged by banks. Higher interest rates encourage people to save rather than borrow and spend; therefore, the money supply decreases. Conversely, a lower discount rate allows banks to charge lower interest. This results in more loans and spending, causing the money supply to go up.

Finally, the Fed uses **open market operations** (the sale or purchase of US treasury bonds) to control the flow of money. When the Fed *sells* securities (bonds), it lowers the money supply and serves to fight inflation. How so? Remember that bonds are a form of saving for investors. They buy the bond to gain interest and then get their money back at a later time. Money that is saved (i.e., invested in bonds) is money that is not spent in the market. Therefore, the more securities sold, the more the money supply decreases. In addition, when the Fed sells securities, bank reserves of money decrease as households and businesses spend more to purchase bonds. This causes a rise in the discount rate as banks have to borrow more from the Federal Reserve to keep the required reserve on hand. This, in turn, raises interest rates and leads to less spending and less money in circulation. However, when the Fed *buys* securities, interest rates drop, spending increases, and more money is pumped into the economy. Can you see now how important the Federal Reserve is?

Practice 6: Effects of Monetary and Fiscal Policy

1. The way the government conducts spending and taxation is called what?

    A. monetary policy
    B. economic policy
    C. free enterprise policy
    D. fiscal policy

2. The way the government chooses to control the money supply is called what?

    A. monetary policy
    B. open market operation
    C. reserve requirement and discount rate
    D. fiscal policy

3. What is the discount rate and how does it affect the money supply?

4. What is meant by "open market operations" and how does the Federal Reserve use it to control the money supply?

9.7 THE IMPACT OF ENVIRONMENT, ECONOMIC CONDITIONS, AND POLITICS

As mentioned before, there are a number of factors that prevent the US economy from simply operating according to the natural laws of a market system. Concerns about the environment, extreme or unusual economic circumstances, and political concerns are all factors that influence the nation's economy.

Chapter 9

ECONOMIC CONDITIONS

One economic problem that faces the nation from time to time is **scarcity** (limited availability of desired products). Despite the demand for a product, there may be reasons why adequate supply is lacking. For instance, the 1973 **OPEC oil embargo** made gasoline very scarce, resulting in long lines at gas stations and extremely high prices. Gas also became scarce after Hurricane Katrina pounded the Gulf Coast in 2005. Once again, high prices resulted as supplies became limited. When scarcity occurs, most individuals find it necessary to alter the way they live. They search for substitute goods that are more available, or seek to eliminate the need for the scarce product altogether. In the case of gas

Gas Lines of the Early '70s

shortages, for example, consumers may walk more, use mass transit, buy gas efficient cars rather than "gas guzzlers", cut back on heat and/or buy more energy efficient windows for insulation, etc. Those that can't cut back on gas (i.e., they can't afford a new car, can't avoid a long commute to work, etc.) find it necessary to cut back in other ways. They might have to limit recreational activities that cost money, shop at a discount grocer, or get rid of cable TV in order to afford gas. In short, scarcity forces consumers to set priorities and make economic choices.

In addition, severe **inflation** (rise in prices), **recession**, and/or **depression** also impact economic choices. (Review Chapter 9, Section 1 regarding economic indicators of the business cycle.) When prices rise, people have to cut back on what they spend (unless, of course, their income increases as well). This means that households and businesses purchase less and the economy slows. A recession means that fewer people are working and raising money. This, of course, means less money is being pumped into the economy as well. If a recession continues to worsen, it can become a depression. People who lose their jobs to a recession have to change their spending habits, dip into savings, and perhaps even depend on government assistance. In addition, some might find that they need to switch careers, go back to school, or acquire new training if they are to have any hope of finding work in a changing market where jobs are suddenly scarce.

The state of the stock market is also an economic factor. When confidence in the stock market is high, people are more likely to invest. This raises stock prices and increases the circulation of money. Therefore, rising stock prices tend to be associated with a growing economy. When the stock market experiences a steady rise in prices over a period of time, it is said to be a **"bull market."** When prices fall steadily and the economy stalls because less money is being invested, it is called a **"bear market."**

Severe circumstances not only affect the way consumers and producers spend money, but also how active the government becomes in the economy. When the business cycle is on the upswing, people tend to want the government to get out of the way and let things take their natural course (forgetting that it may not have been the "natural course" that started the upswing to begin with). However, when inflation rises or recession hits, people tend to call on the government to do something.

ENVIRONMENTAL FACTORS

Since the late 1960s, **environmental concerns** have become increasingly more influential in economic conditions. Because citizens are conscious of the effects that certain industries can have on the environment, corporations now have to abide by government regulations meant to protect the environment, as well as seek to produce goods in the most efficient way possible. They also must be aware of how an environmentally aware public perceives them. Any company seen as not caring about the environment runs the risk of being shunned by consumers in today's market. Laws like the **Clean Air Act** and the **Clean Water Act**, regulate how much pollution companies can legally release into the environment and how they

Recycled Material

dispose of things like radioactive waste. As a result, automakers now must produce cars conscious of how much pollution they emit; companies are limited in how they dispose of waste and tend to recycle more; and advertisers are paid, not only to promote how well products perform their intended function, but also to make known how "environmentally friendly" they are. In addition, the government has declared certain areas as public lands that are "off limits" to development. While environmentalists applaud the government for restricting industrial development, others complain that such measures produce shortages and economic hardship. They point to gas prices caused by oil shortages as an example, claiming that a big part of the problem is that oil companies are not allowed to drill enough off-shore or in places like Alaska. Today more than ever, US consumers tend to make economic decisions based on environmental concerns in addition to price and quality. In fact, in many circumstances, consumers are willing to pay more if they believe that the product they are buying better protects the environment than a cheaper substitute. Some even go so far as to boycott products they feel are harmful (i.e., SUVs that omit a lot of fumes, products that aren't biodegradable, etc.).

POLITICAL FACTORS

Political issues also have economic effects. The United States government has both used and been the target of embargoes. As mentioned above, the OPEC nations of the Middle East imposed an embargo against the US in which it refused to ship oil to the United States; greatly limiting the nation's oil supplies. In the 1930s, the US imposed an oil embargo of its own against Japan that contributed to Japan's decision to invade Indochina and attack Pearl Harbor. For over 40 years, the US has had an **economic embargo against Cuba**. Embargoes limit the supply of certain products, not because of a decline in demand, but by government action meant to punish another country. For example, Cuba may want US goods, but the US won't provide them for political reasons. Conversely, your dad might love a good Cuban cigar once in a while, but he can't get one (at least not legally) because the US will not import Cuban products. Thus, embargoes limit the products that individual consumers are able to buy (thereby limiting competition) and the markets in which producers are able to sell.

Chapter 9

On a local level, political issues also have an impact. One common example is the conflict over **zoning laws** and **building codes**. These laws and codes regulate where commercial facilities and residential housing can be built, as well as the guidelines they must meet. Conflicts sometimes arise between businesses who want to build in a certain area and citizens who don't want their neighborhoods and/or way of life disrupted. The familiar cry of **"NIMBY" ("not in my backyard")** is a phrase used by citizens who oppose unwelcome businesses that want to build close to residential neighborhoods. Why do people sometimes oppose businesses building close to where they live? Sometimes, it is because they fear that property values will drop if the landscape is changed. Other times, it might be because they don't want to see the increase in traffic that accompanies new businesses. As a result, businesses have to worry about more than just money when deciding where to build. They have to make sure that what they want to develop meets local regulations and that they are welcome in the community. Otherwise, they could alienate potential consumers. Such disputes can be tricky for politicians who favor the jobs and other economic benefits that new businesses bring, but don't want to upset residents who might vote against them come election time.

Practice 7: Environment, Economic Conditions, and Politics

1. Paul wants to buy a classic sports car. Unfortunately, only a limited amount of dealers and collectors have the model car he wants. As a result, Paul will have to pay a high price, if he can even get the car at all. Paul is experiencing what?

    A. an embargo on cars
    B. severe inflation
    C. scarcity
    D. depression in the car market

2. Trevor goes to renew his auto tags but is told that he cannot because his car does not meet emissions standards (the car puts out too much pollution). Trevor's car fails to meet standards that were likely put in place because of what?

    A. a recession
    B. environmental concerns
    C. scarcity
    D. zoning laws

3. Explain the difference between a "bull market" and a "bear market."

4. What does "NIMBY" stand for and how can it cause problems for political leaders at the local level?

CHAPTER 9 REVIEW

A. Define the following key terms.

business cycle	comparative advantage	interest rate
expansion/recovery	exchange rate	open market operations
peak/prosperity	tariffs	trough/depression
treaties	scarcity	economic indicators
World Trade Organization (WTO)	per capita gross domestic product	North America Free Trade Agreement (NAFTA)
OPEC oil embargo	European Union (EU)	bull market
standard of living	United Nations (UN)	consumer price index (CPI)
national debt	developed countries	bear market
work place safety	foreign aid	environmental concerns
consumer protection	World Bank	affirmative action
human rights	Clean Air Act	labor disputes
child labor	Clean Water Act	deregulation
fiscal policy		population shifts
monetary policy	economic embargo against Cuba	migration
taxation	immigration	Silicon Valley
"Rust Belt"/"Frost Belt"/"Sun Belt"	personal income, excise, and sales taxes	progressive, regressive, and proportional taxes
Research Triangle Park	government spending	service industries
revenue	zoning laws and building codes	federal reserve
Department of Homeland Security	downsizing (NC's textile and furniture industries)	favorable/unfavorable balance of trade
Patriot Act	reserve requirement	Operation Iraqi Freedom
"tight money" policy	NIMBY	Microsoft™ case
outsourcing	globalization/interdependence	"easy money" policy
multinational conglomerate	discount rate	foreign trade

B. Choose the correct answer.

1. The "ups" and "downs" in the economy are referred to as what?
    A. business cycle
    B. business coaster
    C. prosperity
    D. economic trough

2. GDP, CPI, per capita gross national product, and the national debt are all what?
    A. signs that the economy is peaking
    B. signs that the economy is in contraction
    C. economic indicators used to determine the state and direction of the economy
    D. the results of economic expansion

Chapter 9

3. Economic statistics show that the nation of Zanzio produced 10 million dollars in goods and services last year. Meanwhile, the nation's census shows that it has 100,000 people living in the country. Which of the following statements is true?
   A. Zanzio has a GDP of $1,000,000.00.
   B. Zanzio has a per capita GDP of $100.00.
   C. Zanzio has a national debt of $9,900,000.00.
   D. Zanzio has a per capita GDP of 1,000,000.00.

4. Margaret's company is doing well. However, while Margaret's business is located in and services a community that is mostly African-American and Hispanic, her employees are 90% white. She decides that it is in the best interest of her company to have her workforce reflect the diversity of the population it serves. She decides that out of the 7 new positions she has open, she will hire at least 5 people who are either Hispanic or African-American. Margaret's policy could be BEST described as what?
   A. racism
   B. economic indicating
   C. affirmative action
   D. deregulation

5. The country of Lesinbrow has just taken its first census in ten years. As a result, it discovers that its eastern population has grown by 70%, while its western population has declined by 45%. It also notices that the number of foreigners who have come to the country has remained about the same, if not shrunk, since the last census was taken. Which of the following conclusions is MOST LIKELY accurate?
   A. Lesinbrow has experienced a population growth that is due to immigration.
   B. Lesinbrow has experienced a migration shift from east to west.
   C. Lesinbrow has experienced a population shift from west to east that is due mostly to migration.
   D. Lesinbrow has experienced a population shift from west to east that is due mainly to immigration.

6. Region of the US that has shown the greatest growth in population over the last few decades?
   A. rust belt   B. frost belt   C. sun belt   D. leather belt

7. Which of the following has the LEAST amount of effect on the US economy?
   A. a terrorist attack
   B. legal decisions that affect US businesses
   C. outsourcing by corporations
   D. the closing of a sole proprietorship

8. The High Rock City Shoe Company has been forced to downsize. Which of the following is the most likely effect of such an action?
   A. More of the company's stock will be sold at a higher price.
   B. A number of unskilled laborers who work for the company will likely lose their jobs.
   C. The company will cease outsourcing in favor of handling all aspects of its business itself.
   D. The company will open new facilities and hire more employees.

Factors Influencing the US Economy

9. Phipps Co. is looking for ways to increase efficiency and cut costs. After conducting research, it decides to save money by contracting a separate agency to handle all of its payroll, accounting, record keeping, etc. Phipps Co.'s actions are an example of what?
   A. downsizing   B. outsourcing   C. globalization   D. conglomeration

10. Country A exports 10% more goods than it imports. By contrast, country B imports 15% more goods than it exports. Which of the following statements is obviously true?
    A. Country A has a favorable balance of trade, but country B has an unfavorable balance of trade.
    B. Country A has a comparative advantage over country B.
    C. Country B must rely on foreign aid from country A.
    D. Country B has a favorable balance of trade, but country A has an unfavorable balance of trade.

11. A developing nation in Asia is struggling to obtain enough money to get its economy up and running. Which of the following organizations will it MOST LIKELY turn to for help?
    A. NAFTA   B. EU   C. World Bank   D. EPA

12. The new president proposes an economic plan to Congress. In it, he calls for lower taxes and recommends several programs that he would like the government to spend money on. The president's proposal reflects what?
    A. his monetary policy
    B. his fiscal policy
    C. his desire to reduce inflation
    D. his ability to control the Federal Reserve

13. The Federal Reserve comes to the conclusion that more money must be pumped into the economy in an effort to stimulate economic growth. Which of the following actions could the "Fed" take that would result in increasing the money supply?
    A. raise the discount rate   C. sell securities (bonds)
    B. raise the reserve requirement   D. buy securities (bonds)

14. Jim picks up the morning paper and reads the headline: "Bull Market to Continue!" What can Jim assume from this headline?
    A. Stock prices have been falling and will continue to fall.
    B. Stock prices have been rising and will continue to rise.
    C. Stock prices have been rising but are about to fall.
    D. Stock prices have been falling, but things are about to get better.

15. Which of the following is usually an effect of an embargo?
    A. Prices fall because consumers have more options.
    B. Prices rise because consumers have fewer options.
    C. Countries benefit because open trade is encouraged.
    D. Smaller countries give in to the demands of larger countries.

Chapter 10
Issues and Responsibilities in US Society

This chapter addresses the following competency goal and objective(s):

Competency goal 10	The learner will develop, defend, and evaluate positions on issues regarding the personal responsibilities of citizens in the American constitutional democracy.
Objective 10.01, 10.02, 10.03, 10.04, 10.05, 10.06	

10.1 TENSIONS AND PROBLEMS IN US SOCIETY

CONFLICTING RESPONSIBILITIES

US society depends on citizens who are willing to fulfill their **civic responsibilities.** (Review Chapter 4, Sections 4 and 5 regarding civic responsibility and public service.) These responsibilities include **voting**, **volunteerism**, **speaking to issues** (forming educated opinions about important issues and expressing them) and **community activism** (taking an active role in community improvements and causes). However, civic responsibilities often conflict with *personal responsibilities.* **Personal responsibilities** are those responsibilities one has, not to society as a whole, but to oneself or a select few (i.e., family or co-workers). People have **fiscal responsibilities** (responsibilities related to money), such as supporting one's family, saving for retirement and college, and paying bills. There are also responsibilities involving time. In order for citizens to devote time, energy, and money to fulfilling civic duties, they must sacrifice personal responsibilities to some degree, and vice versa. For instance, time and energy that is spent devoted to civic duties is time that cannot be spent earning money at work, playing with one's kids, cleaning up one's house, or spending quality time with a spouse. Money given to a community project, to support a cause, or donated to a campaign cannot be used to pay bills or college tuition. Citizens have **legal responsibilities** that involve **obeying the laws** of the land. In addition, there are also **moral responsibilities**. These include the responsibilities one feels to live by certain religious convictions, maintain his/her integrity, honor a promise, etc. Sometimes, legal and moral responsibilities can conflict as well. Take,

for instance, the Civil Rights Movement of the 1950s and 60s. Many citizens (black and white) found themselves having to choose between a legal responsibility to obey segregation laws and a moral responsibility to oppose policies which sanctioned racism.

Fulfilling civic responsibilities inevitably requires dealing with people. In order for communities and society to function effectively, citizens must learn to **collaborate** (come together to seek solutions to problems, etc.) in a way that leads to **cooperation** (working together constructively) and **compromise** (citizens who disagree being willing to give up a little of what they want to reach a solution most can live with).

DIVERSITY

The United States has long been a land of **diversity**. In other words, it is home to people from many different cultures, ethnic backgrounds, and belief systems. In fact, the Latin phrase *E pluribus Unum* ("from many, the one") is found on many of the nation's seals, including that of the president. But while many view diversity as something to be celebrated, it also causes divisions and debate. Many US citizens still believe in the *melting pot theory*. This theory states that US society is best served when people abandon their cultural differences. Like a "melting pot" in which all the individual ingredients become indistinguishable in a new, tastier dish, proponents of this position say that a better, more unified society is created when people **assimilate** (become like mainstream US society). By contrast, other citizens hold to what is called the *tossed salad theory*. This theory says that, like a salad in which each ingredient remains distinct as it mixes together, US society benefits most when people keep their cultural identities. Such a view of diversity is often referred to as **multiculturalism** because it encourages cultural differences rather than advocating assimilation. Tension arises because people who believe in the *melting pot theory* and those who hold to the *tossed salad theory* often disagree on issues like immigration, affirmative action, bilingual education (teaching in languages other than English), whether or not English should be made the official language, etc.

While some citizens view diversity more positively than others, just about everyone acknowledges that it creates social problems. **Racism** (viewing people negatively and discriminating against them because of their ethnic race), **sexism** (discrimination or unfair treatment based on gender), **ageism** (discrimination based on age; usually against the elderly), and **bias** (feelings for or against something) against those who practice lifestyles outside the US mainstream (i.e., those with unpopular political beliefs, people with non-traditional views, etc.), are just a few examples of the problems that exist in a multicultural society. To complicate  matters, US citizens often disagree on what constitutes racism, sexism, unfair bias, etc. In addition, there are often **negative stereotypes** (pre-judgments about people) based on a person's race or **nationality** (what nation a person originally comes from). **Religious differences** can also produce tensions. Protestants and Catholics may not get along. Non-Christian faiths might feel that they are treated unfairly by the Christian majority. Jews have traditionally been discriminated against and stereotyped. Many Christians feel that their beliefs and values are mocked and undermined by the media. In addition, even within certain denominations there is often strife as churches deal with questions surrounding the degree to which they believe in the Bible, whether or not to embrace homosexuality as a legitimate lifestyle, and where to stand on issues like abortion. Finally, there are those who may be discriminated against because of their **physical appearance** (how a person looks) or some kind of **disability** (limiting physical or mental condition). For instance, a qualified individual might be overlooked for a job in favor of someone else who better "looks the part" (i.e., more conservative, more mainstream, more attractive, etc.). Meanwhile, someone confined to a wheelchair or who is mentally challenged might not be afforded opportunities to prove themselves. For example, they may be denied jobs that, in reality, they are quite capable of doing. People with certain diseases (i.e., AIDS) often find themselves shunned by members of society, rather than embraced. Although advances have been made in all of these areas, most citizens argue that more needs to change. Exactly *what and how to change*, however, is often a point of controversy.

RECURRING PUBLIC PROBLEMS AND ISSUES

Part of effective citizenship is learning to recognize and help provide solutions to recurring problems in society. In the United States, there are a number of issues and problems that consistently have to be addressed. Below are just a few examples:

- **Discrimination** – Unfairly denying opportunities to otherwise qualified individuals due to race, gender, sexual orientation, nationality, physical condition, appearance, age, etc. Citizens sometimes disagree over what constitutes "discrimination", and charges of discrimination can often be difficult to prove.

- **Unemployment** – Not having enough jobs for US citizens who want to and are able to work.

- **Underemployment education** – Not having enough resources to train and equip citizens to find work and/or advance in the ever technologically changing US workforce.

- **Poverty** – Economic condition in which individuals/families find themselves lacking the money and resources necessary to meet basic needs (food, shelter, clothes, etc.) For some, poverty results in **homelessness** (being without a place to live). Many homeless people rely on charitable shelters for housing. Others simply live on the streets.

- **Substance abuse** – How does society deal with the growing numbers of people addicted to alcohol, illegal drugs, prescription pain killers, and tobacco products which lead to serious health problems (i.e., cancer and heart disease)?

- **Law and order** – What are the most effective ways to deal with **crime** (people committing criminal offenses)? Some citizens believe that society must allocate resources to help rehabilitate criminal offenders. Others believe that crime is best deterred by stiffer penalties. Both sides tend to favor some degree of **prison reform** (improving prison conditions to make for a more effective criminal justice system). In addition, citizens often disagree about what laws are needed and which actions should be considered illegal.

Issues and Responsibilities in US Society

- **Disease** – Like other countries, the US must deal with both the effects and potential threat of serious diseases. Cancer and AIDS are just two examples of diseases that cause the deaths of millions of US citizens every year. How to best fund research and how much of the government's limited resources should go to such research are constant questions facing political leaders. Meanwhile, things like the "bird flu" virus have agencies such as the US Center for Disease Control working on possible vaccines that could be used in the event of a worldwide pandemic (quick spreading of a potentially deadly disease across a large region — possibly several continents).

- **Immigration** – *Immigration* refers to the process of foreigners coming to the United States. In recent years, the vast majority of these immigrants have come from Latin America—normally by way of the US southern border. While many come legally, a growing number tend to be illegal immigrants. Many citizens believe that such people should be arrested and deported back to their original countries. They point out that illegal immigrants cause a drain on the US health care system and other public services without paying enough taxes to cover the costs. Critics of this position respond, however, that most illegal immigrants are decent people simply in search of a better life. They also claim that their presence is necessary to support the US economy because they do  many of the menial tasks and manual labor jobs that most US citizens will not. The terrorist attacks of September 11, 2001 have further ignited debate about immigration because most citizens agree that more must be done to monitor who crosses the US border. Otherwise, the United States leaves itself open to future attacks. What measures should be taken and what this means for illegal immigrants already in the country, however, are issues of controversy.

- **National security** – Since September 11, 2001, US citizens realize the importance of improving national security. Citizens debate, however, how far the government should be allowed to go in limiting civil liberties for the purpose of preventing terrorism.

- **Natural disasters** – The effects and destruction caused by hurricanes, tornadoes, earthquakes, western forest fires, and any other natural disaster that might occur.

- **Pollution** – Potentially harmful chemicals  and gases that are released into the air by factories, cars, etc. Pollution can damage water supplies, cause respiratory (breathing) problems, and kill wildlife. To what degree pollution damages the environment and what can be done to reverse the process is often an issue of intense debate. Questions often arise regarding **waste disposal** (what to do with chemical and other forms of waste). How can industries and individuals dispose of their waste in a manner that has few, if any, harmful effects on the environment? Many citizens also blame man-made pollution for *acid rain* and what they claim to be a *"greenhouse effect."* **Acid rain** is the process in which chemicals released into the atmosphere are absorbed as water droplets in clouds. These chemicals then return to earth in the form of rain, sleet, or snow, thereby increasing the acidity of the soil and altering the chemical balance of lakes and streams. The **"greenhouse effect"** is the name given to what some environmentalists and scientists claim is happening as the result of years of irresponsible pollution. Those who believe in this theory believe that recent global warming can be attributed to a layer of gases produced by pollutants that is holding in heat from the sun rather than allowing it to escape into space after it hits the earth. Proponents of this theory believe that unless measures are taken to reverse this process, catastrophic changes to the environment could occur. While this is a commonly held view, controversies arise because there are scientists and experts who question it. Instead of a layer of gases, they attribute global warming to the sun's increasing temperature in recent years.

- **Taxation** – The degree to which US citizens and businesses are taxed. Conservatives tend to favor tax cuts and believe that the **economic cycle** (periods of economic growth and decline that take place over time) will perform best when policies reduce taxes on wealthy citizens, business owners, and corporations. They believe that such individuals and businesses will spend more money and hire more employees if they pay less in taxes. Conservatives believe this stimulates economic growth and eventually benefits everyone. Liberals, however, tend to favor higher taxes for the purpose of funding government social programs. Any tax breaks they do favor tend to be only for poorer citizens.

- **Graft and political corruption** – Political leaders using their position to make money and serve self-interests rather than the public.

Many problems and concerns center on the **needs of citizens**. For instance, all citizens need income to survive. However, there may not be enough jobs available to provide employment for everyone. Likewise, some citizens may lack health care benefits because they can't afford it. Gas might become less available due to a natural disaster or conflicts in the Middle East, thereby causing prices to rise so high that some people can no longer afford to drive. In short, many of the conflicts that arise in the United States are because of insufficient resources for meeting everyone's needs. One area where this is beginning to become evident

Senior Citizens

is that of *Social Security* (government system that pays income to retired citizens). This is largely because of the **"Baby Boomers"**— the generation of US citizens born in the years following World War II. Because it was a time in which soldiers were returning home from the war and starting/expanding their families, the nation experienced a "boom" in the number of babies being born. Today, this generation is nearing retirement. Because the **"graying population"** is so large and because medical technology now allows most Americans to live many years past retirement, the government anticipates a huge strain on the nation's Social Security System. Some experts have even questioned if the program will survive to exist forty or fifty years from now. As "Baby Boomers" continue to age, the nation's health care system will be challenged as well.

While problems do exist, US citizens can be confident *if* the majority of Americans are willing to become active and informed citizens. The greatest concern, therefore, may not be the controversies that exist, but rather the threat of **citizen apathy** (lack of concern on the part of citizens) that could lead people to do nothing.

Practice 1: Tensions and Problems in US Society

1. Being on time for work, spending time with one's spouse and children, paying bills on time, and saving for retirement are all examples of what?

    A. civic duty

    B. personal responsibilities

    C. issues of diversity

    D. recurring public problems

2. Someone who believes that Chinese immigrants should do their best to assimilate to the US mainstream would MOST LIKELY favor which of the following?
   A. the *melting pot theory*
   B. the *tossed salad theory*
   C. multiculturalism
   D. the "greenhouse effect"

3. Who are the "Baby Boomers" and what problems do they present?

10.2 EFFECTIVE CITIZENSHIP

INFORMED AND EDUCATED

In order for society to function well, citizens must comprise an **informed citizenry**. In other words, they must take time to understand what issues affect them and learn enough to have an intelligent opinion. In addition, citizens must **educate** themselves. This includes both formal education in school and **life long learning** through newspapers, books, magazines, research, electronic media, classes, etc. Of course, in order for a citizen to become informed or adequately educate him/herself, he/she must possess a certain amount of **self-motivation**. People show self-motivation when  they take action on their own to better themselves. No one is going to come along and make someone become an informed citizen. Neither is anyone going to force a person to pursue as much education as they can (although parents might for a while). No, it is up to the individual him/herself to decide if they are going to be an inspiring "difference maker" or an uninformed follower. The degree to which one is informed normally determines how much one cares. The more educated and informed citizens are, the more likely they are to participate in **public service.** (Review Chapter 4, Section 5 regarding public service). Also, the greater one's education, the greater one's *earning capacity*. **Earning capacity** is the amount of income that one is likely to earn in a lifetime. The highest paying jobs normally go to those who are college educated, particularly those with graduate degrees. By contrast, those who fail to finish high school usually earn little more than minimum wage. Therefore, it is critical that citizens be **literate** (able to read and write), finish high school, and—if possible—go on to some form of higher education (i.e., college, an associate degree, training in a particular trade, etc.).

CHARACTERISTICS OF EFFECTIVE CITIZENSHIP

Effective citizenship is citizenship which helps to build up society and enables the US political and judicial systems to function as intended under the Constitution. Below are just a few characteristics of effective citizenship:

- **Voluntary compliance** – Citizens must willingly comply with laws and community standards, recognizing that such standards are essential to maintaining order. Of course, if a law is unjust or discriminatory, then effective citizenship could involve protest of such a standard. However, even then, such actions should be carried out in a civil manner.

- **Volunteerism** – Willingness to volunteer time and energy to worthy causes.

- **Community Spirit** – Having a sense of pride in one's community and a desire to do one's part to make it better. Those with community spirit usually engage in some form of **community service** and often give money and time to **charities** (non-profit organizations established to help the underprivileged in society) because they see it as their responsibility to help others.

- **Patriotism** – a love of and devotion to the United States. Those who engage in effective citizenship tend to appreciate living in the US and feel a deep sense of **duty** (what one is expected or obligated to do) to serve their communities and participate in the political and judicial process.

- **Respecting the rights of others** Good citizens recognize that it is their responsibility to respect the rights of their fellow citizens. This means respecting their **individual rights** (free speech, freedom of religion, etc.) and their **property rights** (the right to own and feel secure in one's property). This requires *tolerance*. **Tolerance** means that one is willing to treat with respect other citizens who choose to live or believe differently.

- **Paying taxes** – Citizens must be willing to pay local, state, and federal governments the taxes they owe. Of course, nothing says you have to smile while you write the check.

- **Voting** – Effective citizens will exercise their right to vote, encourage other citizens to vote as well, and will respect the right of fellow citizens to vote differently from themselves.

- **Responsible behavior** – Effective citizens are citizens that behave responsibly. They are conscious and considerate of their fellow citizens. They recognize the importance of laws and abide by them. They do nothing that would intentionally infringe on the rights of others or endanger their safety. Neither do they do anything that would be reckless or cause damage to public property. They also appreciate and show respect for public servants such as government leaders, police officers, fire fighters, and other emergency and government personnel.

Practice 2: Effective Citizenship

1. Which of the following BEST describes a "self-motivated" person?

   A. Bill's wife drags him out of bed every morning at 6:30am so he won't be late for work.

   B. Janet is so smart that she makes A's on most of her tests at school without ever cracking a book.

   C. George wants to get a scholarship, so he sometimes studies on the weekends when most of his friends are out having fun.

   D. Phyllis goes to the polls and votes even though she really doesn't know what either candidate stands for.

2. Which of the following is NOT a characteristic of "effective citizenship"?
   A. apathy
   B. voluntary compliance
   C. respecting the rights of others
   D. community spirit

3. Why is it important for citizens to educate themselves?

10.3 BENEFITS AND CONSEQUENCES OF FREEDOM

Self-determination is the ability of citizens to act and make their own choices. It is a product of **liberty**, which guarantees that citizens can live their own lives without the arbitrary intervention of government. US citizens are free to make **economic choices.** Other than the obligation to pay taxes, they are free to decide how to spend and invest money, what to purchase, how great an income to pursue earning, which career path to follow, and so on. As a result, citizens need not be confined to one **socio-economic status**. Socio-economic status refers to the social/economic status one is born into or in which they live. In the US, a person born into poverty might attain a higher status in life. Conversely, a person born rich could, due to laziness, irresponsible decisions, or circumstances beyond their control, actually fall to a lower economic status. Citizens are also free to make **political choices.** They are free to educate themselves on issues, form opinions, join political parties, and engage in **political activism**. (Review Chapter 4, Section 3 regarding political activism.) Citizens are also free to make what might be considered **social choices.** So long as their actions are legal, they are free to choose their own lifestyle, what groups they want to be a part of, what religion they wish to practice, where they want to live, and so forth. So long as citizens obey local, state, and federal laws, they enjoy the security of knowing that the government is there to protect them. They need not fear any public authorities. However, citizens who break the law must bear the consequences of **justice.** If caught and convicted, they will have to face punishment for their crime.

BENEFITS OF FREEDOM

Freedom provides obvious benefits. For the most part, US citizens are allowed to live as they see fit. Unlike many other countries, the government does not significantly limit choices in the United States. This allows citizens to set their own goals, dream their own dreams, and seek out the path of their choice. Liberty provides them with the **opportunity to pursue success**. So great are the benefits of freedom that the United States has willingly gone to war from time to time to defend them.

CONSEQUENCES OF FREEDOM

Freedom, however, also comes with consequences. Liberty to make one's own choices also means bearing the **responsibility** of one's own mistakes and failures. An individual is free to invest in the stock market, but if the stock market drops, he/she must be prepared to endure the loss without expecting government to reimburse them. People are free to spend their money on whatever goods and services they desire and can afford. However, other than Social Security, they cannot expect the government to provide money in the future to make up for what they failed to save themselves. For many, one of the greatest economic freedoms is the freedom

to be an *entrepreneur*. **Entrepreneurs** are individuals who organize and start their own business. Accompanying the excitement and opportunity for success, however, is the risk of failure and possible financial ruin.

Political freedom means accepting responsibility for who serves in public office, having to deal with opposition and/or criticism for one's political beliefs, and having to take the time and effort to become informed about issues and take part in the political process. Such freedom also means that people must be willing to **compromise**. Since citizens are free to disagree with one another, they must also learn to modify their positions and reach solutions that can be agreed on and put into practice. Enjoying political freedom means tolerating the political freedom of others who think differently and learning to work together. Society cannot offer personal freedoms to its citizens without demanding that they assume personal responsibilities as well.

Practice 3: Benefits and Consequences of Freedom

1. The opportunity to reach a higher socio-economic status, start one's own business, and practice the religion of one's own choice are each examples of what?

   A. benefits of economic choices
   B. benefits of freedom
   C. consequences of freedom
   D. reasons to oppose self-determination

2. The idea that citizens are free to make their own choices and direct their own lives is known as what?

   A. entrepreneurship
   B. social choice
   C. economic choice
   D. self-determination

3. What are several consequences of economic and political freedom in the US?

Chapter 10 Review

A. Define the following key terms.

civic responsibilities	taxation	opportunity to pursue
personal responsibilities	economic cycle	voting
justice	speaking to issues	community activism
fiscal responsibilities	legal responsibilities	moral responsibilities
collaborate/cooperation/ compromise	bias	physical appearance (discrimination)
diversity	graft and political corruption	success
E pluribus unum	needs of citizens	melting pot theory
baby boomers	responsibility	assimilate
"graying population"	entrepreneur	tossed salad theory
citizen apathy	compromise	multiculturalism
informed citizenry	racism	educated citizenry
ageism	life long learning	sexism
self-motivation	public service	negative stereotypes
earning capacity	literate	nationality
effective citizenship	religious differences	voluntary compliance
volunteerism	disability (discrimination)	community spirit
discrimination	community service/charity	unemployment
patriotism	underemployment education	duty
poverty	respecting the rights of others	homelessness
individual rights	law and order	tolerance
crime	paying taxes	rehabilitate
voting	retribution	responsible behavior
prison reform	self-determination	disease
liberty	immigration	economic choices
national security	socio-economic status	natural disasters
political choices	pollution	political activism
waste disposal	social choices	acid rain
	"greenhouse effect"	

B. Choose the correct answer.

1. Which of the following is an example of fulfilling one's civic responsibilities?

    A. A school teacher decides to run for county commissioner.

    B. A young couple begins saving for their daughter's college education because they don't believe it is the government's role to fund such an expense.

    C. A young woman finally leaves her job to start the business she has always dreamed of.

    D. A nurse works overtime to pay off some of her debt.

Chapter 10

2. Which of the following describes a key difference between personal and civic responsibilities?

    A. Failure to fulfill personal responsibilities never affects others.

    B. Only civic responsibilities are considered important by effective citizens.

    C. Personal responsibilities are not to society as a whole.

    D. Personal responsibilities tend to cause tension, whereas civic responsibilities rarely do.

3. Someone promoting the *melting pot theory* would MOST support which of the following statements?

    A. "Now that these Hispanic immigrants have come to the US, they need to learn English and start acting more 'American' if they want to better our society."

    B. "Due to the various communities within our town, I believe that our annual Christmas parade should include a float honoring Hanukkah and Kwanzaa as well."

    C. "The United States is a land where we should embrace and celebrate our cultural differences."

    D. "Racism is not the evil people claim it is."

4. Which of the following is the BEST example of the tensions that sometimes exist between civic and personal responsibilities?

    A. Mike votes only to have his candidate lose.

    B. Because Jim volunteers to help at a blood drive, he misses the ballgame he's been dying to see.

    C. Karen is paid cash by her employer. Her decision to be honest and declare this money on her tax return, however, prevents her from saving as much money for retirement as she had hoped.

    D. Dana wants to run for governor, however she is unable to win her party's nomination and cannot secure enough signatures to get on the ballot as an independent candidate.

5. Which of the following is the BEST example of the *tossed salad theory* in action?

    A. Hispanics and African-Americans in a community talk about ways to coexist and respect one another's cultural differences.

    B. Students of various nationalities are all expected to learn and communicate in English at school.

    C. Supporters of a political cause decide that those with opposing views are unintelligent.

    D. The cultural majority in a certain country believes that any newcomers must adopt their ways or think seriously about returning to the countries from which they came.

6. Bernardo was born in the US, but his parents are immigrants from Peru. As he walks to school, he meets his friend, Christopher, who is Jamaican. A few blocks away, they pass a local Jewish synagogue and speak to the Rabbi, whom they know very well. Eventually, they reach the Catholic school that they both attend and play soccer with Michael who is Irish, Jose' who is Puerto Rican, and Alfonso, whose family has lived in the city for generations. Which of the following is MOST reflected by Bernardo's morning?

    A. discrimination

    B. nationality

    C. multiculturalism

    D. the impact of physical appearance

7. Which of the following are a pair of recurring problems in US society?
   A. multiculturalism and tolerance
   B. life long learning and discrimination
   C. self-determination and unemployment
   D. substance abuse and controversy over immigration

8. The belief that man-made pollution has created a blanket of gases that hovers above the earth, keeping in heat from the sun that would otherwise have escaped into space, is called what?
   A. *Melting pot theory*
   C. global warming
   B. "greenhouse effect"
   D. acid rain graft

9. Mary was born in St. Louis just a year and a half after her dad returned home from fighting in World War II. She eventually grew up, went to college, became a political activist in the 60s, and got married. After raising two children, she went on to have a satisfying career in teaching. Mary is now nearing the age of retirement. Mary is MOST likely what?
   A. Republican   B. moderate   C. a baby boomer   D. immigrant

10. Which of the following BEST describes someone exhibiting "effective citizenship"?
    A. A soccer mom usually speeds while driving because she is constantly trying to get her kids to activities.
    B. A father of four takes his kids with him to volunteer at a community center every other Saturday for three hours.
    C. A citizen throws cigarette butts into the neighborhood pond because there is no trash can available and he does not want to throw them in someone's yard.
    D. A mother won't let her kids play with the children of another family because the parents practice a different religion.

11. Amanda has long dreamed of starting her own business. She resigns from her well-paying job after securing a loan from the bank. She then throws all of her time and energy into making her business awesome! Amanda is experiencing what?
    A. an economic cycle
    B. the benefits of freedom to make her own social choices
    C. the benefits of freedom to pursue an economic opportunity
    D. the positive effects of compromise

12. Unfortunately, the business started by Amanda in question #11 fails. Amanda has spent large sums of time and money, as well as put her former career on hold while she tried to make her business work. Now, she must start over with very little. Amanda is experiencing what?
    A. self-determination
    B. consequences of freedom
    C. socio-economic liberty
    D. results of political activism

North Carolina Civics and Economics Practice Test 1

The purpose of this practice test is to measure your knowledge of civics and economics. This pretest is based on the **North Carolina Performance Standards** and adheres to the sample question format provided by the North Carolina Department of Education.

General Directions:

1. Read all directions carefully.

2. Read each question or sample. Then choose the best answer.

3. Choose only one answer for each question. If you change an answer, be sure to erase your original answer completely.

4. After taking the test, you or your instructor should score it using the answer key that accompanies this book. Then review and practice for the civics and economics skills tested on the End of Course Test.

1. If one desired to visit a colonial region in the 1600s that offered diversity, religious tolerance, and cities, then which of the following colonies would one have MOST LIKELY gone to?   1.1

   A   Virginia   C   Massachusetts
   B   North Carolina   D   New York

2. Which of the following is FALSE regarding African-Americans in colonial America?   1.1

   A   Many African-Americans arrived in North America by way of the Middle Passage.
   B   Most were slaves, although some occasionally bought their own freedom with money they earned.
   C   In Georgia and South Carolina, the numbers of African-Americans tended to be fewer than in colonies to the north because most blacks left to escape the plantation system.
   D   In the Middle colonies and New England, black slaves were often trained in a craft and put to work in cities and towns rather than on farms.

3. Which of the following represents a cost of jury duty?   4.7

   A   due process of law
   B   preventing a single judge from making decisions about guilt or innocence
   C   time away from family, work, and other pursuits
   D   having no voice in the criminal justice system

4. What is the central problem with which the study of economics is concerned?   7.1

   A   scarcity   C   selfishness
   B   excess   D   altruism

5. In what way did the various acts Parliament passed, such as the Stamp Act and the Intolerable Acts, lead to the colonies' decision to rebel against Great Britain?   1.3

   A   They upset the colonists because Parliament passed them without the king's consent.
   B   They offended the colonies because they did not offer the colonists the taxation without representation that they demanded.
   C   They outraged the colonists because Parliament passed these laws without granting them any representation in the legislative process.
   D   The colonists were angered because they felt that the laws did not go far enough to punish the French following the French and Indian War.

6. An election between candidates from opposing parties for the purpose of choosing one of them to hold a public office is called what?   4.2

   A   primary election
   B   general election
   C   run-off election
   D   recall election

7. Diana leads a political committee which consists of members of both major parties. In addition to party differences, even members of the same party have different views concerning the issue that the committee is facing. Diana must find a way to get everyone to agree enough to move forward with some kind of plan. Diana must engage in which one of the following?   5.1

   A   consensus building
   B   plea bargaining
   C   arbitration
   D   jurisprudence

8. Which of the following BEST describes the difference between "enumerated" and "implied" powers? 2.1

   A   Implied powers are the same as "expressed" powers, while enumerated powers are not clearly expressed.

   B   Implied powers are those powers granted to Congress, while enumerated powers are granted to the courts.

   C   Implied powers are powers assumed under the *Elastic Clause* rather than being specifically stated, while enumerated powers are specifically mentioned in the Constitution.

   D   Implied powers are not supported by the Constitution, whereas enumerated powers are.

9. DVD players are purchased by consumers in what kind of market? 8.3

   A   product market

   B   social market

   C   factor market

   D   mixed market

10. Together, Tim and Mary earn a combined income of $100,000/year. The fact that they decide what to buy, how much to save, and what to invest in shows that Tim and Mary enjoy what? 10.6

    A   socio-economic status

    B   the freedom of economic choices

    C   political freedom

    D   a spirit of entrepreneurship

11. Someone accused of a crime is entitled to due process of law and is protected from *double jeopardy* under which amendment to the Constitution? 1.7

    A   first   C   fifth

    B   third   D   sixth

12. The fact that the Democrats and the Republicans dominate US politics is evidence of what? 4.1

    A   These two parties have existed since the late 1700s.

    B   The US political system is a two-party system.

    C   The US is an absolute democracy.

    D   No third parties exist.

13. What do "freedom of speech", "freedom of the press", "the right to bear arms", and protection against "illegal searches and seizures" all have in common? 1.7

    A   Each is guaranteed in the Preamble to the Constitution.

    B   Each is guaranteed under Article I of the Constitution.

    C   Each is guaranteed in the *Declaration of Independence*.

    D   Each is guaranteed by the *Bill of Rights*.

14. How many senators does each state have in the US Senate? 2.2

    A   2 per state

    B   1 per state

    C   5 per state

    D   It differs from state to state because it depends on population.

15. *Jurisprudence* refers to which of the following? 6.1

    A   the study of law

    B   the study of government

    C   the practice of writing legal briefs

    D   the process by which jurors are selected for jury duty

16. A country's government consists of a 1.2 king, a legislative body with which he shares power, and various other officials. Although the king is the recognized head of state, the nation's constitution requires him to obey certain laws; he cannot do whatever he wants. The same is true for the legislative body and the other officials. Which of the following BEST describes this nation's government?

A   It is an absolute monarchy.

B   It is an oligarchy.

C   It relies on popular sovereignty.

D   It is a limited government.

17. A group of senators are faced with the 2.2 reality that a bill is about to be approved that they adamantly oppose. Although they lack enough votes to defeat the bill, they believe that they can prevent it from passing by one of them taking the floor and continuing to talk so that a vote cannot be called. This strategy is called what?

A   debate defense

B   talking point strategy

C   bill buster

D   filibuster

18. If two-thirds of the senators present vote 2.2 to end discussion on the bill, then debate is closed and the strategy used in #17 does not work. Voting to end debate on a bill in the US Senate by a two-thirds vote is called what?

A   filibuster   C   override

B   cloture   D   veto

19. The EPA has just fined a company sev- 6.2 eral thousand dollars for not following federal guidelines when dumping waste. This represents enforcement of what kind of law?

A   family   C   administrative

B   constitutional   D   tort

20. To stimulate the economy, the Federal 9.7 Reserve decides that the amount of money in circulation needs to increase. Which of the following actions will they be MOST LIKELY to take?

A   raise the reserve requirement

B   raise the discount rate

C   sell bonds

D   lower the reserve requirement

21. The president of the United States 2.2, 2.3 has been accused of violating the Constitution. There is a movement in Washington, DC to remove him/her from office. In order for this to happen, what process will have to occur?

A   The vice president will have to initiate a decree of impeachment. Once this occurs, if a majority of the House and the Senate agree that the president is guilty of the charges, then the president is removed.

B   The president must first be censured. The Senate must then vote on whether or not to impeach the president. If two-thirds of the Senate agrees, then the president is removed from office.

C   The House must bring formal charges against the president. The president then has the right to be heard before the Supreme Court. If the Court finds him/her guilty, then he/she will be removed from office.

D   The House must vote to impeach the president. Once this occurs, the case is then heard in the Senate. Because it is the president, the chief justice will preside over the proceedings. If two-thirds of the Senate finds that the president is guilty, then he/she is removed from office.

22. A system in which power is shared 1.6 between the federal and state governments is referred to as what?

A   federalism

B   bi-partisan government

C   checks and balances

D   separation of powers

23. Which government body/individual has the power to block treaties and presidential appointments? 2.2

    A   the vice president

    B   the US Senate

    C   the House of Representatives

    D   the Supreme Court

24. Under the *Twenty-second Amendment*, how many terms may the president serve? 2.4

    A   One

    B   Two

    C   Three

    D   As many as he/she wants, but no more than two of them may be consecutive.

"Although both houses of Congress have seen fit to pass this bill and send it to the Oval Office for my signature, I cannot sign it. I believe that it is not in the best interest of the American people and I, therefore, am returning it to Capitol Hill. I challenge Congress to come up with a better bill, since I know they do not have the votes necessary to override my decision."

---

25. The above quote is MOST LIKELY from whom? 2.2

    A   the president of the United States

    B   the chief justice of the Supreme Court

    C   the president pro tempore

    D   the speaker of the House

26. Under the US Constitution, certain powers are granted to the president, certain powers to Congress, and still others to the federal courts. This is an example of what? 1.6

    A   federalism

    B   ex post facto government

    C   separation of powers

    D   judicial review

27. The power of *judicial review* refers to the courts's authority to do what? 2.3

    A   declare laws passed by Congress and/or state legislatures unconstitutional

    B   pass laws

    C   impeach the president and/or other puiblic officials

    D   appoint judges

28. In which of the following cases did the Supreme Court rule that a state authorizing the reading of an official school prayer violates the *First Amendment*? 2.6

    A   *Mapp v. Ohio*

    B   *Gibbons v. Ogden*

    C   *Engel v. Vitale*

    D   *Hazelwood v. Kuhlmeier*

29. In which of the following ways are the US Constitution and the NC Constitution DISSIMILAR? 3.1

    A   The US Constitution establishes three branches of government, whereas the NC Constitution only establishes two branches.

    B   The US Constitution grants the president the power to appoint judges, whereas the NC Constitution states that judges shall be elected.

    C   The US Constitution gives military authority to the president, whereas the governor is given no military powers under the NC Constitution.

    D   Amendments can be added to the US Constitution, but there is no process for changing the NC Constitution.

30. The section of the NC Constitution that is MOST similar to the *Bill of Rights* is known as what? 3.1

    A   NC Bill of Rights

    B   NC Articles of Liberty

    C   Declaration of Rights

    D   Article III

31. Jerry has just assumed public office as the head of a particular department of state government. He got the job because he was directly elected to the post by the people of North Carolina. Jerry is part of what? 3.2

A the governor's cabinet

B the Council of State

C the General Assembly

D the judicial branch of state government

32. Melinda is also a new department head. However, Melinda was appointed by the governor rather than elected. Melinda is part of what? 3.2

A the governor's cabinet

B the Council of State

C the General Assembly

D the judicial branch of state government

33. *Green Way* is an organization devoted to protecting the environment. Because they want to ensure that legislation is put in place to prevent pollution, maintain forests, etc. they hire Walter to meet with members of Congress in an attempt to influence votes. Which of the following is true? 4.4

A *Green Way* is a political party and Walter its nominee for office

B *Green Way* is a lobbying firm and Walter its representative

C *Green Way* is an interest group and Walter a lobbyist

D *Green Way* is an interest group and Walter a legislator

34. Which court case helped establish the NC Constitution as being the highest legal authority in the state? 3.5

A *State v. Mann*

B *State v. Marbury*

C *State v. Madison*

D *State v. Plessy*

35. A model of local government in which an elected council hires a manager to oversee the day-to-day administration of city government is called what? 3.2

A mayor-council plan

B council-manager plan

C manager administration plan

D county commission plan

36. The idea that state government must meet its constitutional obligations to its citizens is reinforced by which of the following? 3.5

A The US Supreme Court's decision in *Leandro v. US*

B The NC Supreme Court's decision in *State v. Mann*

C The NC Supreme Court's decision in the *Leandro Case*

D The *Nineteenth Amendment*

37. Someone promoting the "melting pot" theory would most likely support which one of the following statements? 10.2

A "Now that these Latino immigrants have arrived in the United States, they should learn English and try their best to assimilate to the American way of life."

B "Traditional events, such as our town's Christmas parade, should be modified to acknowledge Hanukkah and Kwanzaa, as well."

C "America is best served when we embrace and celebrate our differences."

D "Racism is not a problem in America."

38. What type of income is normally earned by labor? 7.2

A wages   C services

B interest   D goods

39. How many representatives does each state have in the House of Representatives?   2.2

A 2 per state

B 1 per state

C 5 per state

D It differs from state to state because it depends on population.

> "I oppose this action on moral grounds. I do not believe it is right to raise money by exploiting and playing on the fears of the lower classes; who, in vain hope, will lose dollar after dollar in an attempt to beat the odds and ease all their financial woes overnight. How sad it is that the state government of North Carolina has, in effect, become a bookie."

40. The above quote is most likely opposing what?   3.7

A legislative initiative

B charter school education

C state lottery

D regressive taxes

41. In an attempt to help improve schools, the federal government gives the state of North Carolina an education grant. This is an example of what?   3.8

A a federal loan

B a federal bond

C a user fee

D intergovernmental revenue

42. The stage of the business cycle in which the economy is headed towards its peak is known as what?   9.1

A expansion   C recession

B inflation   D contraction

43. When the Republicans meet for their national convention, which of the following actions will they NOT take?   4.1

A nominate a candidate for president

B nominate a candidate for vice president

C hold a primary election

D come up with a list of programs and policies to pursue once the party's candidates are in office.

44. The countries of Tilio and Maximo sign an agreement in which they agree to defend each other if either nation is attacked by an enemy. They also agree not to tax goods imported from the other's country. Finally, they both decide not to trade at all with the country of Sturbo because of that nation's failure to abide by international agreements. Which of the following statements is true?   9.5

A Tilio and Maximo have an embargo with one another in which they have agreed to halt all foreign trade and impose tariffs on Sturbo.

B Tilio and Maximo have agreed to a tariff on each other's products but refused to extend the same tariff to Sturbo.

C Tilio and Maximo have a treaty with one another that eliminates tariffs and imposes an embargo against Sturbo.

D Tilio and Maximo have signed a treaty in which they have sanctioned tariffs with one another and lifted an embargo against Sturbo.

45. A large company has been accused of engaging in false advertising and not fully revealing the possible safety hazards of using their product. Which government organization is MOST LIKELY to investigate these allegations?   6.3

A FCC   C ICC

B CPSC   D FBI

46. Which of the following statements BEST describes how the president of the United States is elected? 4.2

A Whichever candidate gets the most votes nationwide wins.

B Whichever candidate wins a majority vote in the most states wins.

C Whichever candidate wins a majority of votes in the Electoral College wins.

D Whichever candidate wins the most states in the Electoral College wins.

47. In 1941, Japan attacked the US Pacific Fleet anchored at Pearl Harbor. The next day, President Franklin D. Roosevelt went before Congress to ask that Congress declare war on Japan. The fact that Congress has the power to declare war on behalf of US citizens demonstrates that the United States government is which of the following? 1.2

A a republic   C an aristocracy

B a democracy   D an autocracy

48. Which of the following MOST accurately defines the three branches of US government? 2.1

A Congress is the legislative branch, the House of Representatives is the judicial branch, and the president is the executive branch.

B The president heads the executive branch, Congress is the legislative branch, and the federal courts are the judicial branch.

C The federal government is the executive branch, the states are responsible for the legislative branch, and the courts are the judicial branch.

D The Supreme Court is the executive branch, the president is the legislative branch, and Congress is the judicial branch.

49. Marco applies for work at a local business but does not get the job. He later learns that he did not get hired because he is over 60 and the employer is worried that, because of his age, he would miss too much work. Marco is the victim of what? 10.2

A multiculturalism   C ageism

B racism   D gender bias

50. Pablo's congressional campaign has just launched a series of ads. Half of the ads feature his past accomplishments and talk about his patriotism. The other half criticize his opponent and accuse her of misusing public funds. ALL of Pablo's ads are examples of what? 4.2

A negative campaigning

B positive campaigning

C canvassing

D propaganda

51. Which of the following is least associated with costs of running for public office? 4.7

A loss of privacy

B time commitments

C being the target of political attacks

D having to join PACs

52. Dart Industries has been forced to close one of its largest plants and layoff a large number of workers. As a result, not only have Dart employees suffered, but so have many of the business owners and service providers who did most of their business with people who worked at the plant. Both the Dart employees and the surrounding community are experiencing what? 9.4

A the effects of economic expansion

B the effects of downsizing

C the effects of outsourcing

D the effects of price controls

53. Which of the following is a fiscal policy that a Keynesian economist might suggest to avert an economic slow-down? 7.6

    A   increasing taxes

    B   increasing the reserve requirement

    C   printing more currency

    D   increasing deficit spending

54. Sophie and Adam are attorneys representing opposing parties in a civil dispute. After a meeting between the two, Sophie's client agrees to receive somewhat less than what she originally asked for in damages, while Adam's client agrees to pay more than he was originally willing and accepts moving to a different neighborhood. Rather than going to court, this case was resolved in what way? 4.9

    A   arbitration

    B   pre-hearing settlement

    C   plea bargain

    D   mediation

55. In the chart below, which courts should fill in boxes X and Y? 5.2

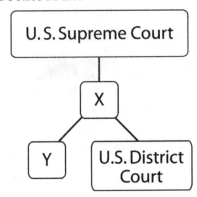

    A   Y = NC Supreme Court, X = US Court of Appeals

    B   Y = NC Court of Appeals, X = NC Supreme Court

    C   Y = US Special Courts, X = US Court of Appeals

    D   Y = US Court of Appeals, X = US Special Courts

56. The role of the judge in an "adversarial system" is MOST like which of the following? 5.3

    A   a coach standing on the sideline while his team plays the game

    B   an umpire in a baseball game, making sure that both teams compete according to the rules

    C   a quarterback, cunningly leading his team downfield

    D   a fan, hoping to see a great game

57. Law enforcement officials are required to have what before they can legally make an arrest? 5.3

    A   an indictment

    B   a summons or a subpoena

    C   evidence

    D   a warrant or probable cause

58. Which statement would an Anti-federalist have MOST agreed with? 1.6

    A   "We must accept the fact that a strong central government is essential to the nation's survival. It is in the hands of a strong president and an empowered legislative branch that our nation will rest the most secure."

    B   "We must not sacrifice state's rights, lest we invite a new tyranny. Likewise, we must not pass this proposed Constitution; that is unless, at the very least, amendments are added securing the rights of citizens."

    C   "Alexander Hamilton's ideas about government are correct."

    D   "The Constitution needs no amending. The rights of citizens are understood and implied in the document."

59. Controversy over the PATRIOT Act is one example of the conflict that sometimes exists between what? 2.7

    A   terrorism and law enforcement

    B   state and federal law enforcement

    C   national defense and domestic spending

    D   national defense and civil liberties

60. Francine shoots and kills her boyfriend. 5.3
However, because the boyfriend has a
history of abusive behavior and was high on
crack at the time, the prosecutor allows Francine to plead guilty to manslaughter rather
than trying her for murder. Francine has benefited from what?

A   the *Second Amendment*
B   a plea bargain
C   an arraignment
D   a pre-hearing settlement

61. Which of the following statements is 5.4
true regarding differences in how the
Senate and the House pass bills?

A   The House only needs a majority vote
in favor of a bill for it to pass, whereas
the Senate requires a two-thirds vote.

B   The Senate requires that a bill go to a
"rules committee" before it goes to the
floor for a vote, whereas the House has
no such committee.

C   Senators may block a vote on a bill
with a filibuster, but representatives
don't have this option.

D   Representatives have been known to
attach riders to bills, whereas senators
are prohibited from such action.

62. An election in which members of the 4.2
same party face one another for the purpose of deciding who will be the party's
nominee for a particular office is called
what?

A   primary election
B   general election
C   run-off election
D   recall election

63. When the president blocks a bill by 5.4
refusing to take action because he/she
knows Congress is not in session, this is
called what?

A   line item veto
B   pocket veto
C   executive privilege
D   executive order

64. Which of the following legal codes 6.1
demonstrates how the ancient Greeks
played a role in the formation of US law?

A   Draconian Laws
B   Justinian Codes
C   Magna Carta
D   Code of Hammurabi

65. Methods which the government can use 6.5
to keep citizens informed include which
of the following?

A   conducting closed sessions
B   speaking in "glittering generalities"
C   engaging in public debate
D   ignoring fiscal policies

66. Which of the following do not have lob- 6.6
byist who work on their behalf?

A   business.   C   doctors.
B   teachers.   D   think tanks.

67. Someone who believes strongly that the 6.8
primary function of the criminal justice
system is to provide retribution would
MOST LIKELY favor which of the following policies?

A   more paroles for prisoners who have
behaved themselves while incarcerated
B   increased use of the death penalty for
those convicted of serious crimes
C   abolishing capital punishment
D   more tax dollars spent on drug rehab
for those in jail

68. When economists monitor the state of 9.1
the economy by keeping track of
changes in the prices of goods and services
typically purchased by consumers, they are
using what economic indicator?

A   gross domestic product
B   per capita gross domestic product
C   stock market
D   consumer price index

69. The United States Census Bureau records that, in recent decades, many people have left the Northeast and Upper Midwest and moved to the South and western states. Numbers also show that many new arrivals from Latin America have helped to increase the populations of these regions as well. Together, these trends suggest what? *9.3*

   A migration

   B immigration

   C population shift

   D a "baby boom"

70. Sam is arrested and charged with attempting to murder a local businessman. Which of the following is true regarding Sam's case? *5.2*

   A state district court will have original jurisdiction, while state superior court will have appellate jurisdiction.

   B because it is a serious charge, it will be tried in federal court.

   C state superior court will have original jurisdiction with the US District Court having appellate jurisdiction.

   D state superior court will have original jurisdiction with the NC Court of Appeals being the first court in line to have appellate jurisdiction.

71. The country of Tilio exports 20% more than it imports on average each year. By comparison, the nation of Maximo imports 10% more than it exports. Which of the following statements is true? *9.5*

   A Tilio has a better exchange rate than Maximo.

   B Tilio enjoys a favorable balance of trade, while Maximo experiences an unfavorable balance of trade.

   C Tilio has an unfavorable balance of trade while Maximo's is favorable.

   D Tilio's exchange rate is less favorable than Maximo's.

72. The nation of Indaraga is incredibly poor. It has very little infrastructure and the national standard of living is much lower than most nations. Indaraga is BEST described as what? *9.5*

   A a command economy

   B a developed nation

   C a developing nation

   D an insignificant nation

73. Which of the following is associated with criminal, rather than civil, court? *4.5*

   A summons   C penal code

   B plaintiff   D lawsuits

74. Congress approves a budget that allocates how much money will be spent on defense, education, social programs, etc. Their plan also calls for an increase in taxes to help pay for all the expenses. This plan defines what? *9.7*

   A the government's monetary policy

   B the government's fiscal policy

   C the government's revenue

   D the government's reserve requirement

75. Margaret has just received a $3000 bonus from work that she was not expecting. Being a very practical person, Margaret does some research and notices that interest rates are currently very high. Because Margaret wants to get as much return from her money as possible, she will be MOST LIKELY to do which of the following? *9.7*

   A She will save her money in a demand deposit account.

   B She will save her money in a time deposit account.

   C She will spend her money while she has enough to pay cash rather than using a credit card.

   D She will spend her money and borrow more before interest rates drop.

76. Which of the following is a modern innovation that has increased productivity? 7.4

A   natural resources

B   the assembly line

C   interest groups

D   opportunity costs

77. Nations that are the target of embargoes are forced to deal with which of the following? 9.8

A   increased scarcity

B   falling prices

C   lower tariffs

D   more foreign competition

78. Which of the following tends to have a positive effect on the economy? 9.8

A   "bull markets"

B   recession

C   environmental disaster

D   embargoes

79. Which of the following is an example of fulfilling civic responsibilities? 10.1

A   A school teacher decides to run for the office of county commissioner.

B   A young couple begins setting aside money for their infant daughter's college education.

C   A banker approves a loan to a charity.

D   A nurse works overtime to pay off some of her debt.

80. Someone who is politically active in environmental causes would be MOST concerned about which of the following? 10.5

A   taxation

B   national security

C   the business cycle

D   the "greenhouse effect"

81. Sylvia and Roman were born in the early 1950s, raised kids in the 70s and 80s, and today are nearing retirement. Sylvia and Roman can BEST be described as what? 10.5

A   lobbyists

B   activists

C   baby boomers

D   Republicans

82. Which of the following is not a characteristic of "effective citizenship"? 10.4

A   apathy

B   volunteerism

C   patriotism

D   paying taxes

83. Which of the following sets of terms can best be used to fill in the blank spaces in the following sentence? "Sarah put her money in a _____ so that she can withdraw it and use it whenever she wanted, but Jennifer put her money in a _____ to earn a higher interest rate, although she will not be able to withdraw it for 5 years." 8.8

A   demand deposit, time deposit

B   pension fund, commercial bank

C   government bond, checking account

D   credit union, savings and loan

> *"Before Congress passed this law, we could take action to penalize workers who joined a union—you know, discourage them. It worked, too. But now they have a legal right to unionize, and there's nothing we can do! I don't know how good this whole 'collective bargaining' idea is going to be for us manufacturers. Now they want us to go before this Board they set up to 'mediate' our disputes. I guess it's a new world now."*

84. To which of the following laws is the above quote MOST LIKELY referring? 8.7

A Social Security Act of 1935

B National Labor Relations Act of 1935

C Fair Labor Standards Act of 1938

D Taft-Hartley Act of 1947

85. Which of the following allows consumers to defer payment until a later date? 8.9

A currency

B demand deposits

C checks

D credit

86. Senator Harksten fears that flower growers in his state cannot afford to stay in business given the low price for tulips. He proposes that lawmakers establish a minimum price for tulips that is above the current equilibrium price. Which of the following would BEST describe this law and its effect? 8.5

A It is a price ceiling that will cause a surplus.

B It is a price floor that will cause a surplus.

C It is a price ceiling that will cause a shortage.

D It is a price floor that will cause a shortage.

87. Which of the following is the BEST description of a political party? 4.1

A They are factions that either favor or oppose taxes.

B They are interest groups that feel strongly about social issues.

C They are organizations that promote political beliefs and sponsor candidates for political office.

D They are action committees that focus on national politics rather than state and local offices.

88. A tax that increases the more one's income rises is called what? 3.8

A regressive tax

B proportional tax

C progressive tax

D excise tax

89. Lola is selling *Happy Teen* magazine at her school to raise money for a trip to Washington, DC. The marginal cost of each magazine she buys is $2.00, and the price she sells them for is $5.00. Yesterday, she got a letter in the mail saying that the magazine was raising its cost per magazine from $2.00 to $3.50. Today, Mrs. Ibarra pulls Lola aside and informs her that, from now on, she will only be allowed to sell the magazine for $3.25 at school. What has happened to Lola's incentive to produce? 7.3

A She will have less incentive to produce because the higher marginal cost lowers her profits.

B She will have more incentive to produce because she will sell more at the lower prices and make more profits.

C Her incentive to produce will remain unchanged because she still wants to go to Washington, DC.

D She will have no incentive to produce because with the change in marginal cost and price, she will be losing money on each magazine.

90. Which of the following sets of terms can can best be used to fill in the blank spaces in the following sentence? "Market economies are known for their _____ in production, whereas command economies produce less goods but have greater _____ in distributing them." 8.1

A efficiency, equity
B private property, laissez-faire
C laissez-faire, private property
D equity, efficiency

91. Which of the following is the assumption of a market economy as promoted by Karl Marx? 7.6

A The means of production will be privately owned.
B Transactions will be voluntary on both the part of the buyer and the seller and government restrictions will be minimal.
C There will be many buyers and sellers all trying to make a profit and get what they want.
D Wealth and resources will be distributed according to need, not ability.

92. Cecilia owns a coffee shop herself, but her shop is part of a national chain which supplies her with products, trains her employees, and gives her name-brand recognition. In return, she pays the chain a fee and agrees to abide by certain rules and guidelines. What type of business does Cecilia own? 8.7

A cooperative   C partnership
B sole proprietor-   D franchise
  ship

93. If the income of consumers declines, what will be the most likely effect on the equilibrium price and quantity of candy produced? 8.4

A Both price and quantity produced will decline.
B Both price and quantity produced will rise.
C Prices will rise but quantity produced will decline.
D Prices will decline but quantity produced will rise.

94. Jeffrey earns a salary of $4,000 per month. He pays $1,500 in income tax, spends $900 on rent, $500 on his car and its insurance, $500 on food, and $200 on entertainment and other. He puts $200 in savings. What is Jeffrey's disposable income? 8.4

A $200   C $2500
B $400   D $4000

95. Which of the following sets of terms can best be used to fill in the blank spaces in the following sentence? "Sole proprietorships have the drawback of _____, while corporations have the advantage of _____." 8.7

A partners, shareholders
B limited life, unlimited life
C limited liability, unlimited liability
D stocks, dividends

96. Douglas owns a cherry orchard. Unfortunately, last February one of his cherry pickers fell off a ladder and broke her collarbone. She decided to sue Douglas because it happened on his property! What kind of insurance is designed to cover Douglas in this situation? 8.8

A life insurance
B medical insurance
C comprehensive liability insurance
D federal deposit insurance

97. A colony founded by a religious group in search of freedom from persecution would be considered which of the following? 1.1

A   a royal colony

B   a self-governing/charter colony

C   a legislative colony

D   a church colony

98. Which of the following BEST describes the role played by the House of Burgesses? 1.2

A   It established a representative form of government in New England.

B   It was the Middle Colonies' first body of representative government.

C   It was the colonies' first representative body of government.

D   If ignited the American Revolution by taxing the colonies without representation.

99. In order for the Constitution to be amended, which of the following must happen? 2.4

A   Either both houses of Congress must pass the proposed amendment and the amendment must be ratified by three-fourths of the states, or a constitutional convention must approve the amendment prior to it being ratified by three-fourths of the states.

B   Both houses of Congress must pass the proposed amendment by a two-thirds vote; the amendment must then be ratified by a majority of the states.

C   Both houses of Congress must pass the proposed amendment, it must be signed by the president, ruled constitutional by the Supreme Court, and ratified by three-fourths of the states.

D   Two-thirds of the states must call a constitutional convention.

100. Jack is a mechanic. He hires an assistant and finds that his profits increase by 60%. He hires another, and his profits increase by 30%. He hires a third assistant, and his profits increase by only 10%. Jack realizes his output versus input ratio is decreasing. He is experiencing what? 7.5

A   the invisible hand

B   the Producer Price Index

C   the law of diminishing returns

D   the benefit of education and training

North Carolina Civics and Economics
Practice Test 2

The purpose of this practice test is to measure your knowledge of civics and economics. This pretest is based on the **North Carolina Performance Standards** and adheres to the sample question format provided by the North Carolina Department of Education.

General Directions:

1. Read all directions carefully.

2. Read each question or sample. Then choose the best answer.

3. Choose only one answer for each question. If you change an answer, be sure to erase your original answer completely.

4. After taking the test, you or your instructor should score it using the answer key that accompanies this book. Then review and practice for the civics and economics skills tested on the End of Course Test.

"Their place in history is interesting. On the one hand, they founded the great colony of Massachusetts and gave us the Mayflower Compact as an early model of government. On the other hand, they themselves could be violently intolerant of other religious beliefs and even hanged people they believed to be witches."

1. What group is the above quote talking about?   1.1

   A   colonial Catholics
   B   the Puritans
   C   the Quakers
   D   founders of Jamestown

2. The United States government most closely resembles which of the following?   1.2

   A   the democracy of ancient Athens
   B   the constitutional monarchy of England
   C   the multi-party system of many of the world's democracies
   D   the republic of ancient Rome

3. Substance abuse, discrimination, disease, and how to deal with illegal immigration are all what?   10.5

   A   results of economic recession
   B   recurring problems in US society
   C   issues on which most citizens agree
   D   problems caused by a market economy

4. Which of the following is necessary to ensure "domestic tranquility?"   4.5

   A   criminal laws
   B   anarchy
   C   mass media
   D   two-party system

5. In what way did the First Great Awakening help shape the *Bill of Rights*?   1.4

   A   It helped establish separation of church and state as a valued principle because passionate preachers challenged many traditional views of what it means to be a Christian.
   B   It helped establish freedom of the press as a crucial right because colonists like John Peter Zenger began printing stories critical of the government for the first time.
   C   Because it was a movement that called for independence, it advocated strong local militias to resist British forces. This eventually led to an amendment guaranteeing the right of citizens to bear arms.
   D   Because it was a philosophical movement that introduced new ideas about government and the rights of citizens, it provided the inspiration for drafting the *Bill of Rights* in order to protect the natural rights of citizens.

6. The "Great Compromise" and the Three-fifths Compromise differed in what way?   1.5

   A   The Great Compromise dealt with how states would be represented in Congress, whereas the Three-fifths Compromise addressed the slave trade.
   B   The Great Compromise addressed the slave trade, whereas the Three-fifths Compromise addressed how states would be represented in Congress.
   C   The Great Compromise addressed how states would be represented in Congress, whereas the Three-fifths Compromise addressed how slaves would be counted in the population.
   D   The Great Compromise addressed the slave trade, whereas the Three-fifths Compromise addressed how slaves would be counted in the population.

7. Someone claiming that the government had passed a law violating the separation between church and state would MOST LIKELY use which of the following as the basis for their claim? **1.7**

A the *Third Amendment*

B the *Establishment Clause*

C the *Necessary and Proper Clause*

D the *Freedom of Faith Clause*

8. Which of the following represents the correct order in which each section appears in the Constitution? **2.1**

A the role and powers of Congress, the role and powers of the president, the Preamble, the *Bill of Rights*, the role of the courts.

B the Preamble, the role and powers of Congress, the *Bill of Rights*

C the *Bill of Rights*, Articles I – III, the Preamble

D the role and powers of the president, the role and powers of Congress, the role and powers of the courts.

9. Which of the following can BEST be described as the federal court systems "trial courts" for criminal and civil cases? **5.2**

A US District Courts

B US Special Courts

C US Circuit Courts

D US Court of Federal Claims

10. Parker is a member of the party that currently controls the House of Representatives. His job is to make sure that party members vote the way the House leadership wants them to. Parker is what? **2.2**

A the minority whip

B the majority whip

C the minority leader

D the majority leader

11. Which of the following is a role of the speaker of the House? **2.2**

A chief diplomat

B commander-in-chief of the armed forces

C leader of his/her party

D appoints committee chairpersons

12. A case comes before the US Supreme Court in which a criminal defendant convicted in US District Court claims she is entitled to a new trial. She claims that FBI agents did not adequately inform her of her rights during their investigation. After hearing the appeal, four of the justices issue an opinion agreeing with the defendant and stating why they believe she is entitled to a new trial. Each of the remaining justices, however, rule that the conviction should stand. Which of the following statements is true concerning the first four justices' opinion? **2.2**

A It is a minority opinion because more justices ruled that the conviction stands than voted to overturn it.

B It is a split opinion, meaning that the other four justices have voted to uphold the conviction.

C It is a majority opinion and her conviction is therefore overturned.

D It is a concurrent opinion.

13. Which of the following cases reversed *Plessy v. Ferguson* and marked the beginning of the end for segregation in schools? **2.5**

A *Brown v. Board of Education of Topeka*

B *Swann v. Charlotte-Mecklenburg Board of Education*

C *Texas v. Johnso*n

D *Engel v. Vitale*

14. The government puts forth a budget for the upcoming year of $5 billion. In actuality, the government ends up spending money on additional programs in the amount of $3 billion. This means that the overall expenditures equal $8 billion while revenue still equaled $5 billion. This adds to the $55 billion that the government already owed entering the year. Which of the following statements is NOT accurate? 2.8

  A The budget deficit equals $8 billion.
  B The national debt equals $58 billion
  C The government engaged in deficit spending during the year
  D The government failed to maintain a balanced budget

15. Which of the following statements regarding the North Carolina Constitution is false? 3.1

  A It is a flexible document.
  B It can be changed by means of either a constitutional convention or legislative initiative.
  C There have actually been three NC constitutions.
  D All changes are attached to the end of the document as amendments.

16. Of the following colonies, which one was LEAST likely to raise tobacco? 1.1

  A North Carolina   C Virginia
  B New York   D Maryland

17. Which of the following bodies of state government MOST resembles the US Congress? 3.1

  A General Assembly
  B Council of State
  C SBI
  D NC House of Legislators

18. Which of the following would a student of jurisprudence be LEAST LIKELY to study? 6.1

  A ancient legal codes
  B the Magna Carta
  C a majority opinion of the Supreme Court
  D grassroots campaign efforts

19. Which of the following is a defining characteristic of a traditional economy? 8.1

  A The means of production are privately owned by the producer.
  B Production is centrally planned by the government.
  C The government sets all prices.
  D The status quo is generally maintained.

20. Paula serves as a law enforcement officer in North Carolina. She works for a department headed by the county's top law enforcement official who is elected every four years. During her ten years with the department, she has worked in the jail, as a courtroom bailiff, and currently serves both criminal warrants and civil orders of the court. Paula works for which law enforcement agency? 3.2

  A police department
  B highway patrol
  C sheriff's department
  D SBI

21. What was established in the case of *State v. Mann* in 1830? 3.5

  A The NC Constitution is the highest legal authority in the state.
  B Residents may sue the state if it fails to fulfill its constitutional responsibilities.
  C The *Bill of Rights* applies to state residents as well.
  D It made slavery illegal in North Carolina.

22. Which of the following taxes can state and/or local government not impose? 3.8
    A sales tax
    C tariffs
    B income tax
    D property tax

23. Which of the following is an example of a personal rather than civic, responsibility? 10.1
    A volunteering for community projects and/or charities
    B going to church
    C obeying local laws
    D educating oneself about important issues

24. Max believes that the government should be very active. He favors more spending and higher taxes to fund important social programs and government run services. Nick strongly disagrees. He thinks that government is best when it remains small and limited in scope. He favors fewer taxes and wants to cut social programs. Donna falls somewhere in between the two, favoring some programs, but also wanting to see government made smaller and more efficient. Which of the following statements BEST describe Max, Nick, and Donna? 4.1
    A Max is conservative, Nick is liberal, Donna is moderate
    B Max is liberal, Nick is moderate, Donna is conservative
    C Max is liberal, Nick is conservative, Donna is moderate
    D Max is a Democrat, Nick a Republican, and Donna an independent

25. The US operates on which of the following party systems? 4.1
    A one-party
    C multi-party
    B two-party
    D free-party

26. At the Republican National Convention, the party delegates nominate Bob Walker for president, Annie Green for vice president, and pass a list of policies the party supports. Among these are longer prison sentences, stricter guidelines governing abortion, increased military spending, and lower corporate taxes. Which of the following is an accurate statement? 4.1
    A Bob is the Republican candidate for president and lowering corporate taxes is the party's platform.
    B Annie obviously came in second in the Republican primaries and therefore is automatically the party's vice presidential candidate.
    C The list of policies that the party passes is the party platform and increased military spending is a plank.
    D Bob and Annie are considered the Republican platform for the election and the list of policies the party passes is considered the party's plank.

27. A good that is used in place of another good to meet the same need is called what? 8.4
    A complementary good
    B capital good
    C substitute good
    D consumer good

28. Governor Mirminghill has been accused of inappropriate—although not illegal—behavior while in office. In addition, his policies have sent the state into a financial crisis. As a result, the voters call a special election to decide whether or not to remove him from office and, if so, to choose a replacement. Governor Mirminghill must face what? 4.2
    A an electoral college
    B a recall election
    C a run-off election
    D a referendum

29. The state of North Carolina has 15 votes 4.2
    in the Electoral College. In the presi-
    dential election, the Democratic candidate
    wins 50% of the vote, the Republican candi-
    date wins 44% of the vote, and the remain-
    ing 6% is split between two additional
    candidates. How are North Carolina' elec-
    toral votes allotted?

    A   The Democrat gets all 15 electoral
         votes.

    B   The Democrat gets 50% of the electoral
         votes, the Republican 44%, and the two
         additional candidates split the remain-
         ing 6%.

    C   The Democrat gets the 50% he/she
         won, plus the 6% won by the two bot-
         tom candidates.

    D   Before any electoral votes can be
         awarded, the Democrat and Republican
         will first have to meet in a run-off elec-
         tion.

30. Which of the following is a strategy 4.2
    used by political candidates during a
    campaign?

    A   annexation
    B   limited government
    C   affirmative action
    D   "stacking cards"

31. The case of John Peter Zenger, 1.3
    England's *writs of assistance* before the
    revolution, and Britain's decision to seize
    arms and ammunition stored by private citi-
    zens at Concord, Massachusetts, each con-
    tributed to what in 1789?

    A   Shay's Rebellion
    B   the *Treaty of Paris*
    C   the *Bill of Rights*
    D   the selection of George Washington as
         commander of the American army.

32. Maggie and Jim lead a group that is 4.4
    devoted to protecting the rights of senior
    citizens. They sponsor programs to educate
    the public about issues that concern seniors,
    raise money, and actively campaign for can-
    didates that support their causes. Recently,
    they got over 10,000 people to sign a docu-
    ment calling for a change in government pol-
    icy. Their group is also big enough that they
    were able to hire the Detmar Group to help
    them influence legislation in the General
    Assembly and Congress. Which of the fol-
    lowing statements is true?

    A   Maggie and Jim lead an interest group
         and the Detmar Group is a PAC.

    B   Maggie and Jim are lobbyists and the
         document they got signed is a petition.

    C   Maggie and Jim lead a PAC, the docu-
         ment they got signed is a referendum,
         and the Detmar Group is an interest
         group.

    D   Maggie and Jim lead an interest group,
         the document they got people to sign is
         a petition, and the Detmar Group is a
         lobbying firm.

33. The study of how firms, nations, and 7.1
    individuals can best allocate their lim-
    ited resources is called what?

    A   circular economic activity
    B   economics
    C   factoring production
    D   supply and demand analysis

34. Brent sues Margaret for $10,000. Which 4.5
    of the following is a true statement?

    A   Brent is the plaintiff in a criminal case.
    B   Margaret is the plaintiff in a civil case.
    C   Brent seeks damages of $10,000.
    D   If she loses, Margaret will have to pay a
         fine of $10,000.

35. Which of the following BEST describes an "informed electorate"? 4.7

 A Voters are aware of current laws/government policies and understand their effects on the world around them.

 B Voters turn out in large numbers to vote on Election Day.

 C Citizens are informed who won an election the same day that they voted.

 D Voters fail to go to the polls in large numbers because they lack confidence in government leaders.

36. Which of the following is a private act rather than a public service? 4.7

 A jury duty

 B filing a lawsuit

 C volunteering at a local VA hospital

 D serving as an alderman

"We must cut taxes imposed on producers! This gives business greater incentive to produce, more money to spend, and more ability to hire workers and invest in capital. This pumps money into the economy. Eventually, it has a 'trickle down effect' that benefits everyone."

---

37. The above quote is advocating what? 8.5

 A supply-side economics

 B deficit spending

 C liberal tax policies

 D increased government revenue

38. Pat and Lin have a dispute to settle. In order to avoid the long process of going through the legal system, they agree to allow a third party to come in and help them resolve their conflict. To take it a step further, they even agree to give the third party authority to reach a decision that will be legally binding on both of them. Pat and Lin are settling their dispute through what method? 4.9

 A mediation   C negotiation

 B collaboration   D arbitration

39. Rick is arrested and charged with a crime. His case is tried in NC superior court and he is found guilty. However, due to alleged improprieties in the case, Rick's attorneys appeal to the NC Court of Appeals. Rick's conviction is upheld, so it is then appealed to the NC Supreme Court. After hearing the case, the NC Supreme Court also upholds the conviction. Which of the following statements is true? 5.2

 A The superior court and the NC Court of Appeals have original jurisdiction, while the NC Supreme Court has appellate jurisdiction.

 B Rick cannot appeal any more since he has already appealed to the highest court in the state.

 C The NC Court of Appeals exercised appellate jurisdiction in the case

 D The superior court and the NC Court of Appeals have concurrent jurisdiction.

40. David is upset because he has to pay taxes to both the federal government and the state of North Carolina. Both the state and the national government have the authority to impose taxes. This is an example of which of the following? 2.1

 A concurrent powers

 B delegated powers

 C reserved powers

 D implied powers

41. Gerald is furious! His friend, Betty, was 5.3 assaulted, raped, and robbed at gunpoint. Now, the man convicted of the crime has just been granted a new trial because the police searched his car without probable cause during the investigation. Gerald is outraged by the decision because he feels that the criminal justice system goes further to protect those who commit crimes than it does to protect people like Betty. Gerald's frustration can BEST be described as what?

A   anger that the police are incompetent

B   anger that the courts discriminate

C   anger that the rights of criminals seem to be more important than the rights of victims

D   anger that the defense attorney pointed out the police department's mistake.

42. Which of the following statements is 3.2 true regarding the governor of North Carolina?

A   He/she alone constitutes the state's executive branch of government.

B   He/she is the last governor in the nation to be granted the power to veto legislation.

C   He/she was originally granted more executive power than any other governor in the nation.

D   NC governors are limited to only one term.

43. In a market economy, what is the pri- 8.4 mary motivation for producers to sell their products at a price consumers can afford?

A   patriotism

B   sense of duty

C   profit

D   fear of government regulations

44. A bill has just been introduced in the 5.4 House of Representatives. Where will the bill go first?

A   to a committee

B   to the House Rules Committee

C   to the floor of the House for a vote

D   to the speaker of the House for his/her signature

45. What do the House of Burgesses, the 1.2 *Mayflower Compact*, and the *Fundamental Orders of Connecticut* all have in common?

A   Each were key parts of colonial governments in New England

B   Each were intended to provide representative governments in the colonies

C   Each originated with the Puritans

D   Each represented a totally new concept in government that had never been practiced before in England

46. The fact that the legislative branch 1.6 makes the laws, the executive branch carries out the laws, and the judicial branch makes sure laws are administered fairly and appropriately, is a reflection of what?

A   separation of powers

B   federalism

C   democracy

D   checks and balances

47. Representative Adkins and Senator Har- 5.4 boken have both added provisions to a bill that was voted on in Congress. Although neither provision is directly related to the matter which the original bill addresses, by attaching them, they have secured passage of provisions that favor their own constituents. The provisions they have added are referred to as what?

A   vetos   C   filibusters

B   clotures   D   riders

48. Congress passes a law making it illegal to call the president a "bonehead". The president, of course, gladly signs it. Eventually, a man convicted of calling the president a "bonehead" appeals to the Supreme Court, which strikes down the law as unconstitutional. What power has the Supreme Court just exercised and what court case established this authority? 2.5

A   Judicial review / *Marbury v. Madison*

B   Judicial discretion / *Gibbons v. Ogden*

C   Jurisprudence / *Mapp v. Ohio*

D   Writs of habeas corpus / *McCullough v. Maryland*

49. The city of Asheburgh is planning to expand and take in additional parts of the county. Some county residents favor this move because it will give them more access to some of the city's benefits. However, others oppose it because they don't want to pay city taxes or open their neighborhoods up to possible industrial development. To address the issue, the city and the county are co-sponsoring a special meeting in which citizens can come and voice their opinions prior to any final decision. Which of the following BEST describes the issue at hand and the meeting? 5.5

A   The issue is a question of infrastructure and the meeting is a council session.

B   The issue is taxation and the meeting is a caucus.

C   The issue is land acquisition and the meeting is an arbitration/mediation.

D   The issue is extra territorial jurisdiction/annexation and the meeting is a forum.

50. Which of the following areas of law is weakened because there is no official means of enforcement? 6.2

A   administrative law

B   constitutional law

C   international law

D   civil law

51. A pharmaceutical company claims that it has developed a revolutionary new drug that slows the growth of cancer cells. Before this drug can be made available to the US public, it will have to be approved by which agency? 6.3

A   EPA   C   FBI

B   FDA   D   FCC

52. Jerry is a lobbyist who has just been hired by the tobacco industry. Which of the following BEST describes Jerry's new role? 6.6

A   educate the public about the harmful effects of tobacco

B   improve the tobacco industry's public image

C   represent the tobacco industry in civil suits

D   convince lawmakers to support policies beneficial to the tobacco industry

53. Amendments 4 – 8 of the Constitution deal with which of the following? 1.7

A   freedom of speech and expression

B   the right to bear arms and practice one's own religion

C   the rights of those suspected, accused, and/or convicted of a crime

D   the rights reserved for the states

54. Of the following actions, which one could be BEST described as "gerrymandering"? 3.7

A The Democrats use their control in the state legislature to push through a new set of tax laws.

B The Republicans use their control in the state legislature to redraw voting districts to their advantage.

C The Republican governor refuses to sign legislation backed by the Democrats because he knows that a new set of representatives will soon be elected.

D The Democrats use their control of the Council of State to reassign voting precincts.

55. Dale is arrested for armed robbery. After six months in prison, he gets out on parole. Within a month, he is arrested and eventually convicted of three more armed robberies. Dale's actions reflect what? 6.8

A the fact that paroles should never be granted

B the fact that rehabilitation works better than retribution

C the reality of recidivism

D the need for restitution

56. Which of the following people is MOST likely to be paroled? 6.8

A a convicted serial killer who is spared the death penalty

B a convicted bank robber who has done well in prison for four years

C someone convicted of a misdemeanor assault

D someone who has abided by the conditions of their house arrest.

57. Which of the following ideas is least associated with the Enlightenment?

A the ideas about church and state expressed in the Justinian Codes

B All human beings have "natural rights."

C Governments which fail to fulfill their role to serve the people can rightfully be resisted and/or replaced.

D Governments get their power from the people.

58. Which of the following advocates the "abolition of private property." 7.6

A Adam Smith's *Wealth of Nations*

B Karl Marx and Frederik Engel's *Communist Manifesto*

C Keynesian Theory

D the *Magna Carta*

59. Each of the following is evidence that the Constitution is a flexible document EXCEPT: 2.4

A congressional actions

B presidential actions

C separation of powers

D judicial review

60. After getting a celebrity athlete to endorse its product, Chocobliss Candy Bars finds that consumer taste favors their candy bars because of the star athlete's popularity. As a result of this popularity, what will happen to the supply and price of Chocobliss bars? 8.5

A Both will fall.

B Both will rise.

C Supply will rise while price falls.

D Supply will fall while price rises.

61. Donald purchases $800 in stock in a company called Magnacorp. If Magnacorp goes into debt and experiences bankruptcy, how much will Donald be liable as a partial owner in the company? 8.7

 A   He has unlimited liability and can be forced to sell all his tangible assets (house, car, etc.) to pay the company's debt.

 B   He has limited liability and will be reimbursed the $800 he invested.

 C   He is partially liable to the point that he is forced to pay a portion of all his future wages/salary until the company's debt is paid.

 D   He has limited liability and will only lose the $800 he invested in the company.

62. Lucy dropped out of school when she was 17 to have a baby. Now 20 years old and the mother of a 3–year–old, Lucy decides it is time to pursue a career. She completes her GED and a 2 year associates degree by going to school at night while her parents watch her daughter. Lucy is exhibiting what? 10.3

 A   citizen apathy

 B   regret

 C   self-motivation

 D   public service

63. By getting her GED and 2 year degree, Lucy is greatly increasing which of the following? 10.3

 A   her love for her daughter

 B   her appreciation of her parents

 C   her intelligence

 D   her earning capacity

64. Costs of production that can change are called what? 7.3

 A   variable costs

 B   fixed costs

 C   marginal costs

 D   total costs

65. Buddy owns an ice-cream parlor at the beach. During the summer months, he spends a lot of money to keep ice-cream and cold drinks in stock. During the winter, however, the cost of maintaining his supply drops because he does not sell as much. Meanwhile, the rent he pays for his store space and the payments he makes on his equipment remain the same year round. Which of the following statements is true? 7.3

 A   The money Buddy spends on his equipment is his variable cost.

 B   The money Buddy spends to keep his store stocked is his fixed cost.

 C   The amount of money Buddy spends on ice-cream, cold drinks, equipment and rent together is his marginal cost.

 D   Buddy's total cost minus his variable costs equals his fixed costs.

66. Theodore has been elected president pro tempore. Which of the following is the BEST description of Theodore's new role? 2.2

 A   He will preside over the House of Representatives.

 B   He will preside over the US Senate.

 C   He is now third in line for the presidency

 D   He will preside over the Senate when the vice president is absent.

67. Michelle is an author who recently finished a new book. In order to make sure that no one else publishes Michelle's work without her permission, her agent helps her obtain which of the following as protection? 8.2

 A   a patent

 B   a copyright

 C   a demand curve

 D   a literary license

68. Dr. Baskin is a dentist whose hobby is restoring vintage cars and entering them in auto shows. On average, Dr. Baskin earns about $240,000/year by working 5 days a week in his dental practice and using Saturdays and Sundays to work on cars and attend shows. About $230,000 of this income is from dentistry and the other $10,000 is in prize money he wins at the auto shows. Because he loves cars so much, Dr. Baskin is considering going to a 4 day work week in his dentist office to give himself an extra day to work on cars. If he does, he estimates that he will make about $190,000/year from his dental practice and probably increase his winnings at car shows to $25,000. If Dr. Baskin goes to the 4 day work week, what will his opportunity cost be?

    7.3

  A   The $25,000 in income he will lose each year.

  B   The day he loses in the dentist office each week.

  C   The additional time spent working on cars.

  D   The fact that he devotes more time to a hobby that he loves.

69. The process by which residents of North Carolina vote on whether or not to accept proposed changes to the state constitution is called what?

    3.1

  A   recall

  B   legislative initiative

  C   referendum

  D   proposition vote

70. Compuhouse is a US technology firm. It recently bought out Indigo Tech, a company in India that produces microchips. As a result of this merger, Compuhouse can BEST be described as what?

    8.6

  A   an oligopoly

  B   a monopoly

  C   an international agency

  D   a multinational conglomerate

71. A delegate from a small state to the Constitutional Convention in 1787 would have MOST LIKELY initially favored which of the following?

    1.5

  A   keeping the Articles of Confederation just as it is

  B   the Virginia Plan

  C   the New Jersey Plan

  D   representation based on population

72. Which of the following is a freedom guaranteed to US citizens?

    10.6

  A   freedom from failure

  B   freedom to say whatever you want, whenever you want

  C   freedom to take whatever property you feel entitled to

  D   freedom to practice your own religion

73. Magnaflare is a corporation that makes road flares. One of the primary components of production is the natural resource, magnesium. Magnesium would be classified as which factor of production?

    7.1

  A   land   C   capital

  B   labor   D   entrepreneurship

74. Which of the following is considered a negative side-effect of a minimum wage?

    8.5

  A   full employment

  B   increased interest rates

  C   unemployment

  D   failure to meet equilibrium production

75. The amount of goods/services that a firm can produce in a set amount of time is known as what?

    7.1

  A   supply-side economics

  B   productivity

  C   capital investment

  D   labor investment

76. Which of the following would be con- 7.4
    sidered an "unskilled worker"?

    A   chef
    B   bank president
    C   delivery truck driver
    D   website designer

77. Galen's company has a great year in 7.5
    which they make record profits. Galen
    decides to use a large percentage of the prof-
    its to purchase new, updated equipment.
    Galen has made what?

    A   an investment in human capital
    B   a profit maximizing decision
    C   a capital investment
    D   a decision based on the law of dimin-
         ishing returns

78. Trent invests $3000 in a company at the 8.7
    beginning of the year. Fortunately, the
    company does well. At the end of the year,
    Trent receives notice that the stock he
    bought for $3000 is now worth $3700.
    Which of the following statements is true?

    A   Trent's surplus is $700.
    B   Trent's dividend is $700 and if he sells
         the stock he stands to make a capital
         gain.
    C   Trent's capital gain is $700 and if he
         sells the stock he will make a dividend.
    D   Trent's profit is $700 and if he sells the
         stock he will likely get a tax break of
         $70.

79. Gene has invested large amounts of 9.8
    money in the stock market. How does
    Gene MOST LIKELY feel about a "bear
    market"?

    A   concerned   C   indifferent
    B   overjoyed   D   optimistic

80. Zack has worked at the same company 8.9
    for 42 years. This Friday he will retire.
    Fortunately, Zack's company has been
    investing a portion of his pay in a mutual
    fund from which he will now draw a
    monthly income. Zack's retirement income
    will come from what?

    A   stock in a single company
    B   a pension
    C   a capital investment
    D   an IRA

81. Which of the following is a phase of the 9.1
    business cycle?

    A   security   C   prosperity
    B   protest   D   migration

82. Joel is an economist who wants to mea- 9.1
    sure the health of the nation's economy
    based on average standard of living. The
    most useful economic indicator that Joel
    could use would MOST LIKELY be what?

    A   GDP
    B   per capita GDP
    C   CPI
    D   measure the national debt

83. Silicon Valley in California and 9.3
    Research Triangle Park in North Caro-
    lina are both evidence of what trend over the
    last few decades?

    A   migration from the South
    B   population shifts to the "Rust Belt"
    C   the increased importance of the US
         technology industry
    D   downsizing

84. Which of the following would involve Anti-trust laws? 8.7

A A US citizen claiming that his civil liberties have been violated by the PATRIOT Act

B A technology company accused of controlling the market and preventing competition

C A company accused of intentionally hiring less qualified minority candidates and not giving qualified white candidates equal consideration

D A company accused of violating an economic embargo

85. A developing nation is in need of help to get its economy moving. It desperately needs foreign money, but it is difficult to get foreign companies to invest in the country because the nation's instability makes investing too risky. What organization will this country MOST LIKELY appeal to for help? 9.6

A EU
B NAFTA
C WTO
D World Bank

86. What effect does a "tight money" policy have on the reserve requirement and the economy's money supply? 9.7

A It raises the reserve requirement, thereby increasing the money supply.

B It lowers the reserve requirement, thereby decreasing the money supply.

C It raises the reserve requirement, thereby decreasing the money supply.

D It lowers the reserve requirement, thereby increasing the money supply.

87. Fiscal policy is concerned with which of the following? 9.7

A government spending and taxation

B consumer spending and productivity

C government spending and the money supply

D taxation and inflation

88. If the Federal Reserve decides to sell bonds, what effect will it have? 9.7

A It will cause the money supply to decrease and inflation to fall.

B It will cause the money supply to increase and employment to rise.

C It will guarantee higher taxes.

D It will extend stagflation.

89. The nation of Tupalow is outraged that the Republic of Za has repeatedly violated international human rights laws. As a result, Tupalow decides not to export products to the Republic of Za until that nation shows evidence that it is complying with such laws. Such action is called what? 9.8

A a tariff
B a trade treaty
C an embargo
D an unfavorable balance of trade

90. When the president appoints a federal judge, only to have the Senate refuse to confirm the nomination, this is an example of what? 1.6

A separation of powers
B federalism
C filibuster
D checks and balances

91. The House of Representatives is established by which of the following? 2.2

A the Preamble of the Constitution
B Article I of the Constitution
C Article II of the Constitution
D Article III of the Constitution

92. Which of the following has the LEAST amount of effect on the economy? 9.8

A stock prices
B concerns about terrorism
C resignation of a bank branch manager
D ruling in an anti-trust case

93. Thad and Nancy are both active citizens who deeply love their country and care about their community. However, they also have very different views. Thad is very conservative, believes in stronger punishments for crime, and favors vouchers for private schools. Nancy is more liberal, wants more money spent to rehabilitate criminals, and believes the government should pump more money into public education. Because of their differences, which of the following is MOST essential in order for Thad and Nancy to work together on matters of public policy?   10.1

A   diversity   C   assimilation
B   debate   D   compromise

94. Multiculturalism is MOST promoted by what?   10.2

A   the *melting pot theory*
B   the *tossed salad theory*
C   nationality
D   assimilation

95. Phil is a 14-year-old African-American. While on the other side of town visiting his friend Vinnie, Phil goes into a convenience store to buy a bag of chips. While he is in the store, Phil notices that the clerk is following him and watching his every move. When Phil asks the clerk what he is doing, the clerk replies, "Just make sure you pay for that." Phil cannot help but notice that the white and Asian kids who are in the store were not treated the same way. Phil most likely believes he has been what?   10.2

A   a victim of multiculturalism
B   a victim of racism and negative stereotypes
C   falsely accused of a crime
D   discriminated against because he is poor

96. Donovan listens to the news everyday and hears about the War on Terror, threats to the environment, economic concerns, etc. However, no matter what is going on nationally or right in his own community, Donovan just doesn't seem to care. He has no strong opinions, he hardly ever votes, and he could care less about community matters. Donovan is guilty of what?   10.5

A   graft
B   self-motivation
C   citizen apathy
D   community withdrawal

97. A formal charge that someone has committed a felony that is issued by a grand jury is called what?   5.3

A   a complaint   C   a summons
B   an indictment   D   a subpoena

98. The idea that citizens are free to make their own choices and direct their own lives is known as what?   10.6

A   entrepreneurship
B   social choice
C   economic choice
D   self-determination

99. How did the invention of money change early economic systems?   8.9

A   It changed what goods people needed.
B   It changed how goods were produced.
C   It provided a medium of exchange that made transactions easier.
D   It created the concept of debt.

100. Connie uses her credit card to buy a $700 dress for a formal occasion. She then pays the credit card company the $700, plus an additional amount a little at a time over the next eight months. The additional amount Connie pays the credit card company is called what?   8.3

A   inflation   C   credit
B   user fee   D   interest

260

S

NOTES

NOTES

NOTES

NOTES

NOTES

NOTES

NOTES

NOTES